BEHAVIOR, HEALTH, AND AGING

BEHAVIOR, HEALTH, AND AGING

Edited by

Stephen B. Manuck
Richard Jennings
Bruce S. Rabin
Andrew Baum
University of Pittsburgh

LEA LAWRENCE ERLBAUM ASSOCIATES, PUBLISHERS
2000   Mahwah, New Jersey   London

Lawrence Erlbaum Associates, Inc., Publishers
10 Industrial Avenue
Mahwah, New Jersey 07430-2262

Library of Congress Cataloging-in-Publication Data
Behavior, health, and aging / edited by Stephen Manuck [et al.]
    p.   cm. -- (Perspectives in behavioral medicine)
    Includes bibliographical references and index.
    ISBN 0–8058–3404–4 (cloth : alk. paper).
    1. Aged—Health and hygiene.   2. Health behavior—Age factors
     3. Aging.   4. Geriatrics.

  RA564.8.B43   2000
  618.97—dc21   99-088820

Printed in the United States of America
10 9 8 7 6 5 4 3 2 1

Contents

Preface

Millennial events are peculiar for many reasons, particularly when they occur in the context of the millions of years that preceded recorded time-keeping and history. They tend to focus attention on long-anticipated outcomes as a fitting conclusion to 1,000-year epochs (this occurs at the end of centuries and decades too, but to a lesser extent) and on the changes that the next epoch promises. They are useful as a way of focusing attention on changes that occur independent of changes in the calendar, taking advantage of the heightened focus on summarizing where we've been and where we are going. So, as a rubric for summarizing changes that may come to dominate our lives in the first 50 to 100 years of the new millennium, they serve a useful purpose. One of the most important changes characterizing the new era is the changing nature of our population and its health care demands. Most prominently, our population is aging as people live longer and remain active longer into their lives. As the population ages it becomes more diverse and our knowledge and priorities must change as well. This book deals with aging in the context of health and health care needs. It considers basic changes that accompany aging and some of the more specific problems that accompany it. Several issues are predominant. Genetics has assumed increasing importance, both in terms of the genomic instability we associate with advancing age and in terms of expression of heritable predispositions and exhibition of predictable behaviors or disorders. Maclearn and Heller review basic tenets of this evolving field, including some of the methods of looking at heritable differences in health and well-being and some consideration of the implications of discovering genes or polymorphisms that appear to be related to accelerated senescence, systemic disease, or depression. Overall, the genetic bases of differences in how quickly people age and/or lose functional competence are of considerable interest as are the environmental conditions that affect the shape such predispositions assume.

The second chapter considers another development that has important implications for health care in the next epoch, adjustment of life expectancy for quality of life. Most of us are aware of changes in the recognition of and emphasis on quality of life in planning therapeutic interventions for disease or disability and most of us can recognize the importance of factoring such concerns into decision-making and research. Kaplan and Erickson discuss the wisdom and value of quality-adjusted survival analysis and describe the findings of a study of such analyses in a large sample of men and women, reporting differences between men and women in overall quality of life. More significantly, quality adjustments had greater impact on life expectancy among women, negating much of the life expectancy advantages typically afforded them. In contrast to mortality-based measures of health outcomes that show women with a clear survival advantage, quality-of-life measures suggest advantages for men.

Issues associated with gender are also a prominent theme of the third chapter. Here, Leventhal argues that gender differences in symptoms, behaviors, and outcomes affect the physical and psychosocial impact of interventions among the elderly, influencing the emergence of frailty or loss of function and, ultimately, use of the health care system. The implications of a view of aging emphasizing multiple systems are considered, and the notion that aging and life span development are really a series of partially independent biological clocks that run at different rates and wind down at different times is discussed. Of necessity, longevity is associated with greater heterogeneity as a variety of factors combine to determine how well people deal with the growth and decline of each of these systems. Gender appears to affect many or most of these systems and implications for behavior, survival, and psychosocial aging are examined.

Chapter 4 continues this focus on gender, focusing on a major life transition among aging women. Matthews, Wing, Kuller, Meilahn, and Owens attack the anecdotal nature of reports of menopause, suggesting that despite negative expectations among premenopausal women, menopause is a complex and potentially positive transition for women that does not necessarily unfold as cultural stereotypes would indicate. The chapter comprehensively reviews the biological bases of menopause, its role in increasing risk for cardiovascular disease, and the emotional and biological changes that accompany it. Importantly, Matthews and her colleagues report evidence that suggests that non-pharmacologic lifestyle interventions may modify risk factors during the menopausal period that reduce potential consequences or health problems later on.

The next four chapters deal with various aspects of aging and the immune system. Some of the primary health-related consequences of aging appear to be mediated by the immune system, and the greater vulnerability of older people to infectious illnesses provides prima facia evidence of declines in immune defenses with age. In chapter 5, Rabin summarizes our knowledge of immune system changes that occur with aging, including autoimmune responses, T-cell function, cytokine activity, and the role of nutrition in aging of immune defenses. This is followed by Robinson-Whelan, Kiecolt-Glaser, and Glaser's chapter on chronic stress as an important immunmodulator in the elderly. This discussion is centered on chronic stress associated with caregiving and its impact on immunity, suggesting health implications and possibilities for intervention in this rapidly growing group of older adults. Chapter 7, by Padgett, Dobbs, and Sheridan, explores the concept of immune senescence from a different perspective, using rodent models to evaluate the immune changes thought to accompany aging. These authors offer a very comprehensive review of findings bearing on clear trends toward the progressive decline of immune functions and corresponding increases in vulnerability to infectious agents. Finally, Solomon and Benton provide a different challenge to the traditional view of immunosenescence. Focusing on healthy behaviors among people doing relatively well in the face of potentially debilitating disease, they found little evidence of substantial immune system decline in a group of healthy older men and women who coped well and maintained good mental health. The implications of this and related findings described in these four chapters are important components of an overall model of health, disease, and outcomes of aging.

The last six chapters evaluate some of the psychosocial implications of aging for health and illness, with emphasis on the contributions of these factors to cardiovascular disease. In chapter 9, Schulz, Heckhausen, and O'Brien address the relations between negative emotional experience and disablement and disability in late life, suggesting that adjustment to limitations on prevailing modes of controlling one's environment is a significant component of the gradual decline many experience. Interventions may address these limitations, facilitating adjustment to them, or may focus on the effects of the disablement process and on secondary prevention. In chapter 10, Williams addresses the dynamic interplay of psychosocial risk factors, biobehavioral mechanisms underlying pathophysiology, and therapeutic interventions in illness across the life cycle. Childhood antecedents of risk are also considered and evidence is presented that suggests that hostility, depression, social isolation, job strain, and SES contribute directly to serious chronic illness, such as cardiovascular disease. Again, the likely value of interventions is described.

Chapter 11 takes this focus a step further, exploring the quality of adjustment to chronic illnessamong the elderly. Helgeson and Mickelson focus principally on self-esteem and the unique threats to self-esteem that chronic illnesses pose for the elderly. The importance of overall adjustment to aging as a factor in coping with illness adds an important dimension to this mix, and the importance of social comparison, denial, and deriving meaning from victimization are compared as means of coping with threats to self-esteem.

Animal models often provide a better context for evaluation of the role of etiological variables in disease onset and/or progression. In chapter 12, Adams, Kaplan, Manuck, Shively, and Williams offer a monkey model of atherosclerosis with sex and psychosocial stress as key components of pathogenesis. Drawing research on psychosocial sources of variability in ovarian function and its effects on atherosclerosis they speculate on mechanisms predicting behavioral disease pathogenesis in female monkeys. The relative advantages or disadvantages of a nonhuman model aside, the issues underlying these observations offer some direct insight into the processes that operate in cardiovascular disease in humans.

Chapter 13 considers a different component or aspect of cardiovascular health and different outcomes. Here, Elias, Elias, DiAgostino, and Wolf explore hypertension and the effects of age and blood pressure on neuropsychological status in the Framingham Study. Traditional perspectives on blood pressure and aging are described and empirical support for these models is reviewed. Evidence is presented of an association between high blood pressure and accelerated age-related declines in fluid, intellectual abilities. Concluding that elevated blood pressure and hypertension have negative affects on cognitive functioning, these investigators offer some evidence of significance of these findings and their implications.

The last chapter in this book, by Muldoon, Kaplan, and Manuck, tackles a timely and provocative issue, the effects of cholesterol lowering strategies on health among the elderly. Cholesterol remains a major risk factor for heart disease and medical interventions over the past decade have focused increasingly on cholesterol-lowering drugs. Underscoring the complexity of these issues is the observation that in a series of major randomized trials reported before 1990, modest decreases in heart offset by increases in noncoronary heart disease-related mortality (due to cancer, accidents, violence, and trauma). Reviewing the effects of cholesterol in aging populations and in the etiology of coronary mortality, the authors conclude that despite the importance of the link between cholesterol and heart disease, cholesterol-lowering interventions should be approached with caution, particularly in the elderly.

This book was conceived as a selective survey of some of the most important developments in research and theory about behavioral aspects of health and illness in aging. Happily, our contributors have risen to the task and provided comprehensive, insightful accounts of a range of important topics. They have engaged in lively and provocative debate about some commonly held assumptions. We are grateful for their efforts in this regard. We are also grateful to Michele Hayward and Lori McBurney, whose editorial assistance was essential to completion of this project.

—Stephen B. Manuck
—Richard Jennings
—Bruce S. Rabin
—Andrew Baum

1

Genetics and Aging

Gerald E. McClearn
The Pennsylvania State University

Debra A. Heller
*The Pennsylvania State University and First Health
Services Corp., Harrisburg, Pennsylvania*

GENETICS AND
GERONTOLOGY

The acceleration of gerontological research in the past few decades has provided a plethora of data and a number of theories, ranging from stochastic to programmed, and engaging molecular, biochemical, physiological and evolutionary levels of analysis and explanation (for recent reviews, see, for examples, Arking, 1991; Rose, 1991; Warner, Butler, Sprott, & Schneider, 1987). The scientific pessimist might lament the absence of a compelling unified theory; the scientific optimist will revel in the richness of the empirical data and the diversity of the current theoretical propositions.

The field of genetics has been prominently and variously featured in gerontological research. Single major genes have been identified whose associated phenotypes are describable as accelerated senescence; interspecific differences in life spans have been attributed to the differing genotypes of the compared species; the possibility that there exists a genetic program for senescence has been explored, as has the possibility that an antisenescing genetic program becomes deficient with advanced age. Of the many genetic perspectives that can be brought to bear on the topic of aging, one of the most engaging concerns the genetic basis of intrapsecific individual differences in rate and pattern of aging. Brief reflection reveals that it is these differences that inspire much of our concern with human aging. We are interested in accounting for the fact that some of us age relatively slowly, retaining functional competence for a long life; others deteriorate rapidly and early; and most of us are located somewhere on the distribution between these extremes. Further, the pattern of age-related decline differs enormously from one individual to another. The point can be appreciated by considering the contrast of the physically intact advanced Alzheimer's patient to the bed-ridden octogenarian with still-sharp intellect. Elucidating the sources of these individual differences not only will contribute to basic scientific understanding of aging processes but also will have significant policy implications for societies faced with problems of welfare and health of rapidly aging populations.

THE QUANTITATIVE
GENETIC MODEL

A valuable perspective on the roots of individuality of any sort is the quantitative genetic differential model (McClearn, 1993). This model had major origins in agricultural application, and in that realm, as well as others, it has demonstrated its general validity and robustness. A classic statement of quantitative genetic theory is that of Falconer and Mackay (1996); application to behavioral phenotypes is described by Plomin, DeFries, McClearn, and Rutter (1997), among others. The essence of the model is the postulation that numerous genetic loci as well as environmental factors may influence the same phenotype. Allelic differences among individuals at the relevant loci, together with differences in exposure to the effective environmental factors, clearly rationalize differences among individuals in phenotypic manifestation. The primary analytic strategy is to decompose the observed phenotypic variance into components due to the genetic differences existing among individuals, to differences attributable to environmental sources, and to the appropriate interaction and covariance terms.

At this level, the conceptualization is basically a "black box" one. The genetic factors are not identified, and the relevant environmental factors are usually similarly anonymous. Yet the great virtue of the analysis is its "bottom line" nature (Plomin et al., 1990). All the genetic influences, regardless of whether they are structural genes or regulatory sequences, and all the environmental influences—familial, peer group, nutritional, disease-exposure, educational, and so on—are included.

A straightforward extension of the purely statistical statement illuminates the properties of the system. The "polygenes" of the quantitative genetic system presumably act through precisely the same mechanism as do the "major" or "Mendelian" genes that are the subject matter of classical genetics and the modern molecular genetic revolution. That is to say, they segregate and assort in Mendelian manner, and they confer specificity on polypeptides that participate in the structural, transport, and catalytic protein functions of the organism. The known intricacies of metabolic sequences ensure that these functions converge and diverge, with the result that a complex "causal field" (Ford, 1987) constitutes the path from gene to phenotype. If we presume, further, that the environmental influences impinge on the same causal field, it becomes obvious that the question of whether some quantitative phenotype is "genetic or environmental" is nonsensical. Any such phenotype is the product of both genetic and environmental factors. The question of what proportion of variance in the phenotype is attributable to genetic and environmental sources, however, is apposite and meaningful.

Quantitative genetic methods are applicable to description of developmental and age-related changes as well as to static characterization of a phenotype. Depending on the context of analysis, several types of change may be relevant, including the following:

1. *Age-related changes in heritability.* Reference to age-related changes in genetic influence most often concerns changes in heritability. Heritability is the proportion of the phenotypic variance that is attributable to genetic variance. At different ages, the relative impact of genetic and environmental variance on population variance may change.

2. *Age-related changes in operative genetic factors.* In addition to age-related changes in heritability, it is possible for different genes or sets of genes to be operative at different developmental points in time. Knowing the estimated heritability of a given phenotype at different ages provides little information regarding whether the same or different sets of genes are relevant. Genetic correlational analysis, however, can be used to address changes in operative genetic factors with age. In a developmental context, the genetic

correlation indicates the extent to which a phenotype is influenced by the same genes at two points in time. Although the study of genetic correlations across time provides much useful information, it requires longitudinal measurements on individuals and family members. For detailed discussions of genetic correlations and developmental change, the reader is referred to Plomin and Thompson (1988) or Plomin (1986). For the present discussion, we focus on age-related differences in heritability.

Because heritability reflects the ratio of genetic variance to phenotypic variance, changes in heritability can result from several types of change. For example, from inspection of the following, simplified equation relating heritability (h^2) to phenotypic variance (V_P), genetic variance (V_G), and environmental variance (V_E),

$$h^2 = V_G/V_P$$
$$= V_G/(V_G + V_E)$$

it is evident that changes in either genetic or environmental variance may affect h^2. For example, genetic variances may remain constant, but changes in phenotypic variance owing to environmental effects may have a profound effect on heritability. Alternatively, phenotypic variance in the population may not differ at different ages, but changes in the relative magnitudes of genetic and environmental variance result in developmental changes in heritability.

Research Strategies

This differential model, addressing interindividual differences as well as intraindividual differences across time, suggests two (at least) different types of research strategy. The quantitative analyses rely on comparisons of degrees of resemblance with respect to the phenotype of relatives of differing degrees. Strong theory (the whole edifice of genetics, really) yields expectations concerning, for example, what the correlation of dizygotic twins should be, given a particular correlation of monozygotic twins, under various conditions of dominance, epistatic interactions, degree of environmental influence, and so on. The empirical results are interpreted in this context. Similar interpretations can be derived from the resemblance of parents and offspring, siblings, and other types of relationships found in a more or less random (or haphazardly) mating population. In experimental animals, of course, matings can be arranged. This assignment of mates constitutes a degree of experimental manipulation of genotype and permits interpretations appropriate to experimental rather than associative research. In the form described, however, it is still "black box" in the sense that input–output relationships are examined, with both genetic and environmental factors constituting the input and the output being the phenotype. The causal field is conceptually overleaped.

With respect to some particular phenotype, an alternate research strategy can be pursued if some entrée can be gained into the causal field. Sometimes this can be accomplished by inspired nomination of some candidate enzyme, biochemical reaction, or physiological process. If this candidate is already known to be, or can be shown to be, related to the target phenotype, then the process of filling in the causal field can be pursued in research on mechanism. A joint strategy is particularly attractive. As elements of the causal field become identified, it is possible to treat them as phenotypes in their own right and address quantitative questions such as degree of genetic correlation among the more proximal and the distal phenotypes. The feasibility of this joint approach is being greatly enhanced with the burgeoning capability of identifying specific quantitative trait loci (QTL) within a polygenic system (see, for example, McClearn, Plomin, Gora-Maslak, and Crabbe, 1991; Plomin, McClearn, and Gora-Maslak, 1991).

Gerontology and Variability

The centrality of variance in quantitative genetics is particularly appropriate for application to gerontology, where the consideration of variance changes with age has been an abiding issue. Much work has been done in recent decades on developmental change from a life-span perspective, focusing on analysis of population variance and individual differences for personality and cognition during aging. Key concepts resulting from this field of study have included the identification of normative and non-normative events, which may be generalized as distinguishing between developmental changes shared by individuals within a cultural unit or cohort, or at a specific developmental stage (normative), and those not common to the cultural unit (non-normative) (Baltes, 1982; Baltes, Reese, & Lipsitt, 1980). Under this rubric, the accumulation of non-normative events across the life span would be theorized to serve as one mechanism responsible for increased variance with age. Results from studies of age-related changes in personality and cognitive ability, however, have been mixed with regard to developmental changes in variance. Although many studies find normative or mean changes during aging, variance and covariance stability differ by phenotype and study (Bornstein & Smircina, 1982; Christiansen, Mackinnon, Henerson, Scott, & Korten, 1994; Hertzog & Schaie, 1986, 1988).

The characterization of the broad domains of genetic and environmental determinants of individuality in age-related processes can thus be seen as important context-building for the interpretation of diverse gerontological data. We report here on some representative research from the Swedish Adoption/Twin Study of Aging (SATSA), one of several projects undertaking such characterization.

SATSA

The Swedish Adoption/Twin Study of Aging (SATSA) is a longitudinal study of mid-life and elder twins based on the Swedish Twin Registry (Cederlöf & Lorich, 1978). A distinctive feature of the study is the inclusion of a substantial number of twin pairs who were separated for some period during their rearing.

Logic of the Separated Twin Design

Twins reared apart provide a comparison that considerably strengthens the inferential power of the basic twin design. In the conventional twin study, the major interpretation derives from comparison of the degrees of similarity of identical (monozygotic, or MZ) and of fraternal (dizygotic, or DZ) twin pairs. The former are identical genetically, and the latter are only as genetically similar as ordinary siblings. In most empirical data, members of the MZ pairs are not phenotypically identical; the difference between the measured similarity and perfect correlation is attributed to environmental influences. Assuming that this environmental influence is the same for DZ as for MZ pairs permits the interpretation of any excess of similarity of the latter over the former as being due to heredity. This assumption is clearly a key element of twin study logic, and in many cases its veracity is not directly demonstrable. Although it appears that this potentially troublesome issue may not be particularly debilitating in practice (see Plomin et al., 1990), some degree of reservation necessarily attaches to results from conventionally reared twins.

The advantage introduced by separated twins is basically the unconfounding of genetic and environmental similarity. In the limiting case, twins separated at birth would be reared by randomly chosen adoptive parents and never interact with each other. Under such circumstances (and ignoring prenatal environmental influences), an excess of MZ similarity over DZ similarity would quite clearly be assignable to genetic factors. In the real world, such separation is extremely rare. More typical is separation after some weeks or months of shared family environment; assignment to rearing parents according to convenience, opportunity, or the criteria of adoption agencies; and postseparation contact of various degrees from occasional phone calls to frequent in-person meetings. Nevertheless, comparison of such (incompletely) separated twin pairs to those reared normally offers considerable interpretational leverage.

The broad-stroke logic in separated twin studies such as SATSA thus includes the following elements:

1. The similarity of DZ twin pairs (measured usually by an intraclass correlation coefficient) gives an indication of general level of genetic influence. A coefficient close to zero implies little or no genetic influence and, similarly, little or no shared environmental influence; the observed variance in the phenotype must be due to environmental influences not shared by the members of a twin pair. An intraclass correlation significantly different from zero represents some degree of familiality. But ordinary DZ twins share a common environment as well as the allelic configuration of one half of their segregating genes. On this evidence only, therefore, genetic influence cannot be distinguished from shared environmental influence.

2. If one is willing to assume that the environmental influences impinging on MZ pairs are not more similar than those impinging on DZ pairs, then the excess of MZ similarity relative to DZ similarity can be interpreted as reflecting the greater genetic similarity of the former. Heritability, the proportion of the phenotypic variance that is attributable to genetic variability, can be estimated as twice the difference between the intraclass correlations of MZ and DZ pairs (Falconer, 1989).

3. For any given "spread" between DZ and MZ similarity, the overall levels are informative. For example, if both are relatively low, the interpretation is that shared environmental influences are minimal. If both are high, shared environmental factors are influential.

4. Greater resemblance of twins reared together than twins reared apart implicates shared environmental influences.

The SATSA Design

Among the items in the establishing questionnaire of the Swedish Twin Registry (which includes twins born between 1886 and 1958; see Cederlöf & Lorich, 1978) was one that inquired if the members of the twin pair were separated during their rearing years. One or both members of 961 pairs indicated that they had been so separated prior to the age of 10 years. After ascertaining which of these pairs were "intact" (both members of the pair alive), we sent a new questionnaire to 591 pairs of these twins and to a sample of 627 conventionally reared twins matched for sex and for county and month of birth.

The numbers of questionnaires returned by both members of pairs of dizygotic twins reared apart (DZA), dizygotic twins reared together (DZT), monozygotic twins reared apart (MZA), and monozygotic twins reared together (MZT) were 182, 175, 83, and 136, respectively.

The mean age of questionnaire respondents was 58.6 years, with a standard deviation of 13.6 years. Mean age at separation of the reared-apart twins was 2.8 years; the distribution is highly skewed, with 48% having been separated prior to 1 year of age and the rest by 10 years of age.

The questionnaire was designed to elicit information pertinent to gerontological issues. The domains investigated include early rearing environment, adult family, social and working environments, personality, activities of daily living, and physical and mental health status.

Following the questionnaire returns, in-person testing (IPT) sessions were arranged for a subset of the twins at their homes or at conveniently located community health centers. The IPT data include measures of cardiovascular function, respiratory function, clinical blood and urine measures, functional capacity, and cognitive functioning. The number of IPT assessments were 100, 89, 46, and 67 pairs for DZA, DZT, MZA, and MZT, respectively. Mean age at testing if IPT participants was 65.6, with a standard deviation of 8.4.

SASTA is proceeding as a longitudinal study with both questionnaire and IPT data collected at 3-year intervals. In this chapter we are concerned only with a few phenotypes from the first waves that are particularly relevant to biobehavioral health.

Selected SATSA Results

The phenotypic data from SATSA are, of course, relevant to the issue of change in variability across the latter part of the life span. The results are very mixed. In one analysis, for example, 22 personality scales from

SATSA were evaluated with regard to age-related variance differences (Harris, Pedersen, McClearn, Plomin, & Nesselroade, 1992; McClearn, Pedersen, et al., 1991). The most common pattern shown was a stable pattern, with no clear variance differences across age groups. Six of the 22 scales displayed the "classic" pattern of greater variance at older ages. Two variables exhibited a constricting pattern, with apparent decreases in variance with age. For three of the scales, variance differences across age groups were either irregular or nonlinear. In aggregate, the findings of studies of age-related changes and differences in phenotypic variance suggest that few, if any, generalizations can be made regarding variance increases or decreases across the life span.

The evidence regarding age-related changes in genetic and environmental components of variance have been even more mixed than that obtained for total phenotypic variance. Although it is tempting to theorize that changes associated with aging should result in decreased heritability owing to the accumulation of environmental experiences, this has not been consistently found in work to date. In fact, as Plomin and Thompson (1988) note, for many phenotypes evincing changes in genetic variance with age, the change is in the direction of increased heritability.

In order to investigate this subject further, we examined several phenotypes from SATSA relevant to behavioral medicine, including two measurements of self-rated health, and three serum lipid measurements. The variables included in the present analyses are:

Self-Rated Health:	A scale including four items relating to self-rated health; assessed by mailed questionnaire (Q1)
Sum of Illnesses (SUMILL):	A scale indexing self-reported chronic illnesses across major organ systems; assessed by mailed questionnaire (Q1)
Serum Cholesterol:	From in-person testing (IPT1)
HDL Cholesterol:	From in-person testing (IPT1)
Triglycerides:	From in-person testing (IPT1)

Several options for analysis exist, given the data available. With twin and family data, structural equation models are typically used to solve simultaneously equations for all groups of relatives and to estimate genetic and environmental parameters (Boomsma, Martin, & Neale, 1989; Neale & Cardon, 1992). To examine age-related trends, alternative hierarchical multiple regression (HMR) models can be used, in which one twin's lipid level is predicted by the cotwin's score, zygosity, sex, and interaction terms. A significant interaction term for zygosity by age indicates that genetic effects vary as a function of age. HMR analyses have been used extensively in twin studies to examine linear differences in genetic influence (Ho, Foch, & Plomin, 1980; Rose, 1991). Structural equation models can also be used to test for group differences in genetic and environmental parameters; however, sample size considerations limit the number of age groups and age ranges that can be tested. For descriptive purposes, we have found it useful to employ alternative analyses using moving intervals as a sampling technique. Moving averages are, of course, frequently used in economic and time-series applications to study temporal trends and to correct for seasonal changes. We used the same concept to divide the SATSA sample into overlapping age bands, enabling us to study multiple age groups while preserving sample size (McClearn, Svartengren, Pedersen, Heller, & Plomin, 1994). Structural equation modeling was performed for each band, yielding estimates of genetic and environmental variance measures. Although the significance of parameter estimate differences across the age bands cannot be evaluated because the age bands are not independent, the moving interval analyses provide useful information regarding age trends in heritability. It is important to keep in mind, however, that the data are cross-sectional.

The results of the moving interval analyses are shown in Figs. 1.1 and 1.2. The five phenotypes can be distinguished by their patterns across age in genetic and environmental variance

In Fig. 1.1, the two self-rated health measures, Self-Rated Health and SUMILL, exhibit a pattern of stable or increasing heritability coupled with early diminution of shared environmental influence. Heritability for SUMILL is somewhat higher (20%–40%) than for Self-Rated Health (10%–20%). SUMILL also shows a larger role for shared environment than does Self-Rated Health, although for both variables, shared environmental effects appear to account for no variance after the early sixties.

In Fig. 1.2, high density lipoprotein (HDL) shows a somewhat different pattern of results, with higher heritability at all ages than that shown by the Self-Rated Health variables. Modest increases in heritability are suggested later in life. Virtually no shared rearing environment (E_S) effect is exhibited throughout the age range.

Total serum cholesterol and serum triglycerides are characterized by apparent dramatic decreases in heritability across the ages studied. In the youngest age band, heritability estimates are between 60 and 70% for both measures, falling to below 20% in the oldest group for cholesterol

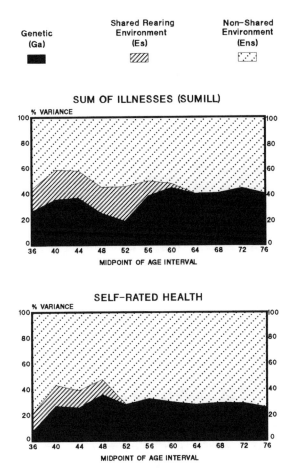

FIG. 1.1. Components of variance for two measures of self-reported health based on moving interval analysis.

and to near zero for triglycerides. The two variables differ, however, in the relative importance of shared rearing environment. The serum triglyceride measure, like HDL, shows little evidence for a role of shared rearing environment. Total cholesterol, in contrast, shows a substantial and even somewhat increasing role for E_S over the range.

Age-related differences in the genetic and environmental components for these five variables have been previously discussed (Harris et al., 1992; Heller, de Faire, Pedersen, Dahlén, & McClearn, 1993). The apparent age differences in heritability for cholesterol and triglycerides may reflect an increase in the importance of accumulated experiences unique to individuals. Alternatively, a decrease in the relative importance of genetic factors

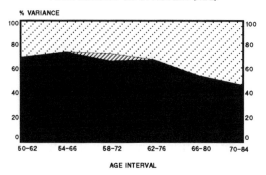

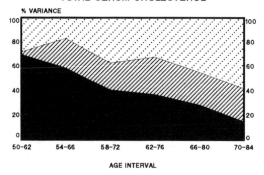

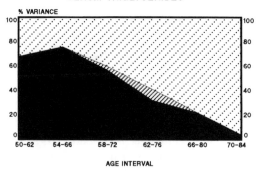

FIG. 1.2. Components of variance for three serum lipid measures based on moving interval analysis.

with age might reflect a survivor effect, in that persons with genetically mediated lipid disorders may die at earlier ages and thus be differentially represented across the age bands (Heller et al., 1993). Harris et al. (1992) have suggested that the apparent increase in genetic influence for SUMILL may be owing to cohort differences in environmental effects between individuals born before the age of industrialization in Sweden and those born later. Cohort effects may also explain the apparent greater magnitude of shared rearing environment effects for total serum cholesterol in older age groups. Such effects may reflect complex relationships among health-related behaviors. For example, older twins reared together may be more alike in behaviors relevant to cholesterol levels, such as diet, due to cohort differences in the likelihood of retaining family dietary or cooking habits (Heller et al., 1993; Whitfield & Martin, 1983). If twin similarity for behaviors learned during childhood is greater in older cohorts than in younger cohorts, the result could be a larger role for shared rearing environment in older age groups, as suggested by these analyses.

The preceding examples and discussion highlight the complex nature of relationships among health and behavior and their mediation by genetic and environmental influences. With the extension of analyses such as the ones presented in this chapter to a longitudinal design, it is likely that in the near future we will learn much more about how genetic and environmental influences affect biobehavioral phenotypes over the course of the life span.

ACKNOWLEDGMENTS

Support of the Swedish Adoption/Twin Study of Aging (SASTA) by the National Institute on Aging (AG-04563, AG-10175) and the John D. and Catherine T. MacArthur Foundation Research Network on Successful Aging is gratefully acknowledged.

REFERENCES

Arking, R. (1991). *Biology of aging.* Englewood Cliffs: Prentice-Hall.

Baltes, P.B. (1982). Life-span developmental psychology: Some converging observations on history and theory. In K.W. Schaie & J. Geiwitz (Eds.), *Adult development and aging.* Boston: Little, Brown.

Baltes, P.B., Reese, H.W., & Lipsitt, L.P. (1980). Life-span developmental psychology. *Annual Review of Psychology, 31,* 65–110.

Boomsma, D.I., Martin, N.G., & Neale, M.C. (Eds.). (1989). Genetic analysis of twin and family data: Structural modeling using LISREL. [Special issue]. *Behavior Genetics, special issue, 19.*

Bornstein, R., & Smircina, M.T. (1982). The status of the empirical support for the hypothesis of increased variability in aging populations. *The Gerontologist, 22*, 258–260.

Cederlöf, R., & Lorich, U. (1978). The Swedish Twin Registry. In W.E. Nance, G. Allen, & P. Parisi (Eds.), *Twin research: Biology and epidemiology* (pp. 189–195). New York: Alan R. Liss.

Christensen, H., Mackinnon, A., Henderson, A.S., Scott, L.R., & Korten, A.E. (1994). Age differences and interindividual variation in cognition in community-dwelling elderly. *Psychology and Aging, 9*, 381–390.

Falconer, D. S., & Mackay, T. (1996). *Introduction to quantitative genetics* (4th ed.) New York: John Wiley and Sons.

Ford, D.L. (1987). *Humans as self-constructing living systems*. Hillsdale, NJ: Lawrence Erlbaum Associates.

Harris, J.R., Pedersen, N.L., McClearn, G.E., Plomin, R., & Nesselroade, J.R. (1992). Age differences in genetic and environmental influences for health from the Swedish Adoption/Twin Study of Aging. *Journal of Gerontology, 47*, 213–220.

Heller, D.A., de Faire, U., Pedersen, N.L., Dahlén, G., & McClearn, G.E. (1993). Genetic and environmental influences on serum lipid levels in twins. *New England Journal of Medicine, 328*, 1150–1156.

Hertzog, C., & Schaie, K.W. (1986). Stability and change in adult intelligence: 1. Analysis of longitudinal covariance structures. *Psychology and Aging, 1*, 159–171.

Hertzog, C., & Schaie, K.W. (1988). Stability and change in adult intelligence: 2. Simultaneous analysis of longitudinal means and covariance structures. *Psychology and Aging, 3*, 122–130.

Ho, H.Z., Foch, T.T., & Plomin, R. (1980). Developmental stability of the relative influence of genes and environment on specific cognitive abilities in childhood. *Developmental Psychology, 16*, 340–346.

McClearn, G.E. (1993). Behavioral genetics: The last century and the next. In R. Plomin & G.E. McClearn (Eds.), *Nature, nurture, and psychology*. Washington, DC: American Psychological Association.

McClearn, G.E., Pedersen, N.L., Plomin, R., Nesselroade, J.R., Friberg, L., & de Faire, U. (1991). *Age and gender effects for individual differences in behavioral aging: The Swedish Adoption/Twin Study of Aging.* University Park: Pennsylvania State University, Center for Developmental and Health Genetics.

McClearn, G.E., Plomin, R., Gora-Maslak, G., & Crabbe, J.C. (1991). The gene chase in behavioral science. *Psychological Science, 2*, 222–229.

McClearn, G.E., Svartengren, M., Pedersen, N.L., Heller, D., & Plomin, R. (1994). Genetic and environmental influences on pulmonary function in aging Swedish twins. *Journals of Gerontology: Medical Sciences, 49*, M264–M268.

Neale, M.C., & Cardon, L.R. (1992). *Methodology for genetic studies of twins and families*. Boston: Kluwer.

Plomin, R. (1986). *Development, genetics, and psychology*. Hillsdale, NJ: Lawrence Erlbaum Associates.

Plomin, R., DeFries, J.C., McClearn, G.E., & Rutter, M. (1997). *Behavioral genetics* (3rd ed.). New York: W. H. Freeman.

Plomin, R., McClearn, G.E., & Gora-Maslak, G. (1991). Quantitative trait loci and psychopharmacology. *Journal of Psychopharmacology, 5*, 1–9.

Plomin, R., & Thompson, L. (1988). Life-span developmental behavioral genetics. In P.B. Baltes, D.L. Featherman, & R.M. Lerner (Eds.), *Life-span development and behavior* (Vol. 8, pp. 1–31). Hillsdale, NJ: Lawrence Erlbaum Associates.

Rose, M.R. (1991). *Evolutionary biology of aging*. New York: Oxford University Press.

Warner, H.R., Butler, R.N., Sprott, R.L., & Schneider, E.L. (Eds.). (1987). *Modern biological theories of aging*. New York: Raven Press.

Whitfield, J.B., & Martin, N.G. (1983). Plasma lipids in twins: Environmental and genetic influences. *Atherosclerosis, 48*, 265–277.

2

Quality Adjusted Life Expectancy for Men and Women in the United States

Robert M. Kaplan
University of California, San Diego

Jennifer Erickson
National Center for Health Statistics

There is a paradox in public health statistics. According to U.S. vital statistics, women have longer life expectancies than do men. Life expectancy for women is 78.2 years, whereas the equivalent figure for men is 71.2 years (Births and Deaths, United States, 1996). On the other hand, studies on health-related quality of life consistently show that women experience greater morbidity than do men (Wingard, 1984). For example, women experience more disabling chronic illnesses such as rheumatoid arthritis. Men are more likely to die suddenly of heart disease or accidents, whereas women are more likely to live longer but experience longer periods of disability (Verbrugge, 1989; Verbrugge & Wingard, 1984; Wingard & Cohn, 1990).

Because women experience lesser mortality but greater morbidity, it is not clear how to provide population-based estimates of health status. If measures of mortality are chosen, women are found to have better health status. However, if measures of morbidity are used, men are found to have better health status. We have proposed measures of survival that

15

make adjustments for quality of life (Kaplan & Anderson, 1990). In order to represent total health status, new methods of analysis known collectively as Quality-Adjusted Survival Analysis are required.

QUALITY-ADJUSTED
SURVIVAL ANALYSIS

The diversity of outcomes in health care has led many analysts to focus on the simplest of measures. Typically, that is mortality or life expectancy. When mortality is studied, those who are alive are statistically coded as 1.0, whereas those who are dead are statistically coded as 0.0. Mortality allows the comparison between different diseases. For example, we can state the life expectancy for those who will eventually die of heart disease and compare it to the life expectancy to those who will eventually die of cancer. The difficulty is that everyone who remains alive is given the same score. A person confined to bed with an irreversible coma is alive and is counted in the same way as someone who is an active jogger.

Traditional survival analysis is problematic in evaluating outcomes when both morbidity and mortality are important because the analysis treats all living patients in the same way. Yet there are biases associated with the exclusive focus on morbidity or quality of life. For example, many quality of life assessments create bias against treatment. This occurs because the sickest patients in the cohort are the ones most likely to die. As they die, the remainder appear to have, on average, improved quality of life.

Consider the analysis of a hypothetical experiment in which patients are randomly assigned to supportive care or to a comparison group. If the patients who die are excluded from the analysis, the results might be represented by the top portion of Fig. 2.1. The figure suggests that there is a slight decline in quality of life for the treatment group whereas there is a slight improvement in the comparison group. Actually, there is significantly higher mortality in the comparison group. The lower half of Fig. 2.1 shows the results of the comparison using a combined index of morbidity and mortality. As the figure shows, there is a slight decline for those in the supportive care (treatment) group but a much more significant decline for those in the comparison group. At follow-up, these groups are significantly different. The reason that these differences are apparent is that the comparison group now includes all subjects. Those who have died are coded as 0.0. In the top portion of Fig. 2.1 those who

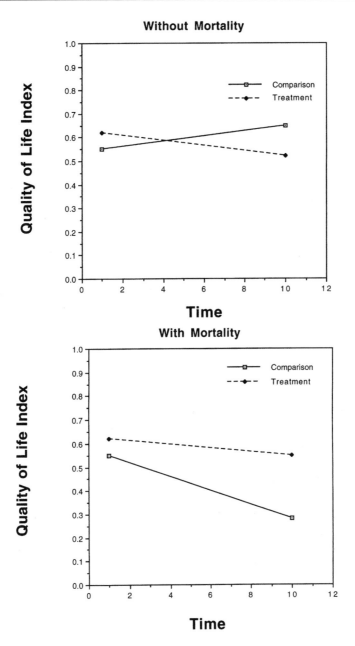

FIG. 2.1.   Outcome of a hypothetical comparison of supportive care and a comparison group in which mortality is eliminated from the analysis (top half) or included in the analysis bottom half). Excluding patients who have died creates bias against the treatment.

died had been removed from the analysis. Thus, the analysis for the comparison group included only the subjects who were initially healthier.

THE PRESENT STUDY

Kaplan, Anderson, and Wingard (1991) reported a study estimating Quality-Adjusted Survival Analysis for men and women. This study demonstrated that the 7-year life expectancy advantage for women is reduced to about 3 years when adjustments for quality of life are made. In other words, the quality adjustment had significantly more impact on women than on men. Analysis suggested that overall health status was better for men until about age 45 and better for women after age 45.

The previous study has several significant limitations. Although the mortality data came from the U.S. population, the morbidity data came from a very small sample of people in the San Diego area. The total sample size for the estimation of quality of life was 867. As a result, the number of individuals in any particular age group was small and potentially unreliable. Another problem is that the analysis was geographically confined to Southern California. It seems unreasonable to estimate U.S. values on the basis of a selected region with limited ethnic variation. A third limitation was that a single measure of health-related quality of life was used. This measure, known as the Quality of Well-Being Scale (Kaplan, 1993), is used in a wide variety of studies. However, many alternative methods are available.

The study reported in this chapter uses data from the United States National Health and Nutrition Examinations Survey (NHANES) Epidemiologic Follow-Up Study. This study is based on a much larger sample size, and it includes more than 12,000 adults. Because the study is based on a representative sample of the U.S. population, generalizations are not restricted to Southern California. Further, the study reports outcomes using the Health Utilities Index (HUI) developed by Torrance and Associates (Torrance, 1987; Torrance & Feeney, 1989.). The HUI is a similar method of providing quality-adjusted survival estimates to that used in the previous study. Variation in the methods helps support the generalizability of the results.

Method

In order to calculate quality-adjusted survival, we used several data sources. First, survival estimates for men and women in the United States were obtained from Vital Statistics of the United States (1985) *Life Tables*. These data are based on the entire U.S. population. Survival estimates described the portion of each birth cohort surviving to particular ages.

National Health and Nutrition Examination Survey (NHANES). Data for the study were obtained from the National Health and Nutrition Examination Survey I Epidemiologic Follow-Up Study (NHANES I). NHANES I was based on a national probability sample of approximately 28,000 persons from the civilian noninstitutionalized population of the United States. Only persons living on reservations for Native Americans were excluded from the sample frame. The survey began in 1971 and was completed in 1974. In order to ensure representation of those at high risk for malnutrition, persons of low income, women of childbearing age, and the elderly were oversampled. Weighting procedures were used to adjust the observations so they would be representative of the U.S. population. Participants in NHANES I were between the ages of 1 and 74 years. The NHANES I sample included 20,729 persons 25–74 years of age, of whom 14,407 (70%) were medically examined.

The analysis reported in this chapter used the NHANES I Epidemiologic Follow-Up Survey (NHEFS), which was conducted between 1982 and 1984. The follow-up study population included the 14,407 participants who were 25 to 74 years of age when first examined in NHANES I. Unlike NHANES I, which had a comprehensive medical examination component, NHEFS is primarily an interview survey that relies on self-reporting of conditions. As of August 1984, 93% of the study population had been successfully located.

Analysis suggests that subjects who were lost to follow-up were more likely to have died than those who were successfully traced. A strong association between smoking and lost-to-follow-up rates indicates that the effects of smoking on mortality, especially at younger ages, should be interpreted with caution. It should be noted, however, that among those age 55 years and over the proportion lost to follow-up is quite small relative to the proportion deceased. Thus, in these age groups there should be relatively little bias as a result of loss to follow-up.

Health Utilities Index–Mark I. The Health Utilities Index-Mark I (Torrance 1987; Torrance & Feeny, 1989) generates scores that can be used to quality adjust survival data. The HUI–Mark I assesses four major concepts of health-related quality of life: physical function, which includes mobility and physical activity; role function, which includes self-care and role activity; social–emotional function, which includes well-being and social activity; and health problems. The concepts and levels of function within the concepts constitute a health status classification scheme. Individuals are categorized into one and only one level within each concept according to their function status at the time the data are collected.

The development of a HUI–Mark I analog using data collected in NHEFS, the NHEFS–HUI, builds on a similar project that was done using data from the National Health Interview Survey. This project developed a 6-step model for conducting retrospective analyses that was used to guide the construction of the health-related quality of life measure used in this analysis to adjust survival data (Erickson et al., 1988; Erickson et al., 1989). Following the steps in this model has been shown to result in a reliable and valid summary of population health status.

Results

In order to estimate Quality-Adjusted Life Expectancy, several calculations were required. First, we estimated life expectancy using the United States *Life Tables*. Next, the NHANES data were broken down by age. The NHANES Epidemiologic Follow-Up Survey includes values for individuals between the ages of 32 and 85. Quality-adjusted survival is the product of the HUI value at each age and the proportion of the population surviving to that age interval. Quality-adjusted survival is shown in one year intervals. Figure 2.2 shows these values for men and women, broken down by age. The mean value for the index for young individuals is near 0.85, whereas those later in the life span have values closer to 0.2. These differences reflect the impact of both death and quality of life.

In order to obtain smooth functions for both men and women, we fit simple polynomials to these curves. For men, a polynomial equation was:

$$\text{Estimated HUI} = 0.55066 + (.0169 \times \text{age}) - (.000259 \times \text{age}^2)$$

For women, the equation was:

$$\text{Estimated HUI} = 0.37293 + (.02126 \times \text{age}) - (.0002737 \times \text{age}^2)$$

The fitted lines are shown graphically in Fig. 2.3. As the figure demonstrates, men score higher on the HUI early in life. However, at about age 48 the curves intersect. Thereafter, the Health Utilities Index is higher for

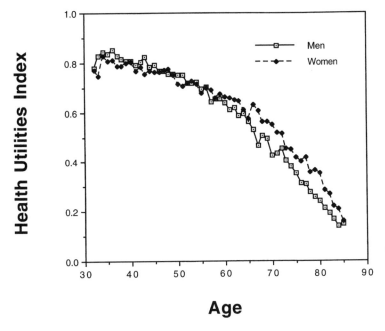

FIG. 2.2. Mortality adjusted HUI by age and sex.

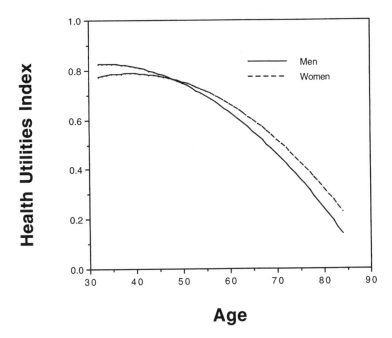

FIG. 2.3. Smoothed and fitted polynomial curves for men and women.

women than it is for men. Overall, women have significantly higher quality of life than do men ($p < .001$), and there is a significant product term for age and gender. Men have significantly higher mortality adjusted quality of life early in the life cycle, while women have higher scores later in the life cycle ($p < .05$).

Figure 2.4 is a different summary of the differences between men and women at different stages of the life cycle. The jagged line shows the raw means. This line was created by subtracting the HUI scores for women from the HUI scores for men at each age. The smooth line on the figure was created by subtracting the differences between the fitted curves at each age. The figure shows the advantage of being male until about age 48, with a female advantage thereafter. Further, the advantage of being female becomes progressively stronger with advancing age.

Using data from the Vital Statistics of the United States, we estimated the current life expectancy for men and women in the NHANES population. The total life expectancy could not be estimated because the NHEFS database did not have information on individuals younger than age 32. The current life expectancy among 32-year-olds was 39.45 years for men and 44.83 years for women. Thus, for 32-year-olds,

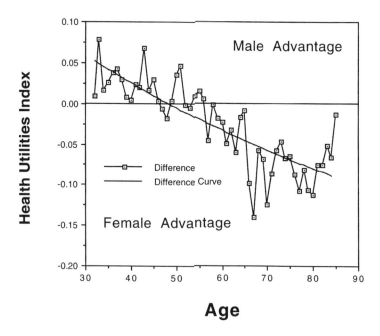

FIG. 2.4. Male minus females differences by age using raw data and fitted curve.

women have a 5.38-year life expectancy advantage. Using quality adjustments, the adjusted life expectancy was 31.8 years for men and 33.1 years for women. In other words, the 5.38-year life expectancy advantage for women reduces to a 1.3-year advantage with adjustments for quality of life.

Discussion

Using data from the National Health and Nutrition Examination Survey, we evaluated differences between the health status for men and women in the United States. These estimates suggest that, on average, women live longer than men. However, during the years that they survive, women experience a lower quality of life than do men. The significant life expectancy advantage for women reduces to a smaller number of years when adjustments for quality of life are made.

This study closely replicates an earlier investigation (Kaplan et al., 1991). However, the earlier study was flawed for several reasons. First, the data were from a single community in California. Further, the earlier study had a small sample and used data from a single quality of life measure. The current study uses a larger sample size and a sample that is representative of the U.S. population. Further, a completely different quality of life index was used. Nevertheless, the results are strikingly similar.

There are many different explanations for these results. In order to evaluate the results, we must first consider the issue of mortality differences. Population statistics show that men are more likely than women to die at all ages throughout the life span. Mortality ratios can be formed by dividing male by female deaths, standardized per 100,000 persons in the population. Figure 2.5 shows these mortality ratios by age. As the figure suggests, the ratio is greater than 1.0 at each age. Even at age 1 year, the ratio is 1.26, suggesting that 1.26 one-year-old males die for each one-year-old female who dies. The peak ratio is during adolescence and early adulthood. Between the ages of 15 and 24, fully 3.1 males die for each female who dies. Thereafter, the ratio falls off as a function of age. Yet even in the 85 year old category, 1.27 males die for each female who dies. It is interesting that our analysis shows there is a male advantage early in the life span, precisely when the male–female mortality ratio is the highest. The reason men have a higher HUI is that men experience higher quality of life during the first four decades of life. Further, the total number of deaths during these decades is very small.

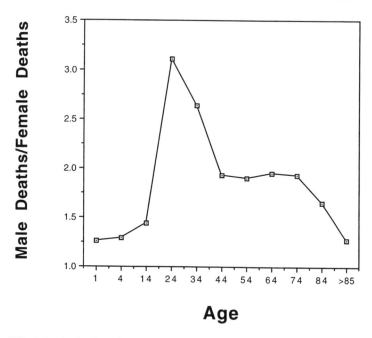

Age

FIG. 2.5.   Male–female mortality ratio by age.

Another explanation for the differences is that men and women are affected by different diseases. Men may make themselves susceptible to a variety of diseases or problems that cause early death. There are differential rates of several causes of death between men and women. Men, for example, are 3.9 times more likely to be victimized by homicide than are women. There are seven causes of death for which men are at least twice as likely to die as women. These are homicide, lung cancer, suicide, chronic obstructive pulmonary disease, accidents, cirrhosis of the liver, and diseases of the heart. Each of these is believed to be related to individual behavior. For example, lung cancer and chronic obstructive pulmonary disease are both primarily caused by smoking cigarettes. Homicide, accidents, and cirrhosis of the liver each have a suspicious association with alcohol use. Suicide is a behavioral act, and the relationship between behavior and heart disease has been discussed previously (Wingard & Cohn, 1990). These data suggest that men are more likely to put themselves at risk for early and sudden death, whereas women live longer to be affected by slow and disabling chronic diseases.

In summary, quantifying health outcomes for men and women can be difficult. Summary measures that emphasize mortality show a strong advantage for women, whereas measures of quality of life suggest some advantages for men. Combined indexes of morbidity show an advantage for men prior to midlife and an advantage for women thereafter. The life expectancy advantage for women is somewhat reduced when there are adjustments for quality of life.

ACKNOWLEDGMENTS

Supported in part by grant PO 1-AR-40423 from the National Institute of Arthritis, Musculoskeletal, and Skin Disorders of the National Institutes of Health. Some of the data presented in this chapter were also published in Kaplan, R. M., & Erickson, P. Gender differences in Quality-adjusted survival using a health-utility index. *American Journal of Preventive Medicine,* 1999, *17*(4).

REFERENCES

Erickson, P., Anderson, J. P., Kendall, E. A., Kaplan, R. M., & Ganiats, T. G. (1988). Using retrospective data for measuring quality of life: National health interview survey data and the quality of well-being scale. *Quality of Life and Cardiovascular Care, 4* (4), 179–184.

Erickson, P., Kendall, E. A., Anderson, J. P., & Kaplan, R. M. (1989). Using composite health status measures to assess the nation's health. *Medical Care, 27* (Suppl. 3), S66–S76.

Feeny, D., Furlong, W., Barr R. D., Torrance, G. W., Rosenbaum, P., & Weitzman, S. (1992). A Comprehensive multiattribute system for classifying the health status of survivors of childhood cancer. *Journal of Clinical Oncology, 10* (6), 923–928.

Feeny, D. H., Torrance, G. W. (1989). Incorporating utility-based quality-of-life assessment measures in clinical trials. Two examples. *Medical Care, 27* (Suppl. 3), S190–S204.

Kaplan, R. M. (1993). Quality of Life Assessment for Cost/Utility Studies in Cancer. *Cancer Treatment Reviews, 19* (Suppl. A), 85–96.

Kaplan, R. M., & Anderson, J. P. (1990). The general health policy model: An integrated approach. In B. Spilker (Ed.), *Quality of Life Assessments in Clinical Trials* (pp. 131–149). New York: Raven.

Kaplan, R. M., Anderson, J. P., & Wingard, D. L. (1991). Gender differences in health-related quality of life. *Health Psychology, 10* (2), 86–93.

Torrance, G. W. (1987). Utility approach to measuring health-related quality of life. *Journal of Chronic Diseases, 40* (6), 593–603.

Torrance, G. W., & Feeny, D. (1989). Utilities and quality-adjusted life years. *International Journal of Technology Assessment in Health Care, 5* (4), 559–575.

Verbrugge, L. M. (1989). The twain meet: Empirical explanations of sex differences in health and mortality. *Journal of Health and Social Behavior, 30* (3), 282–304.

Verbrugge, L. M., & Wingard, D. L. (1987). Sex differentials in health and mortality. *Women and Health, 12* (2), 103–145.

Vital Statistics of the U.S. (1985). *Life tables* (Vol. 2, Sect. 6). United States Department of Health and Human Services (DHHS Publication No. PHS 88-1104). Washington, DC: Government Printing Office.

Wingard, D. L. (1984). The sex differential in morbidity, mortality, and lifestyle. *Annual Review of Public Health, 5*, 433–458.

Wingard, D. L., & Cohn, B. A. (1990). Variations in disease-specific sex morbidity and mortality ratios in the United States. In M. G. Ory & H. R. Warner (Eds.) *Gender, health, and longevity: Multidisciplinary perspectives.* (pp. 25–37). New York: Springer Publishing.

3

Aging Women, Getting Older, Getting Better?

Elaine Leventhal
University of Medicine and Dentistry
Robert Wood Johnson Medical School

Whereas traditional medical research has focused on specific illnesses, geriatrics research, with its life-span perspective, takes a more abstract developmental approach to disease. This life-span perspective is even more important in light of the increasing survival of older Americans, and in particular older women. Until the 1991 NIH Initiative on Women's Health, there had been minimal research on the biological and psychological developmental processes that are important for those diseases that are more common and more serious in women of all ages as well as those that are unique to older women. Such diseases may present atypically, and the resultant diagnostic dilemmas may depend on gender differences in onset and pathophysiology. There are also reported differences in response to and outcomes from treatments in women that may reflect the extrapolation of clinical research findings based solely on research on men to clinical practice in women.

This chapter provides an opportunity to discuss those issues. It is organized to demonstrate gender differences in symptomatology, behavior, and outcome that may affect the physical and psychosocial consequences of "intervention" on health, on the development of frailty or loss of functional independence, and ultimately on the health care system.

First I present a brief discussion of primary aging, secondary aging or senescence, and gender differences in rates of aging. This is followed by an overview of the epidemiological issues such as life expectancy, survival, and mortality and morbidity of the 15 top chronic diseases such as coronary artery disease, stroke, and cancer to help in discussing the phenomenon of "elite" survivors and womens' longevity.

PHYSICAL AGING
AND DISEASE

Many theories have been advanced to account for normal aging; although none has gained universal acceptance, some generalizations are agreed on by most investigators. Growth, development, and senescence are the essence of being alive; they are not static stages in a natural history but represent the continuously changing processes of the life cycle. "Normal" aging, or senescence, is associated with declines in actual numbers of active metabolic cells, receptor numbers, and affinities, and in decrements in the regulation of cellular functions over the life span. Deterioration in overall reserve and declining ability to respond to stress and recover from illness represent losses in regenerative ability and degeneration in function that result eventually in death.

One can think of human aging in terms of multiple biological clocks that start to tick at conception and stop at death. Most cell proliferation peaks around birth, and virtually all growth ceases at puberty. A fraction of prenatal mitotic activity maintains homeostasis in the adult and allows response at times of heightened physiologic demand caused by injury, infection, or other "stress insults." As growth stops, "normal aging" begins. It is characterized by different stem-cell specific as well as gender rates of decline that translate into loss of replicative and repair ability. for some tissues (e.g., the ovary) the aging clock starts in utero. Even though the fetal period is the time of most dramatic growth and cell division, it is also the time of greatest cell loss; the neonate ovary contains 1/1000 of the oocytes that initially populate the fetal gonad.

It is the organism's innate biological plasticity and life-long adaptive history that allows for personalized patterns of accommodation to changes in the body's regulatory system. Thus, aging also produces increasing heterogeneity between individuals as they grow older.

LIFE EXPECTANCY

The chances of reaching the age of 65 have increased from 4% in 1900 to 12% today and are projected to rise to 20% by 2020. Not only are people living longer, but more people are living longer and more of these aging Americans are women. Indeed, women averaged a 2- to 4-year longer life span than men throughout the nineteenth century, and by 1997 the life expectancy of a typical American man was 73.1 years and that of a typical American woman was 79.1 years—though there are clear racial and gender differences in life expectancy, as can be seen in Table 3.1. Mortality also differs by gender and race, with the white male death rate, age adjusted, in 1997 at 573.8 per 100,000 resident population, whereas the white female death rate was 358.8 per 100,000 resident population. For black men, it was 911.9 per 100,000 resident population, and for black women, 545.5 per 100,000 resident population, with a similar gender bias. The five most frequent causes of death are heart disease, stroke (cerebrovascular disease), cancer (lung and breast), and chronic obstructive pulmonary disease (COPD). The gender and racial ratios are presented in Table 3.2, with the contrasts between the genders clearly evident in heart disease and the cancers.

TABLE 3.1
Life Expectancy in Years

Mortality	1970	1980	1989	1990	1996
			Life Expectancy in Years		
Life expectancy at birth	70.8	73.7	75.1	75.4	76.1
Men	67.1	70.0	71.7	71.8	73.1
White	68.0	70.7	72.5	72.7	73.9
Black	60.0	63.8	64.3	64.5	66.1
Women	74.7	77.4	78.5	78.8	79.1
White	75.6	78.1	79.2	79.4	79.7
Black	69.4	73.6	74.9	75.2	76.1

Note. Adapted from U.S. Department of Health and Human Services, Center for Disease Control and Prevention, National Center for Health Statistics, National Vital Statistics System: http://www.cdc.gov/nchswww.

TABLE 3.2
Most Common Chronic Diseases
(Death Rate, Age Adjusted)

Mortality	1970	1980	1989	1990	1991	1993	1995	1997
			Deaths per 100,000 Resident Population					
Heart disease	253.6	202.0	157.5	152.0	148.2			
White male	347.6	277.5	208.7	202.0	196.1	190.3	179.7	168.7
Black male	375.9	327.3	289.7	275.9	272.7	267.9	255.9	236.2
White female	167.8	134.6	106.6	103.1	100.7	99.2	94.9	90.4
Black female	251.7	201.1	175.6	168.1	165.5	165.3	156.3	147.6
Cerebrovascular disease	66.3	40.8	28.3	27.7	26.8			
White male	68.8	41.9	28.4	27.7	26.9	26.8	26.5	25.7
Black male	122.6	77.5	57.3	56.1	54.9	51.9	52.2	48.6
White female	56.2	35.2	24.2	23.8	22.8	22.7	23.1	22.5
Black female	107.9	61.,7	45.5	42.7	41.0	39.9	39.6	37.9
Cancer[a]	129.8	132.8	134.5	135.0	134.5			
White male	154.3	160.5	159.4	160.3	159.5	502.1	452.3	
Black male	198.0	229.9	246.2	248.1	242.4	665.3	584.1	
White female	107.6	107.7	111.1	111.2	111.2	349.9	351.9	
Black female	123.5	129.7	133.5	137.2	136.3	338.5	330.0	
Lung cancer[b]	28.4	36.4	40.8	41.4	41.1			
White male	49.9	58.0	58.3	59.0	58.1	77.2	71.5	
Black male	60.8	82.0	90.8	91.0	88.4	115.7	114.7	
White female	10.1	18.2	25.9	26.5	26.8	43.8	44.2	
Black female	10.9	19.5	26.0	27.5	27.4	46.0	42.9	
Breast cancer[c]	23.1	22.7	23.1	23.1	22.7			
White	23.4	22.8	23.1	22.9	22.5	112.2	115.0	
Black	21.5	23.3	26.5	27.5	27.6	101.0	101.3	
COPD	13.2	15.9	19.6	19.7	20.1			
White male	24.0	26.7	27.2	27.4	27.4	27.2	25.6	
Black male	—	20.9	26.5	26.5	25.9	16.5	16.3	
White female	5.3	9.2	15.2	15.2	16.1	23.3	21.8	
Black female	—	6.3	11.1	10.7	11.3	8.5	8.6	

Note. Adapted from U.S. Department of Health and Human Services, Center for Disease Control and Prevention, National Center for Health Statistics, National Vital Statistics System, 1993.
[a]Death rates for malignant neoplasms of all types.
[b]Cancer of the Respiratory System including lung, bronchus, and trachea.
[c]Female only.

GENDER AND BEHAVIORS

Not only are there differences between the sexes in longevity, but throughout the life span there are many other biological, psychological, and social gender distinctions. For example, in adolescence and early adulthood there are gender differences in diet and exercise practices that reflect current standards of attractiveness and assumptions regarding activities that are life extending. Body building, intense physical exercise, steroid use, and increased caloric intake are adopted for these purposes by men, and fasting and exercise to attain anorectic slimness are frequently adopted by women. These behaviors may persist throughout the life span for women but may decline with age for men.

Complaints and reports of symptoms and the seeking of medical care also reflect concerns about health, illness, and longevity. Such illness behaviors have been described in the medical literature for centuries (Leventhal, 1994). They have been observed more frequently in women than in men and usually are attributed to differences in "socialization." Yet there may be sex specific biological processes such as physical differences in immune resistance or hormonal responsivity, and psychosocial processes such as differential exposure to environmental hazards, and different health habits such as smoking, that are responsible for or that modulate these behaviors for both men and women. This argument has been strengthened as greater numbers of women smoking over the past two to three decades has so increased the incidence of lung cancer (the most common cancer of men) that this disease overtook breast cancer as the most common malignancy for women in 1987. The 1995 age-adjusted incidences of breast cancer were 115.0 per 100,000 resident population in white women, 101.3 per 100,000 resident population in black women. Lung cancer in white women is recorded at a rate of 44.2 per 100,000 resident population, and the rate is 42.9 per 100,000 resident population in blacks (U.S. Department of Health and Human Services, 1998).

WOMEN AND SURVIVAL

The disparity in death rates is dramatic as women outlive their male partners. These older women have more acute and chronic illnesses but die at a lesser rate. The risk for death from coronary heart disease (CHD) is much greater among men, and although overall patterns of morbidity are also similar, clinical pictures vary by sex. Men present most frequently with an acute myocardial infarction, whereas more than half of women with CHD present with symptoms of angina. Silent infarcts are more common in women (Kannel & Abbott, 1984; Kannel & Feinleib, 1972). Women have more hypertension, yet men die more frequently from stroke and hypertensive heart disease. There is a higher incidence of diabetes in women, but their mortality rates are only slightly higher than the rates for men for this disease. Women are commonly thought to be the more frail and less healthy sex, but they live longer than men and many spend a significant portion of their lives alone, coping with the physical as well as the psychosocial changes of isolation, loss, and aging (Stoney et al., 1987).

Thus, although thought to be the "weaker sex," women seem to have a biological and psychological robustness that has provided them with a distinct survival advantage such that throughout the industrialized world there is a gender gap of 4 to 10 years. Women are also less likely to succumb to violent death. They survive "through" the decades that claim their mates from cardiovascular disease and cancer, during which they provide care and succor. But because of their "success," when women develop these illnesses 10 years later they may no longer have social supports or caregivers. Because this survival advantage, which may be related to the cardio-protective effects of estrogen, has been well documented, and although heart disease is the major killer of women and women die as frequently from heart disease as do men, they develop it a decade later. Women have more comorbidity and present with more significant disease (Judge et al., 1991) but are treated less aggressively than men, despite similar complaints of anginal pain and reports of greater functional disability (Khan et al., 1990), and fewer undergo catherization, angioplasty, or coronary artery bypass grafts (CABGs). Although men are twice as likely top undergo catherization, after catherization there are no gender differences in the number of CABG procedures performed (Steingart et al., 1991; Kannel & Abbott, 1987). The barrier is at the referral level (Ayanian & Epstein, 1991; Bickell et al., 1992; Krumholz et al., 1992; Maynard et al., 1992). This "bias" may be unavoidable because diagnosis, usually initiated with exercise stress testing, is less reliable as a predictor of coronary artery disease in women (Barolsky et al., 1979; Detry et al., 1977; Sketch et al., 1975), who may require pharmacological stress testing with agents such as dipyridamole as the first diagnostic measure. Following myocardial infarction (MI), thrombolytic therapy is used less often in women than in men (Maynard et al., 1992). Earlier studies of CABG had operative complications and mortality that appear to have been related to the technical difficulties of operating on small coronary vessels. Increasing surgical skill appears to have obviated this issue, but there is continued concern about the greater mortality risk for women following CABG. This may be related to the greater preoperative risk that accompanies older age; more histories of MIs, hypertension, diabetes mellitus, morbid obesity, unstable angina, congestive heart failure; and perioperative morbidity, generating a referral bias such that patients are evaluated later in the course of disease (Eysmann & Douglas, 1992; Tobin, Wassertheil-Smoller, & Wexler, 1987). These observations raise such questions as: Why is heart disease identified later in course of the illness in women so that women are treated too little and too late? Conversely: Are men treated too early and too vigorously with minimal long-term benefits in terms of quality and reasonable increase in longevity? Or are there psychological barriers to recovery for older women? Table 3.3 presents some findings that are provocative and suggest that older women's health suffers because they may not have access to social supports that facilitate recovery.

If women survive the "common" illnesses such as cardiovascular disease and cancer, they live long enough to develop those devastating illnesses that are unique to the very old: peripheral vascular diseases, geri-

TABLE 3.3
Gender, Myocardial Infarction and Cardiac Surgery:
The Role of "Social" Support

MI Recurrence: Living Alone[a] (n = 202)		
	Men	Women
Hazard ratio	1.24	2.34
Confidence interval (95%)	0.75–2.03	1.17–4.66
Length Of Stay (LOS) in Days: Post Cardiac Bypass Graft Surgery[b] (n = 92)		
Men	14.1	
Women (married)	16.3	
Women (living alone)	26.1	

[a]Adapted from "Living alone after myocardial infarction. Impact on prognosis," by R. B. Case, A. J. Moss, N. Case, M. McDermott, and S. Eberly, 1992, *Journal of the American Medical Association, 267* (4), p. 515–519.
[b]From unpublished raw data, by E. A. Leventhal and R. Contrada, 1991.

atric malignancies, degenerative joint diseases or arthritis that are responsible for pain and immobility, and neurological degenerative diseases such as dementia and movement disorders. Thus, the old-old who reach their eighties or nineties with minimal cardiovascular disease or malignancy are, by definition, "elite" survivors of both biological and chronological aging but may have added years that might not be healthy ones. Throughout the industrialized world the sex ratio of survivors dramatically moves from 1.5:1 women to men over age 65, to 2.5:1 for those over age 85. The mature years are indeed the years of older women.

PSYCHOSOCIAL AGING

In both sexes, there are psychological and social changes that occur across the life span—that is, maladaptive illness and health behaviors, transitions between roles (natural sequences vs. "unnatural" ones, e.g., death of children, parenting parents), premature devastating illness, loss of work-related self-esteem with retirement, and loss of esteem with onset of frailty and dependency. These all have psychological as well as biological implications for the mature woman. Moreover, there are caregiving demands on her from spouse, children, and parents. There are decisions about the need for institutionalization for those she cannot care for, and there is coping with dependency behaviors and dealing with depression in her family or in herself, or both. There are health and risk behaviors practiced earlier in life that have implications for adaptation to serious disease and dysfunction that occur in the mature years. Some of these behaviors specifically put older women at risk for serious disease.

We have some inkling into the biological, "hormonal" elements of the protective aspects of gender and when and how they are lost, as well as some ideas about how they can be modulated. But less is understood about the gender specific behaviors that may relate to longevity, in particular, strategies that may be disease preventatives. Are different interventions needed at different times in the life span, and are there *optimally* effective times at which to initiate interventions? How reasonable is it to expect that diseases are reversible, even very late in life?

What permits women to survive despite an apparent greater degree of frailty has long been a topic of debate. They have a profusion of symptoms from chronic debilitating diseases yet appear to be protected from more deadly illnesses because of their gender specific biology (Stoney et al., 1987). At certain periods in their lives such as menopause, do they report more symptoms and make greater use of the health care system and thus become perceived by investigators as more ill than men? The literature consistently reports that women have lower mortality rates yet more illness. These findings hold with the exclusion of obstetrical and gynecological conditions (Nathanson, 1977). We now need to ask whether there are behavioral models that predict gender differences in health behavior.

AGING, GENDER, AND HEALTH BEHAVIOR

My colleagues and I have conducted several studies that have been directed at examining age and gender effects on illness behaviors. In our early work we asked volunteers to respond to hypothetical health and illness scenarios in various community settings (Leventhal & Prohaska, 1986; Prohaska, Keller, Leventhal, & Leventhal, 1985; Prohaska, Leventhal, Leventhal, & Keller, 1987), and in 1987 we completed a longitudinal investigation of symptomatology, perceptions of health, and utilization of the health care system in a sample of 351 middle aged to elderly (45 to 93 years) community-dwelling respondents. The study sample was recruited from a University Hospital General Internal Medicine and Geriatrics Clinic. Because there were many diseases represented in this patient population, an illness burden index was generated from a comprehensive review of each subject's chart. The score represented a 5-point ranking of diseases by severity, chronicity, and potential for functional compromise and was used as an evaluation of the impact of chronic illness status on a host of health-related behaviors and perceptions. subjects were interviewed five times, with four interviews following the baseline, at 3-month intervals. The interview covered medical history, current symptoms, interpretation of the most significant symptoms, and the unfolding of the most significant symptom episode including the emotional distress and coping responses it provoked and whether it led to the use of health care. Subjects were asked about the presence of major and minor life events, the perceptions that events and age could contribute to the onset of illness, and a number of personality factors. The gender and age differences observed in these data were very similar to those reported from the National Health Survey conducted by the National Center for Health

Statistics (1985). Because our study examined the interpretations and presentations of symptoms in the clinical setting, we were able to examine factors that might account for gender effects. First, we were encouraged to find that subject readily attached disease-related symptoms to specific disease entities whereas ambiguous symptoms were frequently attributed to stress provoked by major or minor life events as mentioned in Baumann, Cameron, Zimmerman, and Leventhal (1989). This allowed us to look at the relationship of age and gender to these different symptom types.

We found significant sex and age differences in illness burden and number of symptoms reported. Although illness burden increased with age for both sexes, there was a crossover with increasing age for men. Whereas younger women had higher illness burdens than did younger men, men over 75 years of age had higher illness burdens and more severe illnesses than did the women of similar age. These differences produced a significant sex by age interaction [$t(348) = 3.22, p < .001$] and a significant contrast in the oldest old group; that is, the illness burden was greater for the oldest old men than for the oldest old women [$t(319) = 4.21, p < .0001$].

Gender differences in symptom reporting paralleled the differences in illness burden. The total number of symptoms increased with age for both sexes, and women had a greater total number of symptoms than did men [$t(337) = -5.57, p < .0001$], with a significant rise for the middle aged women—an effect not seen in men, probably consistent with menopausal symptoms. But the escalation of symptoms with age was significantly greater in the men.

We are now collecting longitudinal data on another community-based sample. This group of 838 subjects was first recruited in 1991. The 504 women and 334 men range in age from 49 to 93, with a mean of 73 years. They are being monitored for 10 years, which will provide an excellent opportunity to follow the effects of acute and chronic illness, age, gender, affect, and social support network on morbidity and mortality. This sample also constitutes a unique clinical "laboratory" in which to discover whether it can be demonstrated that these factors act as moderators of immune function and impact on such morbidities as infections and malignancy and, thus, on mortality.

We challenged a subset of 280 subjects with various antigenic stimuli: influenza and tetanus vaccines and KLH, a benign neo-antigen. We measured both cellular and humoral antibody responses. We also asked subjects to estimate how "strong" their immune system was.

The first set of analyses looked at similar variables that were described for the first community study. As can be seen in Table 3.4 there were no

TABLE 3.4
Gender and Age Differences in
Illness Perceptions and Behaviors

	Women			Men		
Age in years	≤ 69	70–79	≥ 80	≤ 69	70–79	≥ 80
Acute illness	.35	.29	.28	.28	.26	.23
	(.53)	(.54)	(.48)	(.48)	(.50)	(.58)
Illness burden	144.72	166.50	187.19	141.44	173.18	194.21
	(94.13)	(99.44)	(105.65)	(113.35)	(110.27)	(98.53)
Symptoms[b,c]	3.28	4.61	4.95	3.53	3.24	4.66
	(3.31)	(3.75)	(4.20)	(3.35)	(2.57)	(3.51)
Severity of recent illness[a]	3.69	3.58	3.46	3.36	3.54	3.26
	(.91)	(1.19)	(1.25)	(.86)	(1.10)	(1.13)
Worry about illnesses[a]	1.65	1.84	1.65	1.57	1.60	1.47
	(.88)	(.99)	(.92)	(.81)	(.88)	(.83)
Activities of daily living[a]	1.59	1.78	2.22	1.38	1.68	1.98
	(.78)	(.77)	(1.01)	(.50)	(.74)	(.79)
Seeking medical care for recent illness[b]	.43	.55	.73	.31	.46	.62
	(.50)	(.50)	(.45)	(.47)	(.50)	(.49)

Note. SD in parentheses.
[a]5-point scales.
[b]Dichotomous scale.
[c]Based on 363 respondents.

differences in illness burden by gender, but the burden by age interaction was significant ($p < .001$). The interaction by sex and age with illness burden was insignificant. The total number of symptoms reported was the same for both men and women; however, the oldest respondents experienced more symptoms than did the youngest group of subjects ($p < .01$). There were no significant gender by age by symptoms interactions. The findings on perception of immune strength were interesting. Men perceive their immune competency to be slightly stronger than do women ($p < .06$), whereas the younger subjects (up to age 79) believe their immune system is more vigorous than do subjects over age 80 ($p < .003$). There were no second order interactions, and marital status appeared to play no role.

There were no age effects for new onset of diseases in the 3 months preceding the interview, including acute illnesses, infections, gastrointestinal upsets, organic heart disease, or other chronic diseases or injuries.

However, the sum of acute illnesses was higher in women ($p < .07$), and there were more infections reported by the women ($p < .005$). Women worry more about getting ill ($p < .006$), as do the oldest subjects ($p < .05$), but there was no interaction among worry about becoming sick, age, and gender. Women are more likely to report more impairment from illness in their performance of activities of daily living than men ($p < .05$), but illness significantly impairs the oldest subjects with the effect linearly related to age ($p < .00001$) and with gender playing no role. When sick, the oldest subjects seek medical care ($p < .001$) regardless of gender. This finding holds in a regression analysis predicting care seeking, controlling for illness severity, gender, and age. In the regression, age was the most significant predictor of care seeking ($p < .0001$), followed by severity ($p < .00001$) and then gender ($p < .09$). Somatic depression increased with the age of the subjects, whereas somatic anxiety decreased. State anxiety was higher in men than women ($p > .03$), whereas cognitive anxiety, somatic depression ($p > .009$), and somatic anxiety were reported more by women ($p > .006$).

Immune Stimulation

Analyses of the immune challenge data presented in Table 3.5, shows that men have higher baseline titers of tetanus antibody than do women ($p < .001$), and mount a more vigorous response to the antigenic challenge than do women ($p < .001$). When examined by age group, the middle sample (age 70 to 79) had a higher baseline titer than did the most elderly ($p < .034$) and after the antigenic challenge had a more vigorous response ($p < .02$). Using influenza vaccine all subjects had high baseline titers, and after 2 weeks following immunization those under age 69 had the highest response titers ($p < .001$). KLH, a nonedible but benign Pacific mollusk, has been used widely as a neo-antigen demonstrating anergic ability to respond to foreign protein. In this sample all subjects mounted an antibody response to the antigen, with the largest response seen in the 65- to 74-year-olds. When analyzed by gender the patterns are interesting. Young and middle aged persons gave a vigorous response that was greater, although not significant given the sample size, than for women at age 55 to 64, whereas men age 64 to 74 were more responsive.

There are gender effects in cell proliferative responses, as shown in Table 3.6. Women show a higher stimulation index with concanavalin A (ConA) at dilutions of .5 and 2.5 ($p < .033$). There were no ConA age effects and no gender effects with phytohemagglutinin (PHA), although the PHA stimulation index was highest for the oldest subjects ($p < .06$), as was the ConA stimulation index ($p < .10$).

TABLE 3.5
Gender and Age Differences in Antibody Response

	Women (n = 126)			Men (n = 75)		
Age in years	≤ 69	70–79	≥ 80	≤ 69	70–79	≥80
Flu titer: baseline	14.05	14.30	13.93	13.70	14.24	14.29
	(1.54)	(1.16)	(1.36)	(1.81)	(2.29)	(1.16)
Flu titer: 2 weeks post	15.71	15.24	14.56	15.95	15.14	14.88
	(1.63)	(1.29)	(1.31)	(1.15)	(1.93)	(1.45)
Tetanus titer: baseline	5.08	5.44	4.33	9.70	10.34	4.12
	(6.46)	(6.48)	(5.84)	(6.84)	(5.10)	(6.05)
Tetanus titer: 2 weeks post	5.3	5.85	4.37	9.99	10.99	4.38
	(6.54)	(6.42)	(5.89)	(6.84)	(5.10)	(6.05)
KLH titer: baseline	6.97	6.02	5.00	4.60	6.76	7.00
	(5.19)	(5.07)	(5.48)	(5.30)	(5.20)	(5.56)
KLH titer: 2 weeks post	7.71	6.61	6.07	5.95	8.16	8.13
	(5.10)	(5.13)	(5.81)	(5.18)	(4.92)	(5.26)

Note. SD in parentheses.

TABLE 3.6
Gender and Age Differences in
Cellular Proliferative Response

	Women (n = 131)			Men (n = 76)		
Age in years	≤ 69	70–79	≥ 80	≤ 69	70–79	≥ 80
PHA 2.5	551.53	561.64	578.07	524.62	531.03	558.06
	(317.52)	(430.36)	(448.83)	(255.22)	(367.97)	(298.60)
PHA 5.0	780.76	819.02	898.74	750.81	755.21	729.59
	(429.56)	(612.13)	(722.49)	(368.08)	(523.73)	(368.17)
ConA 2.5	430.66	394.95	456.85	438.10	378.68	431.12
	(397.19)	(256.45)	(249.17)	(200.13)	(229.10)	(244.93)
ConA 5.0	512.10	460.44	550.22	490.62	445.24	487.29
	(431.30)	(319.33)	(289.12)	(218.69)	(274.78)	(287.02)

Note. SD in parentheses.

For all subjects, negative affect affected only tetanus titers. Depression was highly correlated with a suppression of antibody response, anxiety did not have a similar effect, and there were no gender effects. The impact of the negative affect appears to be related to chronic exposure to depressed affect.

Emotional State

When asked about current illnesses, women reported more morbidity ($p < .015$), were more worried about getting sick ($p < .006$), had greater impairment per illness ($p < .003$), and made greater use of health care ($p < .037$). Women reported more somatic symptoms of depression than did men ($p < .006$), as well as more cognitive ($p < .001$) and more somatic ($p < .09$) symptoms of anxiety than did the men. It is also interesting to note that there were significant relationships between affect and age. The somatic symptoms of depression were more common in the oldest subjects, whereas the cognitive ($p < .10$) and somatic ($p < .001$) symptoms of anxiety were more common in the younger subjects.

There were no gender differences in ratings of self-assessed health; however, there was a monotonic decline in self-assessed health by age ($p < .003$). In addition, separated or divorced participants reported better assessments of health did married, widowed, or cohabiting participants ($p < .008$). Women were more likely to attribute illness to stress than were men, regardless of age ($F = 10.760, p < .001$).

Discussion

Women have a selective advantage despite a life-long history of body awareness, symptoms, and utilization of the health care system. I suggest that women learn coping skills such that as primary caregivers in most family groups, they are alert to illness and prepared to provide care for others while also being sensitive to their own symptomatology. They make use of the health care system. They utilize illness and wellness behaviors to maintain their own health despite gender biases in the care system because they are more vigilant and open to seeking care (Cameron, Leventhal, Leventhal, & Schaefer, 1993; Leventhal, Leventhal, Schaefer, & Easterling, 1993). Social expectations about behavior and health of women determine what they anticipate from being ill, in terms of clinical treatment as well as how they are treated. The long-term implications of the immune findings remain unclear because there has been no mortality as yet in the immunization subset subjects.

REFERENCES

Ayanian, J. Z., & Epstein, A. M. (1991). Differences in the use of procedures between women and men hospitalized for coronary heart disease. *New England Journal of Medicine, 325*(4), 221–225.

Barolsky, S. M., Gilbert, C. A., Garuqui, A., Nutter, D. O., & Schlant, R. C. (1979). Differences in electrocardiographic response to exercise of women and men: A non-Bayesian factor. *Circulation, 60*(5), 1021–1027.

Baumann, L., Cameron, L. D., Zimmerman, R., & Leventhal, H. (1989). An experiment in common sense: Education at blood pressure screening. *Patient Education and Counseling, 14*, 53–67.

Bicknell, N. A., Pieper, K. S., Lee, K. L., Mark, D. B., Glower, D. D., Pryor, D. B., & Califf, R. M. (1992). Referral patterns for coronary artery disease: Gender bias or good clinical judgement? *Annals of Internal Medicine, 116*(10), 791–797.

Cameron, L., Leventhal, E. A., Leventhal, H., & Schaefer, P. (1993). Symptom representations and affects as determinants of care-seeking. *Health Psychology, 12*, 171–199.

Case, R. B., Moss, A. J., Case, N., McDermott, M., & Eberly, S. (1992). Living alone after myocardial infarction. Impact on prognosis. *Journal of the American Medical Association, 267* (4), 515–519.

Detry, J. M., Kapita, B. M., Cosyns, J., Sottiaux, B., Brasseur, L. A., & Rousseau, M. F. (1977). Diagnostic value of history and maximal exercise electrocardiography in men and women suspected of coronary heart disease. *Circulation, 56*(5), 756–761.

Eysmann, S. B., & Douglas, P. S. (1992). Reperfusion and revascularization strategies for coronary artery disease in women. *JAMA, 268*(14), 1903–1907.

Judge, K. W., Pawitan, Y., Caldwell, J., Gersh, B. J., & Kennedy, J. W. (1991). Congestive heart failure symptoms in patients with preserved left ventricular systolic function: Analysis of the CASS registry. *Journal of the American College of Cardiology, 18*(2), 377–82.

Kannel, W. B., & Abbott, R. D. (1984). Incidence and prognosis of unrecognized myocardial infarction: An update on the Framingham Study. *New England Journal of Medicine, 311*, 1144–1147.

Kannel, W. B., & Feinleib, M. (1972). National history of angina pectoris in the Framingham study: Prognosis and survival. *American Journal of Cardiology, 29*(2), 154–63.

Khan, S. S., Nessim, S., Gray, R., Czer, L. S., Chaux, A., & Matloff, J. (1990). Increased mortality of women in coronary artery bypass surgery: Evidence for referral bias. *Annals of Internal Medicine, 112*, 561–567.

Krunholz, H. M., Pasternak, R. C., Weinstein, M. C., Friesinger, G. C., Ridker, P. M., Tosteson, A. N., & Goldman, L. (1992). Cost effectiveness of thrombolytic therapy with streptokinase in elderly patients with suspected acute myocardial infarction. *New England Journal of Medicine, 327*(1), 7–13.

Leventhal, E. A. (1994). Gender and aging: Women and their aging. In D. M. Reddy & V. J. Adesso, Flemming (Eds.), *Psychological perspectives on women's health* (pp. 11–35). New York: Hemisphere Publishing.

Leventhal, E. A., & Contrada, R. (1991). Unpublished raw data.

Leventhal, E. A., Leventhal, H., Schaefer, P., & Easterling, D. (1993). Conservation of energy, uncertainty reduction and swift utilization of medical care among the elderly. *Journal of Gerontology, 48* (2), 78–86.

Leventhal, E. A., & Prohaska, T. (1986). Age, symptom interpretation and health behavior. *Journal of the American Geriatric Society, 34* (3) 185–191.

Maynard, C., Litwin, P. E., Martin, J. S., & Weaver, W. D. (1992). Gender differences in the treatment and outcome of acute myocardial infarction. Results from the Myocardial Infarction Triage and Intervention Registry. *Archives of Internal Medicine, 152*(5), 972–976.

Nathanson, C. A. (1977). Sex, illness and medical care: A review of data, theory, and method. *Social Science and Medicine, 11*, 13–25.

National Center for Health Statistics (1982). Current estimates from the National Health Interview Survey, 10(150). DHHS Publication No. (PHS) 95-1414, Hyattsville, MD: R. A. Cohen, J. F. Van Nostrand.

National Center for Health Statistics. (1998) GMWK 293. Age Adjusted Death Rates for 72 Selected Causes, US 1979–1997. http://www.cdc.gov/nchswww/data/hus98.pdf.

Prohaska, T. R., Keller, M. L., Leventhal, E. A., & Leventhal, H. (1987). The impact of symptoms and aging attributions on emotions and coping. *Health Psychology, 6* (6), 495–514.

Prohaska, T. R., Leventhal, E. A., Leventhal, H., & Keller, M. (1985). Health practices and illness cognition in young, middle aged, and elderly adults. *Journal of Gerontology, 40* (5), 569–578.

Sketch, M. H., Mohiuddin, S. M., Lynch, J. D., Zencka, A. E., & Runco, V. (1975). Significant sex differences in the correlation of electrocardiographic exercise testing and coronary arteriograms. *American Journal of Cardiology, 36*(2), 169–173.

Steingart, R. M., Packer, M., Hamm, P., Coglianese, M. E., Gersh, B., Geltman, E. M., Sollano, J., Katz, S., Moye, L., Basta, L. L., et al., (1991). Sex differences in the management of coronary artery disease: Survival and Ventricular Enlargement Investigators. *New England Journal of Medicine, 325*(4), 226–230.

Stoney, C. M., Davis, M. C., & Matthews, K. A. (1987). Sex differences in physiological responses to stress and in coronary heart disease: A causal link? *Psychophysiology, 24*(2), 127–31.

Tobin, J. N., Wassertheil-Smoller, S., & Wexler, J. P. (1987). Sex bias in considering coronary bypass surgery. *Annals of Internal Medicine, 107,* 19–25.

U.S. Department of Health and Human Services. (1995). Center for Disease Control and Prevention, National Center for Health Statistics, National Vital Statistics System. Washington, DC: U.S. Government Printing Office.

Vital and Health Statistics. (1995). Trends in the health of older Americans. United States, 1994, Series 3: *Analytic and Epidemiological Studies,* No. 30. Hyattsville, MD: U.S. Government Printing Office.

4

Menopause as a Turning Point in Midlife

Karen A. Matthews
Rena R. Wing
Lewis H. Kuller
Elaine N. Meilahn
Jane F. Owens
University of Pittsburgh

A popular concept of midlife is that it is a critical turning point, a time of abrupt and drastic change. Women are thought to be particularly vulnerable to experiencing midlife as a turning point because of the menopause. Contemporary writers liken the menopause to a tragedy or to a battle. Wilson (1966), the author of *Feminine Forever*, wrote that the menopause led "to a cow-like state, in which women experience the world through a grey veil and they live as harmless, docile creatures missing most of life's values" (p. 347). Sheehy (1991) in *The Silent Passage* likened her menopause to being in a battle. She noted that "a little grenade went off in my brain. A flash, a shock, a sudden surge of electric current that whizzed through my head and left me feeling shaken, nervous, off balance. . . . In the months that followed, I sometimes felt outside my body" (pp. 14–15).

Given these cultural stereotypes and writings by prominent authors, it is not surprising that women expect the menopause to be a negative experience. In the Healthy Women Study, a longitudinal study of the menopause in over 500 initially premenopausal women, subjects expected that the menopause would generally be a negative psycological experience. In addition, they thought that the menopause would have no important or long-lasting effects and would be easier to handle if they had knowledge about it.

In this chapter we suggest that menopause is a major turning point for women, but not in the way these women in the Healthy Women Study or our cultural stereotypes suggest. First, although contemporary mid-dleaged women expect that women experience negative emotions during the menopause, data suggest that this myth is not true. Second, although contemporary middleaged women expect no permanent or long-term biological changes because of the menopause, in fact there appear to be enormously important, permanent changes in terms of altered trajectory of cardiovascular risk. Third, the biological changes might be prevented or at least attenuated by changes in health behaviors prior to or during the menopause. Stated differently, it would be helpful for women to have information about the menopause so that they can promote the highest quality of life. Prior to reviewing the data relevant to each of these issues, we review basic information about the menopause and when it occurs.

WHAT IS THE MENOPAUSE?

During the reproductive years, the hypothalamus releases a hormone called gonadotrophin releasing hormone (GnRH), which is transported to the anterior pituitary. There it stimulates the release of follicle-stimulating hormone (FSH) and luteinizing hormone (LH), which act on the ovary to stimulate growth of the ovarian follicles, induce ovulation, and initiate formation of the corpus luteum. FSH and LH stimulate the production of estradiol, progesterone, and inhibin by the follicle, which act as feedback signals to the brain and pituitary (Speroff, Glass, & Kase, 1983).

After years of aging, regardless of number of pregnancies or use of oral contraceptives, the number of oocytes responsive to FSH and LH declines. In response to the lack of responsiveness, FSH and LH levels increase to attempt to stimulate the growth of ovarian follicles. The follicles, however, release less estrogen and progestin into the circulation, which act as feedback signals to the brain and pituitary to release even more FSH and LH. Eventually there is a complete depletion of responsive oocytes, and the cessation of menses and onset of menopause occur. Diagnosis of menopause is made when FSH is elevated and estradiol level is low ($< 30\ pg/ml$).

On average menopause occurs around the age of 51 (McKinlay, Bifano, & McKinlay, 1985). At the turn of the century, the average age of death and menopause was roughly coincident (see Fig. 4.1). If female children survived the first year of life, they had about 5 years to live beyond the menopause in 1900; in 1982, they had about 27 years beyond the menopause (Table 4.1). Thus, women can expect to live almost one half their adult years beyond the menopause.

MENOPAUSE AND RISK FOR CORONARY HEART DISEASE

The major cause of death in women is coronary heart disease (CHD; Wegner, Speroff, & Packard, 1993), and it has long been thought that the menopause increases risk for CHD. Gender differences are very substantial in midlife in all westernized countries. Tracey (1966) reported that the magnitude of gender differences in risk for CHD peak around the time of the menopause and then decline. He suggested that the reason for the decline after the menopause was related to women's loss of ovarian function. In the Framingham Heart Study, postmenopausal women compared

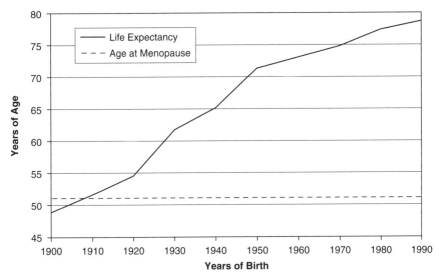

FIG. 4.1. Expectation of life (in years) at birth for U.S. women and average age of menopause (U.S. Bureau of the Census, 1975, 1994).

TABLE 4.1
Years of Life Expectancy of Those Surviving First Year of Life

| | | | Year | | |
Gender	1900	1949	1959	1969	1982
Female	56.1	71.8	73.9	75.0	78.0
Male	54.4	66.7	67.8	67.6	70.8

Note. Data are from the U. S. Bureau of the Census (1984).

to premenopausal women of similar age groups had higher rates of car-diovascular disease (Kannel, Hjortland, McNamara, & Gordon, 1976). However, all data are not uniform in suggesting that menopause confers extra risk. Several studies that statistically controlled for risk factors for cardiovascular disease in comparisons of rates of pre- and post-menopausal women did not find that an early natural menopause increased risk (Colditz et al., 1987).

It is difficult to know how to interpret these latter studies because the age at menopause is not a random event and is earlier among women with high levels of certain risk factors. Perhaps most relevant is that smokers have an earlier menopause than do nonsmokers and that smoking is a risk factor for CHD in women (Willett et al., 1983). In addition, stress may lead to an earlier menopause in women with irregular menses as they approach the menopause (Bromberger et al., 1997), and stress plays a role in triggering CHD events (e.g., Cottington, Matthews, Talbott, & Kuller, 1980). Therefore, it is difficult to disentangle whether or not menopause-related changes in ovarian function do lead to altered risk or whether early menopause is simply a marker of an individual with high levels of other cardiovascular risk factors.

RATIONALE FOR AND DESCRIPTION OF THE HEALTHY WOMEN STUDY

Because of these types of data, we decided to study the natural history of the menopause to observe if and why behavioral and biological risk fac-tors for cardiovascular disease might change during the menopausal tran-sition. We also collected basic descriptive data on the menopausal experience owing to the fact that most studies of the menopause had been flawed because they focused on women seeking treatment for menopausal symptoms, were cross-sectional in design, and often used age as a proxy for the menopause.

In 1983–1984 we recruited 541 women in Allegheny County, Pennsylvania, from a list of women who had driver's licenses. Eligibility criteria included being between the ages of 42 and 50, free of chronic conditions requiring medications that would influence tracking of biological risk factors (e.g., lipid-lowering agents, hormone replacement therapy); below 100 mmHg in diastolic blood pressure; and premenopausal, defined as having menstruated within the last 3 months. Sixty percent of eligible women volunteered to be in the study, with volunteers being better educated than nonvolunteers (Matthews, Meilahn, et al., 1989).

Women were evaluated at study entry after an overnight fast to determine their levels of blood pressure, lipids and lipoproteins, and fasting and 2-hour postglucose load for insulin and glucose; body mass index; dietary intake via a 24-hour food recall by a trained nurtritionist; health behaviors; medical and gynecological history; attitudes toward the menopause; personality characteristics on standardized instruments; and menopausal symptoms (see Matthews, Kelsey, Meilahn, Kuller, & Wing, 1989, for details of measures). Women were re-evaluated within 3 years of entering the study and at years 1, 2, 5, and 8 after the cessation of menses. The evaluation was similar to the baseline evaluation, although new measures were added, such as hemostatic measures (Meilahn, Kuller, Matthews, & Kiss, 1992) and cardiovascular responses to acute laboratory stressors.

Now we are ready to describe our results in relation to women's expectations about the effects of the menopause and its possible effect on risk for CHD. We begin with the possible emotional consequences of the menopause for CHD risk.

Are There Emotional Consequences of the Menopause?

Negative emotional states are linked to cardiovascular disease risk (see Adler & Matthews, 1994 for a summary of current data). Clinical ratings of potential for hostility based on Type A interview responses were significant predictors of CHD morbidity and mortality in the Multiple Risk Factor Intervention Trial and Western Collaborative Group Study data (Dembroski, MacDougall, Costa & Grandits, 1989; Houston, Chesney,

Black, Cates, & Hecker, 1992). Hostile attitudes predicted CHD or total mortality in three of six prospective studies reviewed by Smith (1992). Anxiety scores were related to increases in women's blood pressure and 20-year incidence of hypertension in men (Adler & Matthews, 1994). Depression appears to be a risk factor for complications post-myocardial infarction (Frasure-Smith, Lesperance, & Talajic, 1995). Vital exhaustion, characterized by a feeling of being dejected, increased irritability, and excess fatigue, predicted 4-year incidence of angina and nonfatal myocardial infarction, but not death (Appels & Mulder, 1989).

Recall that women in the Healthy Women Study expected that the menopause would be a negative psychological experience. More specifically, 68% of the subjects thought women would be irritable during the menopause and 82% thought women would get depressed during the menopause. To the extent that this is true, the menopause would not only decrease their sense of well-being but also increase the level of their behavioral risk factors for cardiovascular disease.

Given these negative expectations, do women become anxious, depressed, and hostile during the menopause? The answer is clearly no. We compared the changes from study entry to re-evaluation in scores from standardized measures of these traits or symptoms in the first 69 women who ceased cycling for one year and did not use hormone replacement therapy with the changes in scores of age-matched premenopausal women (Matthews et al., 1990). Postmenopausal women did not report more depressive symptoms or distress, or even total number of menopausal symptoms, than did premenopausal women. These findings are consistent with population-based studies of depressive symptoms and psychiatric disorder from Sweden, Canada, and New England (Hallstrom & Samuelsson, 1985; Kaufert, Gilbert, & Tate, 1992; McKinlay, McKinlay, & Brambilla, 1987).

Why did women expect the menopause to be a distasteful experience, even though the expectation appears to be totally unfounded? Some women did become depressed during the menopausal transition because of stressful life events coincided with the menopause (Bromberger & Matthews, 1996). Some women might have been vulnerable because of their pre-existing traits. Indeed, among women in the Healthy Women Study, those who reported at study entry being anxious, passive, and pessimistic about life had a higher level of depressive symptoms, adjusted for baseline symptoms, than did their counterparts (Bromberger & Matthews, 1996). Perhaps women incorrectly inferred that the menopause was accounting for the depressive symptoms, rather than the stressful events or their personal predispositions, which rendered them vulnerable to depression.

Are There Important Biological Changes During the Menopause?

Women in the Healthy Women Study did not expect important changes to occur during the menopause. At study entry, 60% thought the menopause would not change women in any important way. Available data relative to the effects of menopause on CHD risk come from two types of studies: natural history studies of the changes in risk owing to the menopause, and add-back studies in which hormone replacement therapy (HRT) is given to postmenopausal women, with the inference being that the effects of HRT are similar to those of natural estrogens in younger women. From these types of studies, it is clear that selected cardiovascular risk factors do change in an adverse way during the menopausal transition. We discuss briefly the effects of estrogen exposure via HRT or estrogen deprivation via menopause on lipids, behavior of the vessel wall, blood flow, and clotting factors, as well as on the sympathetic nervous system's response to stress.

Lipids and Lipoproteins. It is generally thought that the favorable effect of estrogen on CHD is primarily owing to lipid metabolism. Indeed, that assertion is consistent with findings from the Healthy Women Study and from the Postmenopausal Estrogen Progestin Investigation (Writing Group for the PEPI Trial, 1995). PEPI is a clinical trial that evaluated the effects of four combinations of hormone preparations on four major risk factors: high density lipoprotein (HDL) cholesterol, systolic blood pressure, fibrinogen, and insulin levels. The results showed that relative to placebo, estrogen replacement therapy alone substantially raised HDL cholesterol, compared to placebo, with the addition of progestins causing a more moderate increase.

Regarding the Healthy Women Study, among the first 69 women who became postmenopausal and were not using estrogen replacement therapy, the increase in low density lipoprotein (LDL) cholesterol was substantially higher than that of age-matched premenopausal women; postmenopausal women on HRT did not show such a great increase (Matthews, Meilahn, et al., 1989). There was also a modest decline in HDL total, and HDL-2. Further follow-up of the sample shows the same pattern of results with LDL increasing and HDL-2 declining across the perimenopausal transition (Matthews, Wing, Kuller, Meilahn, & Plantinga, 1994).

The effects of the transition were not uniform, however. There was substantial variability according to the women's psychosocial characteristics. The change in LDL was most substantial among women who reported at study entry being high in depressive symptoms, menopausal symptoms, and perceived stress. The decline in HDL was most substantial among women who reported at study entry being high in expressing anger outwardly, discussing anger, and experiencing anger frequently. These two clusters of characteristics—reports of negative symptoms and mode of anger expression—are worthy of further investigation in understanding how psychosocial factors may affect change in women's lipids over time.

Endothelial Function. Another proposed mechanism for the protection afforded by estrogen is its favorable effect on the vessel wall of the coronary arteries. It used to be thought that the endothelium, or vessel wall, was passive, like wallpaper. Now it is recognized that it is biologically active and is responsive to local biochemical events, such as release of nitric oxide or prostacycline, which leads to vasodilatation. The endothelium has been studied in the catheterization laboratory using pharmacologic probes, such as acetylcholine. In healthy coronary arteries, acetylcholine is an endothelium-dependent vasodilator manifested by increased coronary blood flow and decreased resistance. In diseased coronary arteries, that is, those narrowed with plaque, there is paradoxical vasoconstriction manifested by decreased blood flow and increased resistance.

Reis et al. (1994) tested the effects of in vivo infusion of ethinyl estradiol into the large coronary arteries of women referred to angiography. Prior to ethinyl estradiol infusion, 8 of 15 women had a normal response to acetycholine, showing an average increase in flow of 44%, whereas 7 showed an abnormal response with an average decline in flow of 33%. After ethinyl estradiol infusion, women with the normal response showed an average increase in flow of 50%, whereas the women with the previous abnormal vasoconstriction showed no change in flow. Similarly, women with the abnormal response to acetycholine increased in resistance in the coronary arteries by almost 40%, whereas after estradiol infusion they showed a nonsignificant decline of 8% in resistance. This study suggests that estrogens can attenuate the effects of abnormal endothelium and change the rate of blood flow. The biochemical mechanisms underlying these effects are not clear, but two candidates are direct effects of estrogen on arterial myoctyes or production of endothelium-derived vasoactive intermediates such as nitric oxide.

Clotting System. One of the many measures of the activity of the clotting system is fibrinogen, an acute phase reactant. Fibrinogen is an important risk factor for CHD and confers about the same risk as lipids. Its role is also controversial because it is not clear if it is a marker of response to endothelial injury or in fact plays a pathogenic role in atherosclerosis. In PEPI (1995), fibrinogen was significantly lowered by estrogen replacement therapy, compared to placebo. In the Healthy Women Study, postmenopausal women not on HRT had elevated levels of fibrinogen, compared to premenopausal women and to postmenopausal women on HRT (Meilahn et al., 1992).

Furthermore, there was substantial variability in fibrinogen levels among the postmenopausal women. Those who had elevated levels of fibrinogen were employed women who reported high levels of job stress or low support from their bosses (Davis, Matthews, Meilahn, & Kiss, 1995). These findings are of interest because a similar association between job stress and fibrinogen has been observed in men by others (Markowe et al., 1985). Take the findings of PEPI and the Healthy Women Study together, it is likely that there are substantial changes in the clotting system during the perimenopausal transition and in women under stress.

Cardiovascular Reactivity to Stress. A final potential risk factor that might change during the menopause is cardiovascular response to behavioral stress. Activation of the sympathetic nervous system in response to repeated stress leads to acute increases in blood pressure and heart rate, which in turn can lead to flow disturbances. Flow disturbances can injure the endothelium, allowing lipid infiltration and platelet aggregation, eventually leading to thickening of the endothelium and development of fibrous plaque.

Several small psychophysiological studies of age-matched pre- and postmenopausal women have shown that postmenopausal women exhibit greater increase in blood pressure and catecholamines during certain types of behavioral stressors (Owens, Stoney, & Matthews, 1993; Saab, Matthews, Stoney, & McDonald, 1989). For example, in Saab et al. (1989), age-matched postmenopausal and premenopausal women were asked to perform a series of tasks, including public speaking, while their blood pressure, heart rate, and catecholamines were measured. Results showed that during the public speaking task, postmenopausal women exhibited enhanced systolic blood pressure, heart rate, and epinephrine responses. Public speaking was considered to be most conceptually relevant to women because of its emphasis on communication and sensitivity to others; it was also the task that elicited the strongest response.

It also appears that adding back estrogen to postmenopausal women results in an attenuation of the stress response. In a recent study by Lindheim et al. (1992), women were randomized to estrogen or placebo patch for six weeks and were evaluated in a stress protocol containing four psychological tasks before and after exposure to the patch. In the estrogen patch group, relative to initial evaluation, there was reduced systolic blood pressure, heart rate, maximal ACTH, cortisol, nonepinephrine, and androstenedione response to mental stress, whereas in the placebo patch group there was no change over time in any of the measures. This suggests that estrogen impacts on the autonomic nervous system's response to acute stress.

In sum, the expectation that women had in our study—that menopause would not lead to any important changes—is unfounded. Rather, it appears that estrogen deprivation may lead to unfavorable alteration in lipid metabolism, endothelium of the coronary arteries, blood flow, hemostatic factors, and sympathetic activation to mental stress. It also appears that subsets of women with specific behavioral characteristics, (e.g., being depressed, angry, and under job-related stress), may experience more adverse changes in cardiovascular risk factors during the menopausal transition than need be. That brings us to the next question.

Can Lifestyle Alterations Prevent Adverse Changes During the Menopause, Especially in Vulnerable Women?

Recall that participants in our longitudinal study thought that if women understood the menopause they would do better during the transition. Specifically, over 90% endorsed, "Women who know what the menopause is all about have less trouble during the change of life." If we could ascertain those lifestyle changes that would be most beneficial, women may be willing to adopt them.

To address this possibility, Owens, Mathews, Wing, and Kuller (1992) examined if women in the Healthy Women Study who made alterations in lifestyle on their own during the menopausal transition would do better in terms of changes in lipids and symptoms of depression and stress. We began our evaluation by examining the extent to which women increased, decreased, or stayed the same across 3 years in physical activity level, estimated by self-reported caloric expenditure in leisure activities. Analyses showed that women who increased their weekly physical activity by 300 Kcal per week did not experience a change in HDL-cholesterol and HDL-2, whereas those who declined even 300 Kcal per week or more in their exercise experienced three times the decline in HDL-cholesterol and HDL-2 as those women who increased in exercise. Caloric expenditure of 300 Kcal weekly is rather small (e.g., walking two to three times per week for 30 minutes). These findings raise the possibility that nonpharmacologic interventions may be an important therapeutic method for altering risk factors during the menopausal transition or in providing an adjunct to pharmacologic treatment. This assertion is tempered by the limitations of the Healthy Women Study design as cohort studies cannot determine cause and effect, although they can determine antecedent and consequent events.

An often prescribed pharmacological treatment for menopausal symptoms and for prevention of coronary heart disease is HRT. The potential benefit of HRT for prevention of coronary heart disease is based primarily on data from observational studies, which suggest that women who use HRT have about half the risk for cardiovascular disease of those who do not (Stampfer & Colditz, 1991). It should be noted that these studies were done at a time when unopposed estrogen replacement therapy was common, typically in higher dosages. In consequence, it is not clear if estrogens opposed by progestins in observational studies would yield the same benefits.

Furthermore, it may be that HRT users have characteristics prior to use of hormones that protect them from CHD. In the Healthy Women Study, relative to nonusers, hormone users have higher levels of HDL and HDL-2 and lower apoB, blood pressure, and weight; they also are more active and consume more alcohol (Matthews, Kuller, Wing, Meilahn, & Plantinga 1996). Although the magnitude of group differences in risk factor profile is specific to our population, it is instructive to consider their potential effect on the estimates of the beneficial effects of estrogen use obtained in observational studies. The difference in HDL-C was 3.9 mg/dl between users and nonusers in the Healthy Women Study. In the Framingham Heart Study, an increment of 1 mg/dl in HDL-cholesterol was associated with a decrement in risk of CHD by 3% and in risk of cardiovascular death by 4.7% in women (Gordon et al., 1989). If this relationship can be applied here, there should be an 11.5% difference in risk of CHD and an 18% difference in risk for cardiovascular death between users and nonusers, attributable to pre-existing characteristics of the women and not owing to the direct effects of hormones. A second example is the 2.4 mmHg differences in diastolic blood pressure between users and nonusers of hormones. Meta-analysis of randomized trials of hypertensives suggests a 2 to 3% decline in risk of myocardial infarction for 1 mmHg decline in diastolic blood pressure (Collins et al., 1990). If this relation can be applied to women, there should be a 5% reduction in risk for myocardial infarction in users, relative to nonusers, attributable to pre-existing characteristics of the women and not owing to the direct effects of hormones.

These findings underscore the need for an accurate evaluation of the benefits and liabilities of HRT, alone and in conjunction with lifestyle changes, such as alteration in diet and exercise patterns. Currently a large scale clinical trial is under way as part of the Women's Health Initiative to meet this need. Forty academic centers are enrolling 64,500 women in three overlapping clinical trials of treatments to reduce the major chronic diseases of postmenopausal women. In one of the treatment arms, women with a uterus are randomized to estrogen plus progestin, or placebo; women without a uterus are randomized to estrogen alone, or placebo. In a second treatment arm, women are randomized to low fat diet and behavioral counseling or usual care. All eligible women are randomized to calcium and vitamin D after one year of enrollment. This study will provide the kind of information that is needed to allow women to decide how to best prevent disease and promote quality of life in the postmenopausal years.

CONCLUDING REMARKS

In this chapter, we review data suggesting that menopause is indeed a turning point, but not in the way our cultural stereotypes portray. First, contemporary women have negative expectations about the emotional changes that they will experience during the menopause, which for most women are totally unfounded. Second, there are important biological changes owing to estrogen deprivation that do increase women's risk for CHD even though women do not believe that the menopause will result in any permanent changes. Finally, women believe that the better informed they are about the menopause the better they will fare, and our data do suggest that women who make positive changes in lifestyle might benefit. Currently our knowledge base is restricted to several observational studies of the menopause and of the health status of users of HRT, and a few clinical trials of the intermediate benefits of various HRT regimens. The Women's Health Initiative Clinical Trials will allow us to learn about behavioral and pharmacologic methods for promoting the health of menopausal women in midlife and beyond. In contrast to the view of midlife as a crisis and the menopause putting women between a rock and a hard place, the menopausal transition may be an optimal time to introduce lifestyle change.

ACKNOWLEDGMENTS

This chapter was supported by NIH grants HL38712 and HL28266 awarded to Karen Matthews and Lewis Kuller and is presented in part elsewhere (Matthews, Kuller, Wing, & Meilahn, 1994).

REFERENCES

Adler, N., & Matthews, K. A. (1994). Health psychology: Why do some people get sick and some stay well? *Annual Review of Psychology, 45*, 229–259.

Appels, A., & Mulder, P. (1989). Fatigue and heart disease: The association between vital exhaustion and past, present, and future coronary heart disease. *Journal of Psychosomatic Research, 33*, 727–738.

Bromberger, J. T., Matthews, K. A., Kuller, L. H., Wing, R. R., Meilahn, E. N., & Plantinga, P. (1997). *A prospective study of the determinants of the age at menopause. American Journal of Epidemiology, 145*, 124–138.

Bromberger, J. T., & Matthews, K. A. (1996). A longitudinal study of the effects of pessimism, trait anxiety and life stress on depressive symptoms in middle-aged women. *Psychology and Aging.* 11, 207–213.

Colditz, G. A., Willet, W. C., Stampfer, M. J., Rosner, B., Speizer, F. E., & Hennekens, C. H. (1987). Menopause and the risk of coronary heart disease in women. *New England Journal of Medicine, 316*, 1105–1110.

Collins, R. Peto, R., MacMahon, S., Hebert P., Fiebach, N. H., Eberlein, K. A., Godwin, J., Qizilbash, N., Taylor, J. O., & Hennekens, C. H. (1990). Blood pressure, stroke, and coronary heart disease: Part 2. Short-term reduction in blood pressure: Overview of randomized drug trials in their epidemiologic context. *Lancet, 335*, 827–838.

Cottington, E. M., Matthews, K. A., Talbott, E., & Kuller, L. H. (1980). Environmental events preceding sudden death in women. *Psychosomatic Medicine, 42*, 467–574.

Davis, M. C., Matthews, K. A., Meilahn, E. N., & Kiss, J. E. (1995) Are job characteristics related to fibrinogen levels in middle-aged women? *Health Psychology, 14*, 310–318.

Dembroski, T. M., MacDougall, J. M., Costa, P. T., Jr., & Grandits, G. A. (1989). Components of hostility as predictors of sudden death and myocardial infarction in the Multiple Risk Factor Intervention Trial. *Psychosomatic Medicine, 51*, 514–522.

Frasure-Smith, N., Lesperance, F., & Talajic, M. (1995). The impact of negative emotions on prognosis following myocardial infarction: Is it more than depression? *Health Psychology, 14*, 388–398.

Gordon, D. J., Probstfield, J. L., Garrison, R. J., Neaton, J. D., Castelli, W. P., Knoke, J. D., Jacobs, D. R., Jr., Bangdiwala, S., & Tyroler, H. A. (1989). High density lipoprotein cholesterol and cardiovascular disease: Four prospective American studies. *Circulation, 79*, 8–15.

Hallstrom, T., & Samuelsson, S. (1985). Mental health in the climacteric: The longitudinal study of women in Gotenburg. *Acta Obstetricia Gynecologica Scandinavica, 130* (Suppl.), 486–491.

Houston, B. K., Chesney, M. A., Black, G. W., Cates, D. S., & Hecker, M. H. L. (1992). Behavioral clusters and coronary heart disease risk. *Psychosomatic Medicine, 54*, 447–461.

Kannel, W. B., Hjortland, M. C., McNamara, P. M., & Gordon, T. (1976). Menopause and the risk of cardiovascular disease. The Framingham Study. *Annals of Internal Medicine, 85*, 447–452.

Kaufert, P. A., Gilbert, P., & Tate, R. (1992). The Manitoba Project: A reexamination of the link between menopause and depression. *Maturitas, 14*, 143–155.

Lindheim, S. R., Legro, R. S., Bernstein, L., Stanczyk, F. Z., Vijod, M. A., Presser, S. C., & Lobo, R. A. (1992). Behavioral stress responses in premenopausal and postmenopausal women and the effects of estrogen. *American Journal of Obstetrics and Gynecology, 167*, 1831–1836.

Markowe, H. L. J., Marmot, M. G., Shipley, M. J., Gulpitt, C. J., Meade, T. W., Stirling, Y., Vickers, M. V., & Semmence, A. (1985). Fibrinogen. A possible link between social class and coronary heart disease. *British Medical Journal, 291*, 1312–1314.

Matthews, K. A., Kelsey, S. F., Meilahn, E. N., Kuller, L. H., & Wing, R. R. (1989). Educational attainment and behavioral and biologic risk factors for coronary heart disease in middle-aged women. *American Journal of Epidemiology, 129*, 1132–1144.

Matthews, K. A., Kuller, L. H., Wing, R. R., & Meilahn, E. N. (1994). Biobehavioral aspects of menopause: Lessons from the Healthy Women Study. *Experimental Gerontology, 29*, 337–342.

Matthews, K. A., Kuller, L. H., Wing, R. R., Meilahn, E. N., & Plantinga, P. (1996). Are users of hormone replacement therapy healthier prior to use than are nonusers? *American Journal of Epidemiology, 143*, 971–978.

Matthews, K. A., Meilahn, E. N., Kuller, L. H., Kelsey, S. F., Caggiula, A. W., & Wing, R. R. (1989). Menopause and coronary heart disease risk factors. *New England Journal of Medicine, 321*, 641–646.

Matthews, K. A., Wing, R. R., Kuller, L. H., Meilahn, E. N., Kelsey, S. F., Costello, E. J., & Caggiula, A. W. (1990). Influences of natural menopause on psychological characteristics and symptoms of middle-aged healthy women. *Journal of Consulting and Clinical Psychology, 58*, 345–351.

Matthews, K. A., Wing, R. R., Kuller, L. H., Meilahn, E. N., & Plantinga, P. (1994). Influence of the perimenopause on cardiovascular risk factors and symptoms in middle-aged healthy women. *Archives of Internal Medicine, 154*, 2349–2355.

McKinlay, J. B., McKinlay, S. M., & Brambilla, D. (1987). The relative contributions of endocrine changes and social circumstances to depression in middle-aged women. *Journal of Health and Social Behavior, 28*, 345–363.

McKinlay, S. M., Bifano, N. L., & McKinlay, J. B. (1985). Smoking and age at menopause in women. *Annals of Internal Medicine, 103*, 350–356.

Meilahn, E. N., Kuller, L. H., Matthews, K. A., & Kiss, J. E. (1992). Fibrinogen and factor VII c levels according to menopausal status and use of hormone replacement therapy. *Annals of Epidemiology, 2*, 445–455.

Owens, J. F., Matthews, K. A., Wing, R. R., & Kuller, L. H. (1992). Can physical activity mitigate the effects of aging in middle-aged women? *Circulation, 85*, 1265–1270.

Owens, J. F., Stoney, C. M., & Matthews, K. A. (1993). Menopausal status influences ambulatory blood pressure levels and blood pressure changes during mental stress. *Circulation, 88*, 2794–2802.

Reis, S. E., Gloth, S. T., Blumentahl, R. S., Resar, J. R., Zacur, H. A., Gernstenblith, G., & Brinker, J. A. (1994). Ethinyl estradiol acutely attenuates abnormal coronary vasomotor responses to acetylcholine in postmenopausal women. *Circulation, 89*, 52–60.

Saab, P. G., Matthews, K. A., Stoney, C. M., & McDonald, R. H. (1989). Premenopausal and postmenopausal women differ in their cardiovascular and neuroendocrine responses to behavioral stressors. *Psychophysiology, 26*, 270–280.

Sheehy, G. (1991). *The silent passage. Menopause.* New York: Random House.

Smith, T. W. (1992). Hostility and health: Current status of a psychosomatic hypothesis. *Health Psychology, 11*, 139–150.

Speroff, L., Glass, R. H., & Kase, N. G. (1983). *Clinical gynecologic endocrinology and infertility* (3rd ed.). Baltimore: Williams & Wilkins.

Stampfer, M. J., & Colditz, G. A. (1991). Estrogen replacement therapy and coronary heart disease: A quantitative assessment of the epidemiologic evidence. *Preventive Medicine, 20*, 47–63.

Tracey, R. E. (1966). Sex differences in coronary disease: Two opposing views. *Journal of Chronic Disease, 19*, 1245–1251.

U.S. Bureau of Census. (1975). *Historical statistics of the United States, colonial times to 1970, Bicentennial Edition, Part 1* (p. 55). Washington, DC: Author.

U.S. Bureau of Census. (1984). *National Center for Health Statistics Statistical Bulletin.* Washington, DC: Author.

U.S. Bureau of Census. (1994) *Statistical abstract of the United States, 1994* (114th ed., p. 87). Washington, DC: Author.

Wenger, N. K., Speroff, L., & Packard, B. (1993). Cardiovascular health and disease in women. *New England Journal of Medicine, 329,* 247–256.

Willett, W., Stampfer, M. J., Bain, C., Lipnick, R., Speizer, F. E., Rosner, B., Cramer, D., & Hennekens, C. H. (1983). Cigarette smoking, relative weight, and menopause. *American Journal of Epidemiology, 117,* 651–658.

Wilson, R. A. (1966). *Feminine forever.* New York: M. Evans Publishing.

Writing Group for the PEPI Trial. (1995). Effects of estrogen or estrogen/progestin regimens on heart disease risk factors in postmenopausal women. *Journal of the American Medical Association, 273,* 199–208.

5

Changes in the Immune System During Aging

Bruce S. Rabin
University of Pittsburgh School of Medicine

As individuals age it is not uncommon for them to become concerned about the mechanisms of the aging process and ways in which the aging process can be delayed. In this regard, it is important to consider what the aging process consists of and to develop a working definition of "age."

The most obvious way to develop a definition of age would be to count the number of years an individual has lived. However, although chronological age is easy to understand, it has very limited usefulness. For example, it is not uncommon to find an individual who is chronologically 70 years old pursuing an active career, exercising regularly, and maintaining social interactions. Another individual of the same chronological age may be debilitated and residing in a nursing home and having no social interactions. Thus, if we regard age as the number of years that one has lived, there is no way to convey information about the quality of the individual's health or, more important, the quality of his or her life.

A way to develop a more biologic concept of aging is related to physiologic changes that occur in the body. For example, two individuals of different chronological ages who develop hypertension at the same time have a similar physiologic age in regard to the pathogenesis of hypertension. This suggests that the subsequent life course of both individuals would be similarly influenced by their physiological alteration. If the subsequent medical complications that occur in these two individuals are similar during their remaining life span, it would be realistic to consider them as having the same physiologic age, even though their chronological ages differ.

A third definition involves the concept of psychologic age. This reflects how one feels about oneself and how one perceives that he or she is regarded by others. Feeling youthful, believing that others think one is youthful, being physically fit, being cosmetically pleasing—all can contribute to the self-perception of one's own age. If an individual has a psychologically young age, the possibility that his or her health will be influenced by this psychologic state is an area of potentially interesting investigation.

AUTOIMMUNE RESPONSES

As individuals age, there is an increased incidence of autoimmune disease and autoantibody formation. On the basis of animal studies, it would be expected to find an association between the presence of an autoimmune response and life span. Strains of animals that spontaneously develop autoimmune diseases have significantly shorter life spans than do strains that do not develop autoimmunity. thus, those individuals who do not develop autoantibodies during the aging process may have potentially longer life spans, and individuals who develop autoantibodies may have shorter life spans.

As an example, the prevalence of autoantibodies to thyroid antigens were measured in 34 centenarians (Mariotti et al., 1992). The prevalence of autoantibodies was significantly greater in subjects age 70 to 85 than in subjects younger than age 50. The prevalence of autoantibodies in the centenarians was the same as in the under 50 age group. Thus, the age-related increase in the prevalence of autoantibodies was not found in subjects in the 9th decade of life. Whether this finding is related to an association of longevity with a decreased predisposition to develop autoantibodies has not been determined in humans but is compatible with observations in animals.

The mechanism for the alteration of life span based on autoimmune processes may relate to the presence of autoantibodies to physiologically relevant proteins. For example, antibodies directed to the adrenergic receptors, endocrine hormone receptors, or transport proteins may later the normal activity of tissues and cells with a resultant alteration of tissue function. Thus, the decreased functional activity of tissue, which occurs during aging, may not merely be a passive wearing out of the tissue. Rather, decreased organ function may be an active process brought about by an autoimmune process. If it is found that autoimmune responses are associated with a shortening of life span and an associated decrease in quality of life, a means of preventing this increase in immunologic autoreactivity should be sought.

T Lymphocytes

The major component of the immune system that tends to change during the aging process is the T lymphocyte population. This particular population of lymphocytes is composed of several subpopulations having different functional activities. The T lymphocyte subpopulation designated as the helper T lymphocyte population, or the helper/inducer T lymphocyte population (also referred to as the CD4 lymphocyte population), is now known to consist of two separate populations of T lymphocytes having different functional activities. The TH1 subpopulation of T helper cells is involved with producing what are termed reactions of cell-mediated immunity. Included in this group of reactions are the delayed hypersensitivity skin responses that occur, for example, following a skin test to determine whether one has been infected with *M. tuberculosis*. The TH1 population is also involved with promoting immune reactions that recruit phagocytic cells to an area where an infectious agent is localized, for the purpose of removing the infectious agent.

The second population of T helper lymphocytes is termed the TH2 population. This population helps the B lymphocytes (lymphocytes that produce antibody) to actually synthesize antibody in response to a specific antigen.

The second major population of T lymphocytes is the cytotoxic T lymphocyte populations (designated the CD8 lymphocyte population). This lymphocyte population directly attacks tissue cells that are infected with a virus or that have been infected with other pathogens. The third population of T lymphocytes is the suppressor lymphocyte population (also designated the CD8 lymphocyte population); it participates in down-regulation of immune responsiveness. Interactions between the various population of T lymphocytes are necessary for maintenance of normal immune function and health. Alterations in the functioning of one of the lymphocyte populations may predispose to disease development.

Both quantitative and qualitative changes occur during the aging process in the T lymphocyte populations. The total number of T lymphocytes is decreased in older as compared to younger individuals, with a decrease being greater in women than in men. In regard to subsets of T lymphocytes, the numbers of T cytotoxic and T suppressor lymphocytes tend to decrease with aging more than does the T helper/inducer population (Hulstaert et al., 1994).

The potential health implications of a decrease of the T cytotoxic population relates to the development of viral infections. As the cytotoxic T lymphocytes are involved in resistance to viral infection, a decrease in their numbers may predispose to viral infections. Thus, older individuals may be more susceptible to illnesses such as mild upper respiratory infections. However, the implications may be greater than the inconvenience of an upper respiratory infection.

The development of an autoimmune disease may occur secondarily to a viral infection in a tissue. Many viruses, by themselves, do not damage tissue but merely sit on the surface of the cell that they infect. An immune reaction may occur to eliminate the virus. If, in the process of eliminating the virus, the cells that have been infected by the virus are destroyed, there is the potential to lose cells that are important for the maintenance of homeostasis. For example, if the insulin-producing cells of the pancreas are infected by a virus that selectively infects such cells, an immune response directed to the virus may destroy all the insulin-producing capabilities of the pancreas. The individual in which this reaction is taking place would then develop insulin dependent diabetes.

A decrease in the functional activity of suppressor cells during aging may also predispose to the development of autoimmunity. During embryogenesis, B lymphocytes form with the capability of producing to self antigens. The autoreactive B lymphocytes usually do not become active because of the influence of the T suppressor lymphocyte population. A decrease in the activity of the T suppressor lymphocytes may allow autoreactive B lymphocytes to become functional. As this population of T lymphocytes decreases in number (and possibly function) as chronological age increases, their loss may participate in the alteration of health that occurs with the development of autoimmunity. Indeed, it may be considered that an individual who is chronologically 15 years old but who has an autoimmune disease may be immunologically equivalent to another individual who is chronologically 60 and who has the same autoimmune disease. In this regard the quality of life, and possibly duration of life, may be the same when comparing the 2 individuals. If immune dysregulation is related to a predisposition to development of an autoimmune disease, mechanisms to prevent such changes should be sought.

There are in vitro measures to determine the function of T lymphocytes. A very simple procedure is to incubate the lymphocytes with agents that bind to receptors on the lymphocyte surface and induce the lymphocytes into mitotic division. These mitosis-inducing agents are commonly referred to as nonspecific mitogens. Individuals who have immune deficiency diseases often have a marked impairment of the ability of their lymphocytes to be induced into mitotic division by nonspecific mitogens. In older individuals without an immune deficiency disease, the inability of peripheral blood lymphocytes to respond to nonspecific mitogens has been associated with increased mortality (Murasko, Gold, Hessen, & Kaye, 1990; Murasko, Weiner, & Kaye, 1988). The cause of death is not necessarily from an immune-related pathogenesis; it may include infection, malignancy, or cardiovascular, neurologic, and pulmonary factors. Thus, decreased responsiveness of lymphocytes to nonspecific mitogens in the elderly may provide a window that allows a comprehensive look at multiple factors associated with longevity.

There are no significant changes in the responsiveness of lymphocytes from young or old individuals to a nonspecific mitogen that selectively induces B lymphocytes into mitotic division. When the number of B lymphocytes that produce immunoglobulin are quantitated, there are no changes in the number of such cells that occur during the aging process. Thus, both the proliferative ability and the ability to synthesize immunoglobulins by B lymphocytes do not appear to change during the aging process.

Following immunization with an antigen, the antibody response decreases as individuals age. This occurs because of the necessity for the TH2 population to help B lymphocytes produce antibody in response to an antigen. Decreases of the functional activity of the T helper cell population would be associated with decreased antibody-producing capabilities. This suggests that the primary immune cell population that is modified during aging is the T lymphocyte and that alterations of antibody production during aging may reflect the necessity for T lymphocytes to provide help to B lymphocytes for normal antibody responses.

Cytokines

Lymphocytes communicate with each other through the production of soluble factors that are termed cytokines. There are at least 13 different types of cytokine molecules, with many others yet to be discovered. Each has a particular function, and different types of cells produce different cytokines. For example, the TH1 lymphocyte population produces a cytokine termed interferon gamma, and the TH2 populations produces a cytokine called IL-4. It is only through the coordinated production of the different types of cytokines that the immune system is able to properly function. If, during the aging process, there is decreased ability to produce some types of cytokines, there will be an imbalance in the immune system and either overactivity or underactivity of some parts of the immune system. As proper functioning of the immune system depends on coordination of the promoting and suppressing activities of different lymphocyte populations, such dysregulation may predispose to disease. In this regard, the production of the cytokine termed interleukin-2 has been studied during the aging process and is found to decrease (Gillis, Kozak, Durante, & Weksler, 1981; Nagel et al., 1988; Thorman & Weigle, 1982). Interleukin-2 is necessary for the proper expansion of activated T lymphocyte populations, and a decreased production of interleukin-2 may be related to the decreased activity of the T lymphocyte population during aging.

At one time it was considered that an individual lived a long life because he or she came from a family of individuals who had long life spans. Indeed, that may be true, but there are reasons why longevity runs in families. And this produces an exciting area of potential investigation. For example, a genetic basis for longevity may be related to the genetic regulation of the immune system, with those individuals having regulatory genes that are associated with sustained normal function of the immune system during chronological aging having healthier and longer life spans. Alternatively, exogenous factors that induce alterations of immune system function during the aging process, if appropriately regulated, may allow the immune system to maintain optimum function. Consideration of factors such as amelioration of stress and proper nutrition that maintains immune system function is necessary, as both are capable of modifying immune system function.

AGING, NUTRITION, AND THE IMMUNE SYSTEM

It is well established, in experimental animals, that alteration of diet can lead to alteration of immunologic responsiveness (Cunningham-Rundles, 1993). Nutritional factors that have been evaluated for their effect on immune system function include the amount of food consumed as well as components of the diet including protein, total calories, minerals, and vitamins. All have been found to exert an influence on the immune system, as manifested by the immune response to exogenous antigens and the development of spontaneous autoimmune disease.

A striking amelioration of the severity and delay in the onset of spontaneously occurring systemic lupus erythematosus in the spontaneously susceptible NZB/NZW mouse has been produced by protein calorie malnutrition. In these animals the concentration of circulating immune complexes is reduced in the serum, which may be a prime factor in the alteration of the clinical course of the disease. Another example of altering an experimentally induced immunologic disease by means of dietary manipulation is suggested by a model of alloxan-induced diabetes. Alloxan injection into rodents leads to destruction of the insulin-producing cells of the pancreas. However, the disease fails to develop in the animals that are maintained on a protein deficient diet. It has been suggested that this experimentally induced disease results from an immune response directed against alloxan-damaged insulin-producing β-islet cells. It is also known that animals lacking normal T cell function fail to develop the disease. Thus, protein calorie malnutrition, which is known to alter cellular immunity, may be influencing the T lymphocyte population and preventing the development of alloxan-induced diabetes. A further example of an immunologically induced disease that is altered by nutritional factors is adjuvant-induced arthritis. This disease does not develop in animals that have been maintained on a diet deficient in copper, magnesium, or zinc.

Several reports have indicated that the concentration of minerals in the diet can induce an effect on the immune system. The element that has been most extensively studied is zinc. Indeed, zinc deficiency leads to a depression of both cellular immunity and antibody production in experimental animals. The weight of the thymus and lymph nodes is usually decreased in zinc deficiency. Thus, consideration has been given to whether supplementation of a diet with zinc can ameliorate the onset or magnitude of a spontaneously occurring autoimmune disease in mice. In this regard my colleagues and I have supplemented the diet of NZB/NZW mice with zinc, raising the concentration from the normal of 15 μg/gm of food to 45 μg/gm of food. Comparing mice on the normal zinc diet with those on the supplemental zinc diet, we found that the mean life span was approximately doubled, the production of autoreactive antibodies not only was delayed in onset but was of a much lower magnitude, and the severity of disease as determined by the pathology occurring in the kidney of the experimental animals was markedly reduced. In essence, this simple procedure of dietary alteration led to a retardation of the development of a spontaneous autoimmune process with a subsequent influence on life span. If dietary factors can be altered during the aging process to maintain the function of the immune system as it is in young individuals, an influence on the quality of health and life span may be achieved.

CONCLUSION

Alterations of immunologic function during aging may be associated with an increased risk for the development of infectious diseases, autoimmune diseases, or malignancy. It is possible, even likely, that there is an interrelationship among the diseases associated with aging and altered function of the immune system. If the cellular immune system is operating at a reduced level of efficiency, an individual would be prone to viral infection, which may predispose to the development of a lymphoproliferative disease, and subsequent further suppression of immune system function. Alternatively, a virus may infect a tissue and, while being presented on the surface of the tissue cell, elicit an antiviral immune response. The immune response to the virus may produce damage to the tissue, which, if rapid and efficient, will eliminate all the virally infected cells; and the tissue will continue to function, although there may be some fibrosis. However, if the immune system is not functioning at an optimal level, the virus may not be rapidly eliminated, and a slow but persistent destruction of the tissue may occur as the immune system keeps destroying tissue cells. Eventually the entire tissue may be destroyed. The sequence of events may be considered analogous to an autologous graft-versus-host reaction in which aging is associated with self-rejection.

There are families that are known to have longevity as a characteristic. The mechanism of the longevity needs to be determined, and it is likely that maintaining a high level of immune system function will be found to contribute to longevity. Thus, a means to keep the immune system functioning at a level that will prevent diseases associated with aging and decreased immune function may contribute to maintaining an optimal quality of health during aging. Coping with stress, adequate nutrition, and moderate amounts of exercise may be found to be beneficial for achieving this goal.

TABLE 5.1
Summary of Age-Associated Immunologic Changes

Thymic Involution

- ↑ thymic hormones

No Real Change in Total Lymphocyte Population, but:

- ↓ in germinal centers of lymph nodes
- ↑ in plasma cells and lymphocytes in bone marrow
- ↑ in CD4 and (in CD8 T lymphocytes

Total Serum Immunoglobulin Changes Little With Age, but:

- ↓ response to foreign antigens
- ↑ production of antibodies to self tissue antigens
- ↑ in monoclonal gammopathies

Many Changes in Cell-Mediated Immunity, Including:

- ↓ response to mitogens
- ↓ capacity to produce cytotoxic T cells
- ↓ production of and response to lymphokines
- ↓ delayed hypersensitivity skin test reactivity

Functional and Postulated Clinical Consequences of Age-Associated Immunologic Changes

- impaired immune response to infection
- impaired response to other foreign antigens
- impaired graft versus host response (lymphocyte transfer test)
- increased response by T cells against autoantigens (autologous graft vs. host reaction)
- increase in autoantibody-producing B cells resulting in:
  - increased autoantibody production
  - increased resistance to tolerance induction

Predicted Clinical Consequences of Functional and Postulated Clinical Consequences of Age-Associated Immunologic Changes

- increased susceptibility to infection with reduced immunologic response
- increased incidence of autoimmune disease
- increased risk of malignancy

REFERENCES

Cunningham-Rundles, S. (1993). *Nutrient modulation of the immune response*. New York: Marcel Dekker.

Gillis, S., Kozak, R., Durante, M., & Weksler, M. (1981). Immunological studies of aging. Decreased production and response to T cell growth factor by lymphocytes from aged humans. *Journal of Clinical Investigation, 67*, 937–942.

Hulstaert, F., Hannet, I., Deneys, V., Munhyeshuli, V., Reichert, T., De Bruyere, M., & Strauss, K. (1994). Age-related changes in human blood lymphocytes subpopulations. II. Varying kinetics of percentage and absolute count measurements. *Clinical Immunology and Immunopathology, 70*, 152–158.

Mariotti, S., Sansoni, P., Barbesino, G., Caturegli, P., Monti, D., Cossarizza, A., Giacomelli, T., Passeri, G., Fagiolo, U., Pinchera, A., & Franceschi, C. (1992). Thyroid and other organ-specific autoantibodies in healthy centenarians. *Lancet, 1*, 1506–1508.

Murasko, D. M., Gold, M. J., Hessen, M. T., & Kaye, D. (1990). Immune reactivity, morbidity, and mortality of elderly humans. *Aging: Immunology and Infectious Disease, 3*, 171–179.

Murasko, D. M., Weiner, P., & Kaye, D. (1988). Association of lack of mitogen-induced lymphocyte proliferation with increased mortality in the elderly. *Aging: Immunology and Infectious Disease, 1*, 1–6.

Nagel, J. E., Chopra, R. K., Chrest, F. J., McCoy, M. T., Schneider, E. L., Holbrook, N. J., & Adler, W. H. (1988). Decreased proliferation, interleukin-2 synthesis, and interleukin-2 receptor expression are accompanied by decreased mRNA expression in PHA stimulated cells from elderly donors. *Journal of Clinical Investigation, 81*, 1096–1102.

Thoman, M. L., & Weigle, W. O. (1982). Cell mediated immunity in aged mice: An underlying lesion in IL-2 synthesis. *Journal of Immunology, 128*, 2358–2361.

6

Effects of Chronic Stress on Immune Function and Health in the Elderly

Susan Robinson-Whelen
Janice K. Kiecolt-Glaser
Ronald Glaser
The Ohio State University

THE RELEVANCE OF AGE
IN STUDIES OF STRESS
AND IMMUNE FUNCTION

There is ample evidence that various stressors can alter immune function (Glaser & Kiecolt-Glaser, 1994a; Herbert & Cohen, 1993b). There is also clear evidence that immune function declines with age (reviewed in Solomon & Benton, 1994). Because immunosenescence occurs in persons with increasing age and is "indistinguishable from immunodeficiency secondary to underlying disease, malnutrition, toxic exposure, or genetic disorder" (Solomon & Benton, 1994, p. 341), older adults may be especially susceptible to the potentially negative effects of stress on immune function.

There are relatively few studies exploring the effects of stress on immune function among older adults. In a recent meta-analysis of the literature on stress-related immunological changes in human beings, Herbert and Cohen (1993b) were limited in their ability to explore age differences because most published studies had used younger subjects (i.e., mean age under 30 years). Older adults appear to show greater immunological impairments associated with clinical depression than do younger adults (Schleifer, Keller, Bond,

Cohen, & Stein, 1989), and a meta-analytic review of the depression and immunity literature similarly suggested that clinical depression had a more negative effect on immune measures among older adults than young adults (Herbert & Cohen, 1993a). Although it seems plausible that stress-related immune changes may become more pronounced with age among nonclinically depressed adults, further research is clearly needed.

THE RELEVANCE OF
STRESSOR DURATION

It is particularly important to explore the effect of chronic stress on older adults in view of the glucocorticoid cascade hypothesis, which suggests that chronic stress may have persistent negative effects on immune function in older adults and may actually accelerate immunosenescence (Sapolsky, Krey, & McEwen, 1986). This hypothesis was generated from animal studies that found that aged rates were impaired in their ability to terminate glucocorticoid secretion at the end of a stressor relative to young rats. By analogy, because glucocorticoids down-regulate immune function, chronic stressors may have persistent and severe consequences for immune function in the elderly.

Although most studies have examined the immunological consequences of acute rather than chronic stressors, there are exceptions. Baum and his colleagues conducted an elegant series of studies using people who lived near the Three Mile Island (TMI) nuclear power plant (Baum, 1990; McKinnon, Weisse, Reynolds, Bowles, & Baum, 1989). They compared psychological stress, endocrine function, and immune function in people living near TMI after the nuclear power plant sustained damage with a demographically comparable control group. TMI-area residents and controls had comparable blood pressure in the years before the TMI accident as reflected in records obtained from their physicians; in contrast, blood pressure data collected by the research team several years after the accident showed higher blood pressure in TMI residents as compared to controls (Baum, 1990). Chronic stress was implicated as a factor in enhanced cardiovascular reactivity as well as in higher levels of urinary catecholamines (Fleming, Baum, Davidson, Rectanus, & McArdle, 1987; McKinnon et al., 1989). TMI residents had more neutrophils and fewer B lymphocytes, T suppressor/cytotoxic lymphocytes, NK cells, and higher antibody titers to latent herpes simplex virus (HSV) than did controls.

Higher antibody titers to latent HSV are thought to reflect poorer control of the latent virus by the cellular arm of the immune system (Glaser & Jones, 1994). Herpesviruses are different from many other viruses in that they remain in a latent state in the body after the primary infection subsides. The competence of the cellular immune response is a critical factor in the control of herpesvirus latency. When cellular immunity is compromised, the immune system's control over latent herpesvirus replication is impaired, and there are characteristic elevated herpesvirus antibody titers (Glaser & Kiecolt-Glaser, 1994b).

In addition to the studies on the long-term effects of living near TMI, several investigators have examined the consequences of caregiving for a relative with a progressive dementia (e.g., Irwin et al., 1991; Kiecolt-Glaser et al., 1987; McCann, 1991; Reese, Gross, Smalley, & Messer, 1994). These studies have provided data on the immunological consequences of a persistent stressor in older adults.

THE CHRONIC
STRESS OF CAREGIVING

Caring for a family member with a progressive dementing illness is an extraordinarily long-term, unpredictable, and uncontrollable stressor. The progressive cognitive impairments characteristic of Alzheimer's disease (AD) lead to gradually increasing needs for care and assistance with daily living. The irreversible deterioration of brain tissue eventually progresses to the point at which the AD patient is unable to provide even the most basic self-care. Caregivers have described the process as a kind of living bereavement as they watch their relative's intellect and personality gradually disintegrate (Light & Lebowitz, 1989).

It is not possible to accurately predict or anticipate the time course of the disease. The modal survival time after onset is quite variable, ranging from 5 to 10 years (Hay & Ernst, 1987). Because of the long-term course of the disease, caregiving for a friend or relative with AD has been conceptualized as a chronic stressor (Fiore, Becker, & Coppel, 1983).

There is ample evidence that the stress of caring for a relative with AD adversely effects caregivers' mental health (Light & Lebowitz, 1989). The literature clearly shows greater self-reported psychiatric symptomatology among caregivers (Schulz, Visitainer, & Williamson, 1990) and suggests that caregiving places individuals at risk for developing syndromal depressive disorders (Cohen & Eisdorfer, 1988; Dura, Stuckenberg, & Kiecolt-Glaser, 1990, 1991; Fiore et al., 1983; Gallagher, Wrabetz, Lovett, Del Maestro, & Rose, 1989).

Although the effects of caregiving on psychological health have been well documented, much less is known about the effects of caregiving stress on physical health. Most studies assessing physical health have relied on self-report measures. In their review of the literature, Schulz et al. (1990) noted that caregivers consistently report poorer self-rated health than do matched controls. Schulz et al. (1990) cautioned, however, that it is difficult to draw conclusions and causal inferences from such studies. Few researchers have used longitudinal designs to study the physiological consequences of caregiving stress. In the sections that follow, we review the results of a series of investigations addressing the effects of caregiving on health.

The Impact of Caregiving on Immune Function

Cross-Sectional Data. In the first study to assess the immunological consequences of AD caregiving, measures of psychological health, physical health, and immune function were collected from a group of 34 caregivers and a group of 34 matched noncaregivers (Kiecolt-Glaser et al., 1987). Participants were generally well educated, with a mean age of 60 years. The caregivers had been providing care for their impaired family member for an average of 5.5 years; thus caregivers were facing a chronic, rather than an acute, life stressor. The majority were caring for a spouse; the remainder provided care for a parent or parent-in-law. Half the caregivers lived in the same residence as the relative for whom they were caring, but the caregivers' psychological well-being was unrelated to living arrangement. Consistent with previous studies demonstrating negative psychological consequences of family caregiving, these caregiving subjects reported significantly greater depressive symptomatology, poorer self-rated mental health, and lower levels of life satisfaction than did sociodemographically matched comparison subjects.

Comparisons of immunological data revealed significant differences between caregivers and control: caregivers had lower percentages of total T lymphocytes (CD3+) and helper T lymphocytes (CD4+) than did noncaregiving comparison subjects. Although the two groups did not differ in the relative percentages of suppressor T cells (CD8+ cells), caregivers had a significantly lower CD4+/CD8+ ratio. No differences were found in the percentages of NK cells.

In addition to the differences observed in relative percentages of lymphocytes, caregivers had significantly higher antibody titers to latent Epstein–Barr virus (EBV) than did comparison subjects. Taken together with the quantitative immune measures, elevated EBV antibody titers (similar to the discussion for HSV) suggest that caregivers had poorer cellular immune function than that of noncaregivers.

In contrast, Reese and her colleagues (1994) compared three groups: 25 AD caregivers, 25 caregivers of stroke patients, and 25 noncaregivers. Of the AD caregiver sample, 56% were caring for a parent, 36% were caring for a spouse, and the remainder were caring for some other friend or relation. AD caregivers were significantly younger (mean age of 56) than the subjects in the other two groups (means of 64 and 61), and AD caregivers were slightly better educated with higher incomes. Reese et al. (1994) found no differences among groups on a battery of quantitative immunological assays, even though the AD caregivers reported more distress than did the other two groups.

The absence of significant immunological differences may be related to the exclusive use of quantitative assays by Reese et al. (1994). Meta-analyses have shown stronger and more consistent stress-related differences in qualitative or functional measures than have quantitative assays (Herbert & Cohen, 1993b). Indeed, although pilot work showed significant differences between caregivers and controls (Kiecolt-Glaser et al., 1987), a subsequent longitudinal study with a larger and more homogeneous sample did not yield significant differences in quantitative immunological data, but it did continue to demonstrate differences on functional assays (Kiecolt-Glaser et al., 1991).

Other researchers have also found differences on functional immunological assays between caregivers and controls. For example, McCann (1991) found that the response to delayed hypersensitivity skin testing was significantly poorer among older adult spousal caregivers than among noncaregivers. Whereas 12% of the control subjects in her study were categorized as totally or relatively anergic compared to normal age and gender standards, 50% of the caregivers were so categorized. Caregivers in this study not only showed immunologic deficits relative to a comparison sample, but demonstrated deficits compared to age-based norms as well.

Irwin et al. (1991) investigated the effects of AD caregiving stress on sympathetic nervous system activity and NK cytotoxicity. Plasma levels of neuropeptide Y (NPY) were significantly elevated in older spousal caregivers as compared to those of older controls, and NPY was negatively correlated with NK cell activity among caregivers. NK activity itself, however, was not significantly different between spousal caregivers and controls. In summary, data from several cross-sectional studies suggest that individuals facing the chronic stress of caring for a relative with AD do not show physiological adaptation (i.e., caregivers do not appear to return to the level of well-matched controls).

Longitudinal Studies. In a longitudinal study of the immunological consequences of caregiving stress, 69 spousal caregivers and 69 matched controls were examined on two occasions an average of 13 months apart (Kiecolt-Glaser et al., 1991). The caregiver group consisted of all spousal caregivers who were continuing to provide care for their spouse and were available for follow-up assessment. Caregivers had been providing care for an average of 5 years prior to the initial assessment. Most caregivers were caring for their impaired spouse at home across both times of testing. The mean age was 67 years.

Between the two times of measurement, caregivers showed declines relative to controls on all three functional measures of cellular immunity included in the study: antibody titers to latent EBV, and the ability of lymphocytes to proliferate when exposed to the mitogens concanavalin A (Con A) and phytohemagglutinin (PHA). Caregivers showed increased antibody titers to EBV over time, whereas controls evidenced minimal change. Caregivers showed a decreased proliferative response to both Con A and PHA over time relative to controls, with differences most pronounced at the highest mitogen concentrations. In contrast, caregivers and controls did not differ significantly on quantitative immune measures. There were no group differences in CD3+, CD4+, or CD8+ cells at intake into the study, nor were there any significant differences in change over time on these measures.

Data on infectious illnesses showed differences between caregivers and controls. The Health Review (Jenkins, Kraeger, Rose, & Hurst, 1980), a checklist of specific illness symptoms related to infectious diseases, was administered every 3 months to assess illness episodes. Although caregivers did not report greater frequency of infectious illnesses, they reported illnesses of longer duration and were more likely to have visited their physician as a result of their illness.

Health behaviors were assessed in order to explore their contribution to the immunological differences observed between caregivers and controls. Similar to the results of the cross-sectional study, caregivers and controls did not differ on health behaviors (i.e., use of alcohol, tobacco, and caffeine), nor did they differ in nutritional status as assessed by plasma albumin levels. Recent amount of sleep differed between the two groups, but sleep was not reliably related to any of the immunological data. Therefore, differences between groups in immune function and infectious illness could not be explained by recent health behaviors.

In an attempt to better understand factors contributing to observed immunological changes, participants were divided into those who showed overall down-regulation of cellular immunity (i.e., those showing decrements on the three functional immunological assays) and those who did not. Nearly one third of the caregivers were classified as "at risk" because of their uniform declines on functional immune measures. "At risk" caregivers did not differ from the remaining caregivers in the length of caregiving, amount of time per day spent caregiving, or extent of their spouses' cognitive impairment, but they were significantly more likely to have institutionalized their spouse between the initial assessment and follow-up than those not classified as "at risk." "At risk" caregivers also reported more distress in response to dementia-related behaviors and lower levels of helpful social support at the initial assessment. Although caregivers as a whole had substantially higher rates of syndromal depressive disorders than did controls at both times of assessment, negligible differences between depressed and nondepressed caregivers' immune data suggested that immunological down-regulation was not simply related to syndromal depression.

These data should not be taken to indicate that caregivers show continued declines in immune function related to years of caregiving. In fact, the best evidence is more consistent with the adaptation hypothesis, that is, that caregivers eventually stabilize in their responses to the stresses of caregiving (Townsend, Noelker, Deimling, & Bass, 1989). The "at risk" caregivers showed the largest declines, and the characteristics of this group are particularly important in this regard. As described previously, these individuals were more likely to have institutionalized their spouses in the intervening year. Caregivers who decided to place their spouses in a nursing home often made this decision because behavioral or other problems had become so severe that they could no longer cope. The decision to move the spouse was often a wrenching one, and caregivers frequently found themselves conflicted over nursing home placement, a condition that continued well after the initial move. Thus, rather than simply reflecting down-regulation related to chronicity, these caregivers appear to have been adapting to a new set of caregiving strains. Indeed, in the longitudinal data from this sample we have not observed continuous downward change in immune function, but rather stabilization at levels below those of control subjects.

Post-Stressor Functioning: Caregivers After Bereavement. Relatively few studies have explored the psychological recovery of care-givers after bereavement; even fewer have addressed the question of physiological recovery. Preliminary evidence on psychological recovery following bereavement suggests that, unlike the psychological rebound observed in "normal" bereavement (Harlow, Goldberg, & Comstock, 1991; Lund, Caserta, & Dimone, 1989; Thompson, Gallagher-Thompson, Futterman, Gilewski, & Peterson, 1991), caregivers' distress and depression are not substantially alleviated in the year following the death of their relative (Bass & Bowman, 1990; George & Gwyther, 1984). Recent research using structured psychiatric interviews to assess clinical depression revealed that former caregivers did not differ from continuing care-givers in their incidence of syndromal depression or in their level of depressive symptomatology an average of 2 years after the death of their impaired relative (Bodnar & Kiecolt-Glaser, 1994); both continuing and former caregivers were significantly more depressed than were noncare-givers.

The longer-term physiological consequences of caregiving were examined in a study that compared three groups of subjects: a group of 14 care-givers currently caring for an impaired relative, a group of 17 former caregivers, and a group of 31 noncaregiving control subjects (Esterling, Kiecolt-Glaser, Bodnar, & Glaser, 1994). Participants in the study were the first 62 subjects from the longitudinal project to receive their fifth annual appointment. Continuing caregivers were those who had been caring for a demented relative throughout all 5 years of the longitudinal study. At the time of the Year 5 assessment, they had been providing care for an average of 10 years. Approximately half of them continued to provide care for their family member at home. Former caregivers were those who had been caregiving when they initially joined the study but whose caregiving had ceased because of the death of their family member. The average length of time since the death of the family member was a little more than 2 years (26.57 months). The average age of the continuing caregiver, former caregiver, and noncaregiver groups was 68, 72, and 71, respectively.

The immunological question of interest was whether caregivers and controls differed on three NK cell assays: NK cell cytotoxicity and NK cell cytotoxicity after enhancement with two cytokines, recombinant interferon-[γ] (rIFN-γ) and recombinant interleukin-2 (rIL-2). These cytokines enhance NK cell cytotoxicity in vitro (Herberman & Ortaldo, 1981), and there is evidence that stress can modulate the synthesis of these cytokines by nitrogen-treated peripheral blood leukocytes (Dobbin, Harth, McCain, Martin, & Cousin, 1991; Glaser, Rice, Speicher, Stout, & Kiecolt-Glaser, 1986).

Consistent with the data from Irwin et al. (1991) discussed earlier, current caregivers, former caregivers, and noncaregivers did not differ in NK cell cytotoxicity. However, differences were observed in NK cell responses to rIFN-γ and rIL-2. Although current and former caregivers did not differ from each other in their response to these two cytokines, both groups demonstrated significantly poorer responses to these cytokines than did controls (Easterling et al., 1994).

When continuing and former caregivers were divided into low-cytokine responders (i.e., those responding below the median to both cytokines) and high-cytokine responders (i.e., those responding above the median to either or both cytokines), low responders reported less positive social support from their networks and described less closeness in their important relationships. High- and low-cytokine responders did not differ significantly in depressive symptomatology or health behaviors.

Consistent with data on psychological adaptation following long-term caregiving stress, these data suggest that former caregivers do not show physiological recovery in the years immediately following the cessation of caregiving. On a more positive note, there was some evidence indicating eventual adaptation and recovery. Relative to caregivers who were more recently bereaved, those who had been bereaved for longer periods had significantly higher levels of NK cell cytotoxicity after rIFN-γ stimulation and a similar trend after rIL-2 stimulation. Further study is required to determine the length of time required for recovery and whether or not a complete recovery of immune function is possible. A better understanding of what factors may assist and what factors may hinder the recovery process is also needed.

HEALTH IMPLICATIONS

It is often mistakenly believed that changes in immune function translate directly into changes in physical health. Although gross impairments in immune function such as those found in AIDS patients are clearly associated with increased morbidity and mortality, the effects of less extreme immune changes on physical health are largely unknown. Two recent studies, however, provide evidence that stress-related immune changes are relevant to protection against infectious illness.

In a carefully controlled prospective study, Cohen, Tyrrell, and Smith (1991) examined the relationship between stress and susceptibility to several different respiratory viruses. After completing measures of psychological stress, volunteers were inoculated with one of five viruses or a placebo. They were subsequently quarantined and monitored for the development of both respiratory infections and clinical colds (i.e., presence of cold symptoms in addition to the presence of infection). The researchers found that the incidence of respiratory infections and clinical colds increased in a dose-response manner with increases in psychological stress across all five viruses they studied.

Consistent with these results, Glaser, Kiecolt-Glaser, Bonneau, Malarkey, and Hughes (1992) found that stress interfered with the immune system's ability to generate an immune response to a primary antigen. Over 6 months, 48 medical students were given a series of 3 hepatitis B vaccine inoculations, each on the last day of a 3-day exam period. The 25% of the sample who seroconverted (i.e., produced a measurable antibody response to the vaccine) after the first inoculation were significantly less stressed and less anxious than those who did not seroconvert until after the second injection. In addition, students who reported greater social support demonstrated a stronger immune response to the vaccine at the time of the third inoculation, as measured by antibody titers to a hepatitis B surface antigen (HBsAg) and the blastogenic response to the viral peptide. These data suggest that the immunological response to vaccination can be modulated by a relatively mild, time-limited, commonplace stressor, a finding replicated in another population (Jabaaij et al., 1993). These studies demonstrated that the effects of stress on the immune system are significant enough to affect the ability of healthy young or middle aged adults to respond to an infectious pathogen.

However, susceptibility to an infectious agent is more relevant for older adults. Pneumonia and influenza together constitute the fourth leading cause of death among individuals over age 75 (Yoshikawa, 1983), and mortality from influenza infection is four times higher among those over age 60 than among those under 40 (Burns, Lum, Seigneuret, Giddings, & Goodwin, 1990). Immune senescence is thought to be associated (in part) with the greatly increased morbidity and mortality from infectious illness in the elderly and is thought to be related to the poor response of many older adults to vaccines (Phair, Kauffmann, Bjornson, Adams, & Linnemann, 1978). Older adults achieve lower peak antibody levels following vaccination and show more rapid decline of antibody levels over time (Burns et al., 1990). If chronic stress accelerates age-related declines in immune function, as the glucocorticoid cascade hypothesis suggests, chronic stress could have serious health consequences for older adults, including increased risk and severity of infectious illness.

Potentially even more serious than an increased risk of infectious illness, Murasko, Weiner, and Kaye (1988) suggested that immunological changes may reflect changes in other systems as well and thus may provide a marker of physiological aging. They found that older adults who did not show lymphocyte proliferation in response to three mitogens were twice as likely to die over a 2-year period than were those showing a proliferative response. The major cause of death among their sample of older adults was sudden death or a diagnosable cardiovascular-related disease.

A 20-year longitudinal study of healthy older adults showed that poorer cell-mediated immunity was associated with subsequent morbidity and mortality (Wayne, Rhyne, Garry, & Goodwin, 1990), and a 16-year longitudinal study of healthy elderly men found that decreases in the absolute number of peripheral blood lymphocytes during the 3 years prior to death were related to subsequent mortality (Bender, Nagel, Adler, & Andres, 1986). These studies suggest that immunological decrements among older adults may be related to more than just increased infectious illness. Such suggestions heighten concern about the immune down-regulation observed among older adults experiencing the chronic stress of caregiving.

POTENTIAL DIRECTIONS FOR INTERVENTION

Psychological intervention studies that include measures of immune function are relatively rare (Kiecolt-Glaser & Glaser, 1991). One intervention study conducted with an older adult sample, however, did find positive changes in immune function following the intervention. Older adults living in retirement homes were randomly assigned to one of three conditions: a progressive relaxation training condition, a social contact condition, or a no contact control condition (Kiecolt-Glaser et al., 1985). Older adults in the relaxation and social contact conditions were visited by a student three times a week for one month. Participants were seen individually by the same student on each visit. Blood samples and self-report data were collected at baseline, at the end of the intervention, and at the 1-month follow-up.

Individuals in the relaxation condition showed significant increases in NK cell lysis at the end of the intervention (but not at follow-up) and a decrease in antibody titers to HSV both at the end of the intervention and at the 1-month follow-up. Subjects in the social contact and no contact control conditions did not show significant changes on these measures.

Relaxation was also incorporated into a 6-week structured group intervention for patients with Stage I or II malignant melanoma (Fawzy et al., 1990). Although the mean age of the sample was 42 years, the sample included some older adults (age range 19 to 70 years). Fawzy et al.'s brief intervention (consisting of health education, enhancement of problem-solving skills regarding diagnosis, psychological support, and additional stress reduction techniques) produced beneficial psychological and immunological changes in treatment group members relative to controls. Despite the brevity of the intervention, intervention subjects showed increases in the percentage of large granular lymphocytes (NK cells), increases in NK cell cytotoxicity, and small decreases in the percentage of CD4+ T cells. These changes were not observed immediately after the intervention but became evident at the 6-month follow-up.

Although these studies demonstrate that immune function in older adults may be enhanced through psychosocial interventions, it remains to be seen whether interventions can counteract the toll that years of chronic stress takes on older caregivers' immune systems. An exploration of the ability of caregiver interventions to enhance immunity may have to wait until the efficacy of specific caregiver interventions has been better established. Given the recent findings that psychological and physiological impairments persist even after caregiving has ceased (Bodnar & Kiecolt-Glaser, 1994; Esterling et al., 1994), programs designed for recently bereaved caregivers may offer a more fruitful opportunity to evaluate the immune-enhancing capability of psychosocial interventions. Intervention programs designed for bereaved caregivers that are less likely to be fraught with the challenges of caregiver interventions (e.g., limited caregiver availability, profound daily stressors) may offer valuable insights into the plasticity of the long-term immunological down-regulation in older adults following chronic stress.

REFERENCES

Bass, D. M., & Bowman, K. (1990). The transition from caregiving to bereavement: The relationships of care-related strain and adjustment to death. *Gerontologist, 30*, 35–42.

Baum, A. (1990). Stress, intrusive imagery and chronic distress. *Health Psychology, 9*, 653–675.

Bender, B. S., Nagel, J. E., Adler, W. H., & Andres, R. (1986). Absolute peripheral blood lymphocyte count and subsequent mortality of elderly men. *Journal of the American Geriatric Society, 34*, 649–654.

Bodnar, J., & Kiecolt-Glaser, J. K. (1994). Caregiver depression after bereavement: Chronic stress isn't over when it's over. *Psychology and Aging, 9*, 372–380.

Burns, E. A., Lum, L. G., Seigneuret, M. C., Giddings, B. R., & Goodwin, J. S. (1990). Decreased specific antibody synthesis in old adults: Decreased potency of antigen-specific B cells with aging. *Mechanisms of Ageing and Development, 53*, 229–241.

Cohen, D., & Eisdorfer, C. (1988). Depression in family members caring for a relative with Alzheimer's disease. *Journal of the American Geriatric Society, 36*, 885–889.

Cohen, S., Tyrrell, D. A., & Smith, A. P. (1991). Psychological stress in humans and susceptibility to the common cold. *New England Journal of Medicine, 325*, 606–612.

Dobbin, J. P., Harth, M., McCain, G. A., Martin, R. A., & Cousin, K. (1991). Cytokine production and lymphocyte transformation during stress. *Brain, Behavior, and Immunity, 5*, 339–348.

Dura, J. R., Stukenberg, K. W., & Kiecolt-Glaser, J. K. (1990). Chronic stress and depressive disorders in older adults. *Journal of Abnormal Psychology, 99*, 284–290.

Dura, J. R., Stukenberg, K. W., & Kiecolt-Glaser, J. K. (1991). Anxiety and depressive disorders in adult children caring for demented parents. *Psychology and Aging, 6*, 467–473.

Esterling, B., Kiecolt-Glaser, J. K., Bodnar, J., & Glaser, R. (1994). Chronic stress, social support, and persistent alterations in the natural killer cell response to cytokines in older adults. *Health Psychology, 13*, 291–299.

Fawzy, I. F., Kemeny, M. E., Fawzy, N. W., Elashoff, R., Morton, D., Cousings, N., & Fahey, J. L. (1990). A structured psychiatric intervention for cancer patients. *Archives of General Psychiatry, 47*, 729–735.

Fiore, J., Becker, J., & Coppel, D. B. (1983). Social network interactions: A buffer or a stress. *American Journal of Community Psychology, 11*, 423–439.

Fleming, I., Baum, A., Davidson, L. M., Rectanus, E., & McArdle, S. (1987). Chronic stress as a factor in physiologic reactivity to challenge. *Health Psychology, 6*, 221–237.

Gallagher, D., Wrabetz, A., Lovett, S., Del Maestro, S., & Rose, J. (1989). Depression and other negative affects in family caregivers. In E. Light & B. D. Lebowitz (Eds.), *Alzheimer's disease treatment and family stress: Directions for research* (pp. 218–244). Rockville, MD: National Institute of Mental Health.

George, L., & Gwyther, L. (1984, November). *The dynamics of caregiver burden: Changes in caregiver well-being over time.* Paper presented at the annual meeting of the Gerontological Society of America, San Antonio, TX.

Glaser, R., & Jones, J. (Eds.). (1994). *Human herpesvirus infections.* New York: Marcel Dekker.

Glaser, R., & Kiecolt-Glaser, J. K. (Eds.). (1994a). *Handbook of human stress and immunity.* San Diego, CA: Academic Press.

Glaser, R., & Kiecolt-Glaser, J. K. (1994b). Stress-associated immune modulation and its implications for reactivation of latent herpesviruses. In R. Glaser & J. Jones (Eds.), *Human herpesvirus infections* (pp. 245–270). New York: Marcel Dekker.

Glaser, R., Kiecolt-Glaser, J. K., Bonneau, R., Malarkey, W., & Hughes, J. (1992). Stress-induced modulation of the immune response to recombinant hepatitis B vaccine. *Psychosomatic Medicine, 54*, 22–29.

Glaser, R., Rice, J., Speicher, C. E., Stout, J. C., & Kiecolt-Glaser, J. K. (1986). Stress depresses interferon production by leukocytes concomitant with a decrease in natural killer cell activity. *Behavioral Neuroscience, 100*, 675–678.

Harlow, S. D., Goldberg, E. L., & Comstock, G. W. (1991). A longitudinal study of risk factors for depressive symptomology in elderly widowed and married women. *American Journal of Epidemiology, 134*, 526–538.

Hay, J., & Ernst, R. L. (1987). The economic costs of Alzheimer's disease. *American Journal of Public health, 77*, 1169–1175.

Herbert, T. B., & Cohen, S. (1993a). Depression and immunity: A meta-analytic review. *Psychological Bulletin, 113*, 472–486.

Herbert, T. B., & Cohen, S. (1993b). Stress and immunity in humans: A meta-analytic review. *Psychosomatic Medicine, 55*, 364–379.

Irwin, M., Brown, M., Patterson, T., Hauger, R., Mascovich, A., & Grant, I. (1991). Neuropeptide Y and natural killer cell activity: Findings in depression and Alzheimer caregiver stress. *FASEB Journal, 5*, 3100–3107.

82   ROBINSON-WHELEN, KIECOLT-GLASER, GLASER

Jabaaij, P. M., Grosheide, R. A., Heijtink, R. A., Duivenvoorden, H. H., Ballieux, R. E., & Vigerhoets, A. J. J. M. (1993). Influence of perceived psychological stress and distress of antibody response to low dose rDNA Hepatitis B. vaccine. *Journal of Psychosomatic Research, 37*, 361–369.

Jenkins, C. D., Kraeger, B. E., Rose, R. M., & Hurst, M. W. (1980). Use of a monthly health review to ascertain illness and injuries. *American Journal of Public Health, 70*, 82–84.

Kiecolt-Glaser, J. K., Dura, J. R., Speicher, C. E., Trask, O. J., & Glaser, R. (1991),.Spousal caregivers of dementia victims: Longitudinal changes in immunity and health. *Psychsomatic Medicine, 53*, 345–362.

Kiecolt-Glaser, J. K., & Glaser, R. (1991). Stress and immune function in humans. In R. Ader, D. Felten, & N. Cohen (Eds.), *Psychoneuroimmunology II* (pp. 849–867). San Diego: Academic Press.

Kiecolt-Glaser, J. K., Glaser, R., Dyer, C., Shuttleworth, E., Ogrocki, P., & Speicher, C. E. (1987). Chronic stress and immunity in family caregivers for Alzheimer's disease victims. *Psychosomatic Medicine, 49*, 523–535.

Kiecolt-Glaser, J. K., Glaser, R., Williger, D., Stout, J., Messick, G., Sheppard, S., Ricker, D., Romisher, S. C., Briner, W., Bonnell, G., & Donnerberg, R. (1985). Psychosocial enhancement of immunocompetence in a geriatric population. *Health Psychology, 4*, 25–41.

Light, E., & Lebowitz, B. D. (1989). *Alzheimer's disease treatment and family stress: Directions for research.* Rockville, MD: National Institute of Mental Health.

Lund, D. A., Caserta, M. S., & Dimone, M. F. (1989). Impact of spousal bereavement on the subjective well-being of older adults. In D. A. Lund (Ed.), *Older bereaved spouses: Research with practical implications* (pp. 3–16). New York: Hemisphere.

McCann, J.J. (1991). *Effects of stress on spouse caregivers' psychological health and cellular immunity.* Unpublished doctoral dissertation, Rush University College of Nursing, Chicago.

McKinnon, W., Weisse, C. S., Reynolds, C. P., Bowles, C. A., & Baum, A. (1989). Chronic stress, leukocyte subpopulations, and humoral response to latent viruses. *Health Psychology, 8*, 389–402.

Murasko, D. M., Weiner, P., & Kaye, D. (1988). Association of lack of mitogen-induced lymphocyte proliferation with increased mortality in the elderly. *Aging: Immunology and Infectious Disease, 1*, 1–6.

Phair, J., Kauffmann, C. A., Bjornson, A., Adams, L., & Linnemann, C. (1978). Failure to respond to influenza vaccine in the aged: Correlation with B-cell number and function. *Journal of Laboratory and Clinical Medicine, 92*, 822–828.

Reese, D., Gross, A. M., Smalley, D. L., & Messer, S. C. (1994). Caregivers of Alzheimer's disease and stroke patients: Immunological and psychological considerations. *Gerontologist, 34*, 534–540.

Sapolsky, R. M., Krey, L. C., & McEwen, B. S. (1986). The neuroendocrinology of stress and aging: The glucocorticoid cascade hypothesis. *Endocrine Review, 7*, 284–301.

Schleifer, S. J., Keller, S. E., Bond, R. N., Cohen, J., & Stein, M. (1989). Depression and immunity: role of age, sex, and severity. *Archives of General Psychiatry, 46*, 81–87.

Schulz, R., Visitainer, P., & Williamson, G. M. (1990). Psychiatric and physical morbidity effects of caregiving. *Journal of Gerontology, Psychological Sciences, 45*, 181–191.

Solomon, G. F., & Benton, D. (1994). Psychoneuroimmunological aspects of aging. In R. Glaser & J. K. Kiecolt-Glaser (Eds.), *Handbook of human stress and immunity* (pp. 341–363). San Diego; Academic Press.

Thompson, L. W., Gallagher-Thompson, D., Futterman, A., Gilewski, M. J., & Peterson, J. (1991). The effects of late-life spousal bereavement over a 30-month period. *Psychology and Aging, 6*, 434–441.

Townsend, A., Noelker, L., Deimling, G., & Bass, D. (1989). Longitudinal impact of interhousehold caregiving on adult children's mental health. *Psychology and Aging, 4*, 393–401.

Wayne, S. J., Rhyne, R. L., Garry, P. J., & Goodwin, J. S., (1990). Cell mediated immunity as a predictor of morbidity and mortality in subjects over sixty. *Journal of Gerontology, Medical Sciences, 45*, M45–M48.

Yoshikawa, T. T. (1983). Geriatric infectious diseases: An emerging problem. *Journal of the American Geriatrics Society, 31*, 34–39.

7

Neuroimmune Interactions: Implications for Aging and Immunosenescence— Rodent Models

David A. Padgett
Cathleen M. Dobbs
John F. Sheridan
The Ohio State University

One of the long-term objectives of research on aging must be to define the mechanisms underlying age and stress-related changes in immunocompetence and susceptibility to infection. For example, why do the elderly remain at risk for influenza infection despite years of intense research the efficacy of influenza viral vaccines? Similarly, how does behavior (stress) increase the occurrence of respiratory infections in the elderly, seen in such circumstances as caregiving to patients with Alzheimer's dementia? It is important to address both aging and stress in the same breath, as some of the underlying mechanisms are shared with regard to modulation of immunity. The rationale behind this connection derives from observations in experimental models that (a) stress-induced alterations in microbial pathogenesis and cellular immunity are caused by both adrenal-dependent (glucocorticoid) and -independent (sympathetic nervous system) mechanisms (Bonneau, Sheridan, Feng, & Glaser, 1993), (b) virus-infected, aged rodents have reduced virus-specific T cell responses and higher levels of morbidity and mortality, (c) aging is associated with altered glucocorticoid responses, and (d) aging is also associated with a decline of sympathetic non-adrenergic innervation of secondary lymphoid organs.

Until recently, systemic theories of aging were based on regulatory networks that are responsible for integrating and adapting the functions of cells, tissues, and their responses to internal and external stimuli. The major systemic theories are typically restricted to two physiologic networks, the neuroendocrine and immune systems. Aging, according to these theories, represents poor or lost regulation of these networks. The neuroendocrine theory is based on the notion that this system (hypothalamus, pituitary, pituitary-dependent target glands, and other neurosecretory components) modulates many physiological functions in the body and that this system deteriorates progressively with advancing age. The immunologic theory of aging is based on the notion that the immune system is essential for maintaining the "health" of the body. This system also undergoes a progressive decline with age: immunosenescence. However, the discovery of complex interactions among the nervous, endocrine, and immune systems have revealed that some age-associated alterations in both systems are mutually interdependent. Therefore, as an alternative to an "either–or" hypothesis wherein aging results from a decline in either the neuroendocrine or the immune systems, the dysfunctions associated with aging may instead be a result of a loss of interactions among these systems during the aging process.

Here, we describe several animal models of aging and immunosenescence, while giving particular attention to neuroimmune mechanisms by which age and behavior affect viral pathogenesis and immunity. Behavior-induced responses, at least in terms of the response to stress, are mediated via the sympathetic nervous system (SNS) and the hypothalamic-pituitary-adrenal (HPA) axis. Therefore, we describe experimental animal models in which the impact of these systems has been analyzed during infection. Specifically, we detail the roles of secretory products of the SNS and HPA, namely catecholamines and glucocorticoids (GC), in the underlying mechanisms by which age and stress modulate immunity and pathogenesis during infectious diseases.

AGING AND THE
IMMUNE RESPONSE

As individuals age, they tend to become increasingly susceptible to infection. Some of this increased susceptibility has been attributed to senescence of cell-mediated, humoral, and nonspecific host immune defenses. Normal aging is accompanied by many different dysfunctions impacting immune function that can be associated with illness. These alterations have long been recognized as a correlate of advancing age and have even been postulated as the primary determinants of biologic senescence. Although this theory of aging, with impaired immune function as the focus, can be debated, it is apparent that many diseases of the elderly are associated with alterations in immune function. The senescence of health in adults is accompanied by a number of quantitative and qualitative changes in the activity of both T and B lymphocytes, NK cells, and macrophages. However, longitudinal studies of healthy subjects have shown that the total number of lymphocytes in peripheral blood does not change over time (Sparrow, Silbert, & Rowe, 1980). In addition, no consistent changes have been shown for the numbers or relative proportions of CD4+ or CD8+ T cell subpopulations (Nagel, Chrest, & Pyle, 1983). Similarly, B lymphocyte numbers do not change significantly throughout aging, nor do the serum levels of total immunoglobulin or of the major immunoglobulin subclasses (IgG, IgM, IgA).

In addition to the adaptive arm of the immune response, composed chiefly of T and B lymphocytes, there are a number of innate, nonspecific elements—both cellular and humoral. These include natural killer cells as well as cells mediating antibody-dependent cell-mediated cytotoxicity, reticuloendothelial cells, polymorphonuclear leukocytes, and serum complement. Because age-related changes in the activity of these nonspecific elements are much less apparent than those of T and B lymphocytes, data on their status in older individuals is often conflicting. However, it has been generally agreed that absolute numbers of peripheral blood polymorphonuclear leukocytes and levels of serum complement do not undergo major changes in a healthy elderly patient (Nagaki, Hiramatsu, & Inai, 1980).

Although the number of cells remains relatively stable throughout life, the decrease in the immune response is mediated by a decline in function of those cells. Herein, we describe the functional alterations associated with age-related immunosenecence. Although there are many abnormalities associated with age, including an increased frequency of both monoclonal gammopathies and autoantibodies (Saltzman & Peterson, 1987), many of the age-related changes in both the adaptive and innate branches of the immune system can be related either directly or indirectly to T lymphocyte dysfunctions. Therefore, current research in many laboratories is directed toward establishing the definition of the defect or defects intrinsic to T lymphocytes that alter their functional abilities. Early on in this pursuit, evidence suggested that decreased signals by regulatory helper T cells contributed to the decline of T cell activity. However, as we detail in the subsequent discussion, these findings merely represented the complications of more basic age-related changes in cellular physiology. At present, research focuses on ligand–receptor interactions, particularly those involving a group of membrane phospholipids and their transmembrane signaling. In the discussion that follows we characterize the changes in the immune system that accompany progressive age. While available, we include pertinent data from animal models.

Thymic Involution

The thymus, a primary lymphoid organ, may play a central role in some age-associated changes of immune functioning. In all mammalian species studied, including human beings, there is a progressive involution of the thymus. A major loss of thymic tissue begins at puberty and is completed by middle age. The involution of the thymus gland is accompanied by a decline in serum thymic hormone activity, which becomes undetectable in human subjects over 60 years of age (Lewis, Twomey, Bealmear, Goldstein, & Good, 1978). The thymus gland is essential in providing an environment that facilitates the modification of T cell function. Because of its involution, thymuses from older individuals express an inability to support differentiation of immature lymphocytes into mature or immunocompetent cells. Although there is a great interindividual variability in the degree of immunosenescence among aged individuals, there is a remarkable consistency in the reduction in the mass of the thymus and the decline in the thymic hormones in the blood. This involution appears to be a strict consequence of age, dependent on the endocrine milieu of the body. To support this hypothesis, Hirokaw and Makinonan (1975) illustrated that thymuses transplanted from old mice into thymectomized young mice could restore the T cell population to the young recipients. However, if the researchers transplanted young thymuses into old animals, the transplant failed to restore T cell numbers and their associated functions.

Age-Associated Alterations in Lymphocyte Numbers

The number of lymphocytes in the peripheral blood tends to remain the same in healthy older individuals. The ability of the bone marrow to generate B cells does not diminish with aging. Studies quantitating age-related changes have generated divergent results. Some researchers have reported a decline in both the absolute number and proportion of T lymphocytes

(Nagel, Chrest, & Pyle, 1983) whereas others detected no change (Terpenning & Bradley, 1991). The most common finding is a decrease in the proportion of T lymphocytes with a decrease in both CD4+ and CD8+ cells. The magnitude of the differences between older and younger human subjects is less than 20%, which may be too small to account for the functional decline of the immune system with aging. Thus, it is generally believed that the quantitative changes in the lymphocytes do not play a major role in immunosenescence. However, during aging, the fraction of naive CD4+ T cells (CD45RB^{high}, CD44^{low} Pgp-1$^-$, Mel-14$^+$) decreases in favor of memory CD4+ T cells (CD45RB^{low}, CD44^{high}, Pgp-1$^+$, Mel-14$^-$) (Lerner, Yamanda, & Miller, 1989).

Analysis of T cell function, until recently, has been carried out almost entirely in vitro; thus, the physiologic relevance of these assays has limited interpretation. However, they have uncovered several functional impairments associated with aged T cells. Measurements of proliferative responses to the following stimuli are commonly formed: nonspecific mitogens (e.g., phytohemagglutinin, concanavalin A, pokeweed), specific recall antigens (e.g., tetanus, Candida), and allogenic cells (i.e., mixed lymphocyte responses). Responses to each of these are diminished in cells from aged persons as compared with cells from young persons (Miller, Jacobson, Weil, & Simons, 1987). More specifically the age-related shift in phenotype to the memory CD4+ T cell is reflected in a loss of mitogenic responsiveness, low Ca^{2+} fluxes, low IL-2 production, and increased production of IL-4 (Grossmann, Ledbetter, & Rabinovitch, 1990; Lerner et al., 1989).

Humoral Immunity in the Aged

Humoral immunity was the first component of the immune system in which an age-related impairment was noted (Callard & Basten, 1978; Effros & Walford,1987). When compared to young healthy subjects, the antibody response to pneumococcal capsular polysaccharide was diminished in aged, healthy individuals (Ammann, Schiffman, & Austrian, 1980; Wade & Szewczuk, 1984). Likewise, the antibody response to an influenza vaccine or tetanus toxoid was also reduced (Effros & Walford, 1987; Makinodan & Kay, 1980). Even when produced, the specific antibodies secreted in vitro by cells from aged persons are less heterogeneous and have reduced antigen avidity (Proust, Bender, & Nagel, 1989). In short, these cells make less antibody, and that which is produced in less able to bind antigen. This decline may have additional relevance with regard to the efficacy of immunization.

One of the paradoxes of the alterations in immune function with age is the increased frequency of monoclonal immunoglobulins in older human beings despite the reduced capacity to mount an antibody response to specific antigens (Crawford, Eye, & Cohen, 1987). There is also an increased frequency of autoantibody levels in the old human being and rodent populations (Borghesi & Nicoletti, 1994; Kato & Hirokawa, 1988). Furthermore, in vitro proliferative responses of B lymphocytes to both nonspecific and antigen-specific stimuli decline with age (Thoman & Weigle, 1989).

What factors are responsible for the impaired humoral response seen with aging? Weksler (Hu, et al., 1993) explored the underlying mechanisms for the age-associated impaired production of antibodies to foreign antigens. Those studies suggest a cellular basis for the age-associated shift in the expressed antibody repertoire, namely, an increased activity of the CD5+ relative to the CD5– B cell subsets. The CD5+ population is skewed to polyreactive, natural autoantibodies whereas the CD5– B cell population produces most antibodies to foreign antigens (Hayakawa & Hardy, 1988). The impaired response of elderly human beings to many antigens, including influenza vaccine, may reflect a defect in the CD5– B cell population. However, does this represent an inherent defect of the B cell, or is there an underlying mechanism indirectly responsible for this dysfunction?

Many researchers believe that the major defect in antibody production by lymphocytes from elderly persons is not owing to the B cell itself but most likely owing to altered T lymphocyte functions. Evidence for this comes from cell transfer studies in mice (Goidl & Innes, 1976). When T-dependent antigens such as sheep erythrocytes are mixed with mouse lymphocytes, the amount of antibody response generated from 18-month-old mice is only about 5% of that seen when cells from 3- to 6-month-old mice are used. Spleen cells from old mice transfer the age-associated defects in immunity to young irradiated, thymectomized mice. The young recipients of spleen cells from old mice express a reduced immune response to foreign antigens with a preferential loss of high affinity and IgG antibodies typical of the immune response in older mice. When transfer studies were performed in which B lymphocytes and T lymphocytes from old and young mice were mixed in various combinations, the predominant defect was shown to reside in the T lymphocyte population, specifically helper T cells. Thus, the weight of the current evidence lends support to the concept that B cell changes are secondary to age-associated changes in T cell function.

Cell-Mediated Immunity

In regard to the components of the immune system, cell-mediated immunity exhibits the most profound dysfunction associated with aging. Evidence for the severe functional decline of the cellular immune response comes from both in vivo and in vitro analyses of T cell function. Delayed hypersensitivity, mediated by cell-mediated immunity and demonstrated by skin testing with ubiquitous antigens, is depressed with advancing age. Elderly humans have a less frequent and less vigorous response to antigens. In one study, 279 healthy elderly individuals underwent skin testing with four common antigens (Goodwin, Searles, & Tung, 1982). One third of the patients had no induration after 2 days to any of the antigens, whereas all young subjects showed at least 5 mm or greater induration to at least one or more of the antigens. In addition to an impaired immune response to previously exposed skin antigens, there is an impaired ability of the elderly to develop a new hypersensitivity response. Dinitrochlorobenzene (DNCB), which usually sensitizes an individual on first contact, will stimulate contact sensitivity after a second application. However, when young and older human beings were challenged with DNCB, 30% of individuals over 70 years of age failed to respond to the re-application while only 5% of subjects under 70 years of age failed to respond (Waldorf, Wilkens, & Decker, 1968).

As mentioned, the majority of the research demonstrating decreased T cell function with age has relied on in vitro studies. Although there are some inconsistencies from different labs, in general the proliferative capacity of human peripheral lymphocytes in response to T cell mitogens is reduced in older subjects. In one study, the proliferative response to both phytohemagglutinin (PHA) and concanavalin A (ConA), each a T cell mitogen, was reduced by approximately 50% in older individuals as compared to younger control subjects (Murasko, Nelson, & Silver, 1986). Furthermore, among those cells that do proliferate, the number of sequential divisions for each cell declines with age (Thoman & Weigle, 1989). In contrast, there was no decreased response to a B cell mitogen such as pokeweed mitogen, supporting the concept that the T cell response is diminished whereas the B cell response remains relatively intact with age.

Lymphokines are essential for the generation and recruitment of cytotoxic T lymphocytes (CTLs). IL-2, secreted by T lymphocytes in response to antigenic stimulation, promotes proliferation of both CD4+ and CD8+ T cells. Such secretion declines with age (Gillis, Kozak, & Durante,

1981). The decreased production of IL-2 appears to result from the reduced function of T-helper-1 cells, which are responsible for the majority of its production (Mosmann & Coffman, 1989). However, exogenous IL-2 is incapable of fully restoring the defective T cell response in aged cells, perhaps owing to a parallel age-related defect in the expression of the IL-2 receptor (Nagel, Chopra, & Chrest, 1988).

To summarize, the diminished proliferative response of aged T cells is owing to a limited numbers of cells entering the cell cycle. That is, aged lymphocytes are a mosaic of normal, active cells and those that are defective. The reason why some cells retain their youthful vigor and others become inactive is unknown.

Signal Transduction and Activation Defects

Although at any stage in life there are cells that do not respond to activation, there is an age-related accumulation of these cells such that most T lymphocytes do not respond at all to mitogenic or antigenic stimulation. What distinguishes these cells from those that do respond in earlier life? In other words, what is preventing the transition from the G0 to G1 and S stages in the cell cycle?

Extensive studies to identify why aged T cells fail to properly respond to antigenic stimuli has demonstrated that multiple defects impair this process. The activation of T cells requires a primary signal through the Ag-specific receptor (TCR) and a second costimulatory signal through such a surface molecule as CD28. The initial binding of the mitogen or antigen to the TCR appears to be normal. However, transduction of this signal may be impaired owing to hyporesponsiveness to costimulation through CD28 by B7 on antigen-presenting cells. Engwerda and colleagues (Engwerda, Handwerger, & Fox, 1994) showed that although aged T cells expressed comparable levels of CD28, they were indeed less responsive to costimulation by anti-CD28 mAb as compared to younger control cell populations. Further analysis of lymphocyte activation has shown that there is an age-associated defect with regard to Ca^{2+} mobilization after mitogen or anti-CC3 antibody stimulation (Miller et al. 1987). both CD4+ and CD8+ T lymphocytes appear to be affected by this early activation signal. The mobilization of Ca^{2+} is believed to play an important role in helping to initiate later and more committed steps of the activation process. Supporting this concept, Miller and colleagues (1987) have shown that a calcium ionophore (ionomycin), which bypasses the need for a ligand-induced signal for Ca^{2+} mobilization, provided a good proliferative stimulus for T cells from old mice. However, they further showed that there is an age-related decline in the extent to which mouse T cells can accumulate intracellular Ca^{2+}.

In addition to these initial activation signals, there exist many levels of control in which age-dependent alterations such as cell membrane composition and cytoplasmic levels of IP3, DAG, and PLC may interfere with proper signal transduction for activation and proliferation (Utsuyama, et. al., 1993). Extensive research focusing on the many signal transduction systems has shown similar dysfunctions associated with advancing age (Miller, 1989; Nordin & Proust, 1987). Thus, because of the number of defects associated with cellular activation, perhaps the individual findings only represent the complications of more basic age-related changes in physiology.

Natural Resistance Mechanisms

Although immune responses to many pathogenic microorganisms and tumors decline with age, it would be reasonable to assume that the first line of defense also may be compromised owing to age. The function of natural killer cells, thought to contribute to immunosurveillance against tumors and viruses, declines with age, although frequency analysis has not shown a significant difference (Mikael et al., 1994). Albright and Albright (1985) showed that mouse strains with high endogenous natural killer cell (NK) activity such as C3H show a more rapid decline in NK function than do strains exhibiting medium NK activity such as the C57BL/6 mouse. Because of their similar killing mechanisms, the decline in cytotoxic activity of NK cells as well as that of CTLs may be owing to decreased serine esterase or perforin release, or both. In light of this speculation, could the same mechanism lead to the decline in both NK and CTL function?

As another of the first lines of defense, macrophages, particularly alveolar macrophages, play critical roles in several important ways. First, macrophages kill microorganisms through phagocytosis; second, the mamacrophage is a principal antigen-presenting cell for education of the T lyumphcytes; third, cytokines secreted by these activated macrophages function to activate appropriate lymphocytes to mount an attack against the foreign insult. Fukuchi (Fukuchi et al., 1993) showed that alveolar macrophages from aged mice, as compared to their young controls, had a lower phagocytic capacity and produced lower levels of tumor necrosis factor alpha (TNF-α).

Others have shown that peritoneal macrophages from aged animals produced low levels of IL-1 (Bradley, Vibhagool, Kunkel, & Kauffman, 1989). In addition, interferon-γ activation leading to upregulation of MHC class II molecules and TNF-α production from peritoneal rate macrophages also decline with age (Davila, Edwards, Arkins, Simon, & Kelley, 1990). Another potent cytokine produced principally by macrophages (also by B cells and peripheral adherent cells) is interleukin-12 (IL-12). IL-12 augments natural killer cell activity and synergizes with IL-2 to increase the proliferation of both NK and T cells in response to mitogens and phorol esters (Gately, Wolitzky, Quinn, & Chizzonite, 1992; Perussian, et al., 1992). It also stimulates IFN-γ production by both the NK and CD8+ and CD4+ T-helper-1 cells. As we have detailed previously CD8+ CTL responses requiring CD4+ T cell help are severely compromised with age. Bloom and Horvath (1994) showed that (a) cells from young and aged mice responded to IL-12 in a qualitatively similar manner, and (b) IL-12 restored allo-specific CTL generated by cells from aged mice to approximately the level generated by cells from young mice in its absence. These decreased functions inherent to macrophage from elderly individuals may relate to the poor inflammatory response in elderly individuals. Without a proper inflammatory response, the initial reaction to an invading pathogen is slow to start, poorly managed, and insufficient to combat microbial replication.

NEUROENDOCRINE–IMMUNE INTERACTIONS

The immunologic theory of aging is based on the notion that the immune system is essential for maintaining the "health" of the body. This system undergoes a progressive decline with age, as we have briefly detailed. However, while reviewing the data concerning age-related immunosenescence, one should question whether the changes within the immune system are inherent or are a result of age-associated changes in systems that interact with the immune system. Another theory of aging, the neuroendocrine theory, is based on the notion that the nervous system (hypothalamus, pituitary, pituitary-dependent target glands, and other neurosecretory components) controls many physiological functions of the body and that this system deteriorates progressively with advancing age. However, the discovery of the complex interactions among the neuroendocrine and immune systems has revealed that some age-associated alterations in both systems are mutually interdependent. Therefore, as an alternative to an "either–or" hypothesis wherein aging results from a decline in either the neuroendocrine or immune systems, the dysfunction associated with aging may instead be a result of a loss of interactions between these two physiologic systems during the aging process.

Evidence from a wide variety of fields indicates that neuroendocrine–immune interactions provide a biological mechanism for resistance or susceptibility to disease. Although specific central pathways through which the neuroendocrine system interacts with the immune system have not been completely elucidated, two important efferent pathways involve hormonal mediators and autonomic innervation. Given the interactions that exist between the neuroendocrine and immune systems, age-associated alterations in the neuroendocrine system are predicted to contribute to declining immune responses in the aged.

Glucocorticoids and Immune System Interactions

Glucocorticoids are perhaps the best studied neuroendocrine substances that have been shown to exert pronounced effects on immune responses. Although GCs may exert stimulatory effects on certain immunologic responses, the effects are most often inhibitory. The immunomodulatory effects of GC are owing, in large part, to interactions of GC with specific receptors on mononuclear cells (Crabree, Munck, & Smith, 1980; Werb, Foley, & Munck, 1978). Immunosuppressive effects of GC on lymphocytes include inhibition of: (a) cytokine production, (b) antibody formation, (c) natural killer (NK) cell activity, (d) delayed type hypersensitivity responses (Cupps & Fauci, 1982; Munck & Guyre, 1991), and (e) chemotaxis and trafficking (Dobbs, Vasquez, Glaser, & Sheridan, 1993; Hermann, Beck, & Sheridan, 1995). Immunosuppressive effects of GC on monocytes and macrophages include decreased: (a) cytokine production (e.g., IL-1 and TNF), (b) phagocytosis, and (c) MHC class II expression (Cupps & Fauci, 1982; Munck & Guyre, 1991).

SNS and Immune System Interactions

Both primary and secondary lymphoid organs are directly innervated by nonadrenergic postganglionic nerve fibers of the SNS, which often end in regions where lymphocytes are clustered. These fibers are dispersed throughout the cortex and medulla of the thymus and traverse the stromal-cell matrix of the bone marrow (Felten & Felten, 1991). The spleen and lymph nodes are similarly innervated by nonadrenergic nerve fibers. In the periarteriolar lympohoid sheath of the spleen, for example, these nerve fibers form intimate anatomic associations with T lymphocytes and interdigitating dendritic cells (Felten & Olschowka, 1987). However, in Fisher rats, an age-related decline in noradrenergic innervation of secondary lymphoid organs has been documented (Bellinger, Ackerman, Felten, Lorton, & Felten, 1988). T lymphocytes express adrenergic receptors (Fuchs, Albright, & Albright, 1988) and are, thus, poised to respond to neuronally released catecholamines such as norepinephrine (NE). In vivo studies in rodents using chemical sympathectomy or surgery to remove noradrenergic innervation of lymphoid organs demonstrated the important role of the SNS in the control of immune responses (Felten, et al., 1987). For example, treatment of animals with 6-hydroxydopamine has been found to suppress alloantigen-induced CTL activity and reduce primary antibody responses. Chemical sympathectomy has also been used to alter mitogenic responses and enhance NK cell activity in the spleen. In vitro studies indicate that catecholamines can enhance NK cell activity in the spleen. In vitro studies indicate that catecholamines can enhance primary antibody responses and alloantigen-specific CTL generation when present at the initiation of culture, but they can inhibit effector cell function (reviewed in Madden & Livnat, 1991). As can be seen from these studies, it is difficult to assign a strictly immunosuppressive or immunoenhancing role to products of the SNS.

Stress Response

The close functional relationship between the neuroendocrine system and the immune system is highlighted during the stress response. The neuroendocrine responses to stress, mediated through the activation of the HPA axis and SNS, intersect and modulate immune response pathways, and, through the mechanisms delineated previously, after cellular and humoral immunity. Significant interactions among these important physiological systems are predicted to impinge on the pathophysiology of disease processes increasing susceptibility or severity, or both.

Generally defined, a stressor is any stimulus that disrupts normal physiologic equilibrium or homeostasis. Through neural circuits and hormonal secretions, all living organisms strive to maintain homeostasis in the face of both externally and internally generated stressors. Both physiological and behavioral challenges trigger stress-response mechanisms. The stress response is the entire set of neural and endocrine adaptations directed at restoring homeostasis. This response is a disparate body-wide set of adaptations, responding to a specific challenge and to the stimulus. Neuroendocrine changes set and reset priorities for organs throughout the body and confer a survival advantage in the face of a stressor (Chrousos & Gold, 1992). Glucose and free fatty acids are mobilized from storage tissues and made available for energy production within critical tissues (brain, heart, skeletal muscle); further energy storage is halted. Blood is shunted from the skin, mucosa, connective tissue, and kidneys; blood flow to the heart and skeletal muscle is increased. Digestion, growth, reproduction, and immunity are suppressed. During a short-term stressor, the costs associated with suppression of these systems can be contained, but, as expected, these responses can be deleterious if activated chronically.

The most important facts about stress physiology are that (a) if an organism cannot appropriately initiate a stress response during an acute stressor, the consequences can be deleterious, and (b) if an organism cannot appropriately terminate a stress response at the end of stress, or if it is hyperresponsive because of repeated or chronic stressors, numerous stress-related diseases can emerge. Thus, the stress response is a vital set of adaptations on the part of the body, but a potentially dangerous one if not closely regulated.

Age-Related Changes in the Stress Response

Aging may be thought of as a time of decreased capacity to respond appropriately to stressors; the aged individual may require less of an exogenous insult for homeostasis to be disrupted or may require longer to re-establish homeostasis once the stressor has occurred. In addition, aging may be associated with a lost ability to turn off the neuroendocrine response to the stressor. This is observed in the HPA axis system in which against is associated with prolonged stressor-induced plasma glucocorticoid levels (Lorens et al., 1990). Such dysregulation is also seen with regard to the nervous system after the end of a stressor. Perego and colleagues (Perego, Vetrugno, De Simoni, & Algeri, 1993) have shown that stress-induced noradrenaline levels in rat hypothalamus that, in young animals, returned to normal shortly after removal of the stressful stimulus, remained elevated significantly longer in old rats subjected to the same stressor. This response is not limited to the hypothalamus; plasma carecholamines persisted longer in old than in young rats following acute stress (DeTurck & Vogel, 1980; McCarty, Horwatt, & Konarska, 1988). Thus, there is evidence that aged organisms respond to stress less adaptively than do young organisms. Exposure to a stressor may lead to more pronounced effects on the immune system of aged organisms. These findings indicate that aging impairs the capacity to recover from stress and return to homeostasis.

AGING, STRESS AND
VIRAL INFECTION

Experimental Murine Viral Infections:
Influenza A Virus and HSV-1 Models

Influenza virus is a "replicating antigen" that initially infects both the upper and lower respiratory tract in the mouse. For an immune response to effectively terminate viral replication in a nonlymphoid organ such as the lung, effector T and B lymphocytes must be recruited to the site of infection. The accumulation of antigen-reactive cells occurs as a consequence of both the inflammatory process and antigen-specific recruitment (Huneycutt, 1990; Yong-He & Nai-ki, 1986; Hopkins, McConnell, & Lachman, 1981; Wells, Albrecht, & Ennis, 1981). Regional draining lymph nodes and the spleen provide the appropriate microenvironments for antigen presentation and stimulation of virus-specific lymphocytes. both CD4+ and CD8+ lymphocytes are stimulated by influenza virus, and antigen-specific lympohocytes traffic to sites of inflammation by recognizing adhesion molecule expression and responding to chemotactic signals; once at the inflammatory site, they become fully activated effector cells.

Experimental innoculation of herpes simplex virus type-1(HSV-1) into the skin of mice results in viral replication in the epithelium. As a consequence of infection, the draining popliteal lymph nodes increase in size and cellularity owing to several events such as an influx of lymphocytes, the proliferation of virus-specific lymphocytes, and the retention of lymphocytes within the nodes. The ability of HSV-1 to spread by direct cell-to-cell contact and become latent necessities a cellular immune response for control of infection. Virus-specific CLTs are essential for resolution of the infection and can be detected in the popliteal nodes within 4 days of infection (Bonneau et al., 1993).

Anti-Viral Immunity and Importance in Aging

Advancing age brings an increased vulnerability to infectious agents. Infection is the fourth most common cause of death in older people, with pneumonia leading the last (Anonymous, 1994). The decline in immunocompetence with increasing age is certainly a major factor in the high incidence of pneumonia in the elderly population (Murasko et al., 1986).

Evidence from experimental animal studies suggests that age-associated decrements in cell-mediated immunity are particularly important in the increased susceptibility to infections with intracellular pathogens (Effros & Walford, 1987; Louria, Sen, & Buse, 1982). Murine models of influenza have been used extensively to study the effects of aging on the immune response to infection. In aged mice, immunity to influenza is characterized by diminished CTL and cytokine (IL-2) responses (Bender, Johnson, & Small, 1991; Bender & Small, 1993; Effros & Walford, 1983a, 1983b). Aged mice demonstrate a decreased frequency of influenza-specific CTL precursors in comparison to younger mice (Ashman, 1982; Effros & Walford, 1984). The reduced frequency suggests an age-associated defect in the clonal expansion of influenza virus-specific CTL. However, the inability of exogenously added IL-2 to fully restore CTL responses in cultures from aged mice indicates that reduced cytokine is not the only reason for limited clonal expansion of anti-viral CTL (Effros & Walford, 1983a). There is evidence to suggest that defective antigen presentation by splenic adherent cells from aged mice may contribute to the age-related decrease in anti-influenza CTL activity (Effros & Walford, 1984). In contrast to reduced T lymphocyte responses to influenza, aging is not associated with an altered anti-influenza antibody response (Bender et al., 1991; Zharhary & Klinman, 1984). These studies clearly document a relationship between immunosenescence and increased infectious disease susceptibility, and they point out the utility of the model of influenza infection in studies of aging and the immune response to intracellular pathogens.

Animal Models to Examine the Neuroendocrine Influences on Viral Infections

Experimental stressors have been used to activate neuroendocrine pathways and facilitate the study of immunomodulation. Parametric variations of a stressor (physical restraint) were tested for effects on the cellular immune response during viral infection. Activation of T cells (cytokine-secreting and cytolytic T cells) was examined in restraint-stressed animals. Short cycles of restraint (< 6 hours) briefly elevated plasma corticosterone levels but had not effect on the IL-2 response to influenza virus, nor did they alter the pathophysiology of the infectious process (Feng, 1992). Similarly, a low number (< 4 cycles) of longer cycles of restraint (> 12 hours) did not affect these parameters. However, when the number of restraint cycles was greater than or equal to 4 (cycle length 10 to 16 hours), the IL-2 and CTL responses were significantly depressed in both influenza and herpes simplex viral infections (Bonneau, Sheridan, Feng, & Glaser, 1991b; Sheridan et al., 1991).

Effects of Stress on the Cellular Immunity

To examine the effects of physical restraint on a viral infection in the respiratory tract, a series of experiments was conducted in which C57BL:/6 male mice were infected intranasally with 32 hemagglutinating units (HAU) of influenza A/PR8 virus, and restraint (16hr/cycle) was started 1 or 2 days prior to infection and continued throughout the infection period. Physical restraint significantly altered the inflammatory response during infection; the extent of inflammation was greater in the nonrestrained/infected group, suggesting that restraint resulted in diminished pulmonary inflammation (Hermann et al., 1995). Cellular immune responses by virus-specific T cells from lymph nodes and spleens were also significantly depressed in restraint-stressed animals (Sheridan et al., 1991). Furthermore, IL-2 responses from these lymphocyte populations were still depressed as late as 25 days following the last cycle of restraint. The depressed IL-2 response to influenza virus was not owing to a diminished frequency of virus-specific cytokine secreting T cells, as limiting dilution analysis indicated similar frequencies in restrained and control mice. However, the reduced cell density in the draining lymph nodes of restrained mice probably was responsible for the diminished IL-2 response, as the absolute number of virus-specific T cells in the nodes was significantly lower than that of the virus-infected controls (Feng, 1992).

The effects of restraint stress on a mouse footpad infected model with HSV-1 strain Patton have also been shown (Bonneau et al., 1991a). Restraint reduced the cell yields from the draining lymph nodes (popliteal) as well as the virus-specific T cell IL-2 responses. Cytotoxic responses of natural killer cells and CD8+ T cells were also suppressed by restraint (Bonneau et al., 1991b). This probably accounted for higher titers of HSV-1 in the footpads of the restrained mice. Restraint had a differential effect on the T cell subsets (CD4+ and CD8+ T cells). Restraint diminished the IL-2 responses in the draining lymph node, but the frequency of virus-specific IL-2 secreting T cells was similar in control and restrained groups as observed in the influenza model. Restraint also diminished the cytolytic activity of class I-restricted CTL recovered from the nodes; however, the frequency of CTL precursors in the node was reduced. The effect of restraint on the development of HSV-specific memory CTL (CTLm) responses was examined, as well as was the effect of stress on HSV-specific CTLm localization and proliferation in the popliteal lymph node following re-exposure to HSV. Restraint stress did not inhibit the generation of CTLm; however, it did inhibit the ability to activate CTLm to the lytic phenotype. Furthermore, in mice primed to HSV prior to restraint, the application of the stressor prevented in vivo activation or migration or both of HSV-specific CTLm in the popliteal lymph nodes (Bonneau et al., 1991a). These findings suggest that virus-specific immunological memory can be inhibited by physiological changes associated with experimental stressors. Further, it is possible that such immune inhibition may provide a mechanism that accounts for the development of recrudescent herpetic disease.

Effect of Stress on Lymphocyte Trafficking

The ability of lymphocytes to enter a lymph node draining the site of a viral infection plays a critical role in the development of the anti-viral cellular immune response. The regional draining lymph node provides the appropriate microenvironment for antigen presentation to naive, virus-specific lymphocytes that results in lymphocyte activation, differentiation, and clonal expansion. Reflective, in part, on an influx of mononuclear cells and the clonal expansion of virus-specific lymphocytes, a massive increase in the cellularity of the draining lymph node occurs during the primary immune response to viral infection (Hermann, Tovar, Beck, Allen, & Sheridan, 1993; Huneycutt, 1990; Lynch, Doherty, & Ceredig, 1989). Following clonal expansion and differentiation, virus-specific T lymphocytes exit the draining lymph node and traffic to the site of infection.

The trafficking of virus-specific effector lymphocytes to a site of virus replication plays a critical role in the eradication of virus. Restraint stress decreased the cellularity of the draining lymph nodes in both HSV and influenza virus infections of mice; and in the influenza model, restraint reduced mononuclear cell infiltration in the lungs of virus-infected animals. Additionally, reduced cellular accumulation was owing to restraint-induced elevations in plasma corticosterone, as treatment of stressed animals with RU486, a glucocorticoid receptor antagonist, restored lymphadenopathy to draining lymph nodes and lymphocyte trafficking to the infected lung (Dobbs et al., 1993; Hermann et al., 1995). One mechanism by which activated effector T lymphocytes are directed to an inflammatory site is thought to be the differential regulation of lymphocyte adhesion molecules (Mobley & Dailey, 1992). Therefore, it is proposed that the altered pattern of mononuclear cell trafficking observed in restrained mice was owing to the inhibition of lymphocyte, or endothelial cell, adhesion molecule expression. Furthermore, the elevated plasma corticosterone induced by restraint may be the mechanism that decreases lymphocyte localization to sites of virus replication by inhibiting adhesion molecule expression either directly or indirectly through cytokine modulation. Although cytokines have been associated with induction or enhancement of adhesion molecule expression, Glucocorticoids have been shown to inhibit the synthesis of cytokines that upregulate expression of ICAM-1 and VCAM-1 (IL-1, and TNF-a) (Lee et al., 1988; Beutler, Krochin, Milsark, Leudke, & Cerami, 1986). In addition, glucocorticoids have been shown to directly inhibit both constitutive and cytokine-induced expression of ICAM-1 in vitro (Sadeghi, Feldmann, & Hawrylowicz, 1992; Rothlein et al., 1988; Cronstein, Kimmel, Levin, Martinuik, & Weissmann, 1992). Experimentation is currently ongoing to test the mechanisms by which stress might modulate adhesion molecule expression.

Effect of Stress on Humoral Immunity

Viral infections induce specific antibody responses that can be measured systemically in plasma or locally in mucosal secretions. Isotype specific enzyme-linked immunosorbent assays (ELISA) have been used to study the kinetics, magnitude, and isotypes of anti-viral antibody responses and assess the effects of stressors on the responses (Feng, Pagniano, Tovar, Bonneau, & Sheridan, 1991; Kusnecov et al., 1992). In an HSV rodent model, mild electric footshock depressed serum igM anti-HSV antibody titers (Kusnecov et al., 1992). In the influenza viral infection model with physical restraint as the stressor, little or no effect of stress on the humoral immune response was seen when virus-specific IgG titers were measured 14 days post-infection (Sheridan et al., 1991). However, in subsequent experiments designed to assess the kinetics and class switching of the anti-influenza antibody response, stress altered the kinetics of the antibody response, and seroconversion in the IgM isotype was delayed by restraint. In addition, isotype switching from IgM to IgG, and IgG to IgA, was significantly delayed, perhaps owing to suppression of T cell cytokine responses necessary to support B cell activation and differentiation. Again, restraint did not alter the magnitude or class of the humoral response (Feng et al., 1991).

Neuroendocrine Immune Interactions During Viral Infection

Surgical adrenalectomy (ADX) and the administration of exogenous corticosterone were used to examine the effects of adrenal hormones on the restraint-induced suppression of virus-specific lympohocyte activation and lymphocyte trafficking. ADX inhibited the stress-induced suppression of HSV-specific CTL activation (Bonneau et al., 1993). However, administration of exogenous corticosterone to adrenalectomized mice was insufficient to suppress CTL activation, suggesting that adrenal medullary hormones, or other non-glucocorticoid hormones of adrenal origin, mediated this response during stress. ADX did not affect the restraint-induced suppression of lymph node cellularity. However, exogenous corticosterone combined with restraint stress reduced the cellularity of the draining lymph nodes in HSV-infected, adrenalectomized mice. This suggested that corticosterone and an adrenal-independent, stress-induced component were responsible for the suppression of lymph node cellularity (Bonneau et al., 1993).

In an effort to move specifically delineate the role of endogenous glucocorticoids, mice were treated with RU486, a potent glucocorticoid receptor antagonist (Moguilewsky & Philibert, 1984), to study the effects of glucocorticoids in the presence of intact adrenal catecholamine secretion. RU486 treatment of C57BL/6 mice did not restore the restraint-induced suppression of HSV-specific CTL activation (Dobbs et al., 1993). These results corroborate those of the ADX study by demonstrating that corticosterone alone was insufficient to mediate the stress-induced suppression of CTL activation. However, treatment of C57BL/6 mice with RU486 did reverse the restraint-induced diminution of cellularity in response to local HSV infection. These results strengthen those of the ADX study by confirming a role for endogenous corticosterone in the reduction of lymph node cellularity.

To assess the contribution of the SNS to restraint-induced immunosuppression, the adrenergic neurotoxin 6-OHDA was used to selectively eliminate terminals of the SNS in mice prior to influenza infection and restraint (Hermann, et al., 1994). Pretreatment of mice with 6-OHDA abrogated the restraint-induced reduction in lymph node cellularity. These results suggest that SNS-derived neurotransmitters may play a role in the stress-induced suppression of lymph node cellularity. However, to more directly assess the effects of catecholamines on the modulation of anti-viral cellular immune responses, without interfering with central adrenergic responses to stress (Stone, 1987), restrained mice were treated with nadolol, a peripherally acting, β-adrenergic antagonist (Lee, Evans, Baky, & Laffan, 1975). Nadolol treatment of C57BL/6 mice partially restored the restraint-induced suppression of HSV-specific CTL activation (Dobbs et al., 1993) but failed to restore the cellularity of the draining lymph nodes. Thus, these data confirmed a role for catecholamines in the restraint-induced inhibition of lymphocyte activation. Furthermore, the results suggested that the restraint-induced decrease in cellularity was not mediated by the actions of catecholamines at peripheral β-adrenergic receptors. the data do not, however, rule out a role for catecholamines acting at α-adrenergic receptors in the diminution of lymph node cellularity.

An effective anti-viral CTL response requires the clonal expansion and differentiation of antigen-reactive lymphocytes within the draining lymph nodes. It has been hypothesized that the inability of nadolol to completely restore the restraint-induced suppression of CTL activation was owing to a corticosterone-dependent decrease in HSV-1 specific lymphocytes in the draining popliteal lymph nodes. In support of this hypothesis, it was determined that simultaneous treatment of mice with RU486 and nadolol fully abrogated the restraint-induced suppression of HSV-Specific CTL activation. These data, along with data from the ADX studies, support the concept that both glucocorticoids and catecholamines mediate the restraint-induced suppression of CTL activation. Overall, these studies on the mechanisms of neuroendocrine immune interactions during viral infection indicate roles for both glucocorticoids and catecholamines in the modulation of anti-viral cellular immune responses.

CONCLUSION

Advancing age brings an increased vulnerability to infectious agents. The decline in immunocompetence with increasing age is certainly a major factor in the high incidence of pneumonia in the elderly population.

However, virtually every human being who survives into adulthood expresses an age-related state of immunodeficiency. Therefore, in discussing the effects of age on the immune system it is necessary to emphasize that other factors such as age-related changes in various organ systems (which might affect immune–endocrine interactions), diminished nutritional status (which might have a direct effect on immunity), and the frequent presence of chronic debilitating diseases (particularly those with inflammatory or autoimmune components) may all impact on an individual's state of immunocompetence.

Considerable evidence documenting correlations among neuroendocrine alterations, immunosenescence, and increased infectious disease susceptibility is accumulating from human research (Kiecolt-Glaser, Dura, Speicher, Trask, & Glaser, 1987; Kiecolt-Glaser, Glaser, et al., 1987). further research is needed to elucidate the significance of these observations. To accomplish this goal, animal models of infectious disease provide the tools to explore neuroendocrine–immune interactions in the context of aging. They allow for the identification of significant age-related alterations in interactions among physiological systems that impinge on susceptibility to infectious disease.

REFERENCES

Albright, J. W., & Albright, J. F. (1985). Age-associated decline in natural killer (NK) activity reflects primarily a defect in function of NK cells. *Mechanisms of Aging and Development, 31*, 295–306.

Ammann, A. J., Schiffman, G., & Austrian, R. (1980). The antibody responses to pneumococcal capsular polysaccharides in aged individuals. *Proceedings of the Society for Experimental Biology and Medicine, 164*, 312–316.

Anonymous. (1994). Update: influenza activity—worldwide. *Morbidity Mortality Weekly Report, 43 (38)*, 691–693.

Ashman, R. B. (1982). Persistence of cell-mediated immunity to influenza A virus in mice. *Immunology, 47*, 165–168.

Bellinger, D. L., Ackerman, K. D., Felten, S. Y., Lorton, D., & Felten, D .L. (1988). Noradrenergic sympathetic innervation of thymus, spleen, and lymph nodes: Aspects of development, aging and plasticity in neural immune interaction. In J. W. Hadden, K. Masek, & G. Nistico (Eds.), *Proceedings of a Symposium on Interactions Between the Neuroendocrine and Immune Systems* (pp. 35–66). Rome/Milan: Pythagora Press.

Bender, B. S., Johnson, M. P., & Small, P .A. (1991). Influenza in senescent mice: Impaired cytotoxic T-lymphocyte activity is correlated with prolonged infection. *Immunology, 72*, 514–519.

Bender, B. S., & Small, P.A. (1993). Heterotypic immune mice lose protection against influenza virus infection with senescence. *Journal of Infectious Diseases, 168*, 873–880.

Beutler, B., Krochin, N., Milsark, I. W., Luedke, C., & Ceramin, A. (1986). Control of cachectin (tumor necrosis factor) synthesis: Mechanisms of endotoxin resistance. *Science, 232*, 977–980.

Bloom, E. T., & Horvath, J. A. (1994). Cellular and molecular mechanisms of the IL-12–induced increase in allospecific murine cytolytic T cell activity. *Journal of Immunology, 152*, 4242–4254.

Bonneau, R. H., Sheridan, J. F., Feng, N., & Glaser, R. (1991a). Stress-induced effects on cell-mediated innate and adaptive memory components of the murine response to herpes simplex virus infection. *Brain, Behavior and Immunity, 5*, 274–295.

Bonneau, R. H., Sheridan, J. F., Feng, N., & Glaser, R. (1991b). Stress-induced suppression of herpes simplex virus (HSV)–specific cytotoxic T lymphocyte and natural killer cell activity and enhancement of acute pathogenesis following local HSV infection. *Brain, Behavior and Immunity, 5*, 170–192.

Bonneau, R. H., Sheridan, J. F., Feng, N., & Glaser, R. (1993). Stress-induced modulation of the primary cellular response to herpes simplex virus is mediated by both adrenal-dependent and adrenal-independent mechanisms. *Journal of Neuroimmunology, 42*, 167–176.

Borghesi, C., & Nicoletti, C. (1994). Increase of cross (auto)-reactive antibodies after immunization in aged mice: A cellular and molecular study. *International Journal of Experimental Pathology, 75*, 123–130.

Bradley, S. F., Vibhagool, A., Kunkel, S. L., & Kauffman, C. A. (1989). Monokine secretion in aging and protein malnutrition. *Journal of Leukocyte Biology, 45*, 510–514.

Callard, R. E., & Basten, A. (1978). Immune function in aged mice. IV. Loss of T cell and B cell function in thymus-dependent antibody responses. *European Journal of Immunology, 8*, 552–558.

Chouros, G. P., & Gold, P. W. (1992). The concepts of stress and stress system disorders: Overview of physical and behavioral homeostasis. *Journal of the American Medical Association, 267*, 1244–1252.

Crabtree, G. R., Munck, A., & Smith, K. A. (1980). Glucocorticoids and lymphocytes. I. Increased glucocorticoid receptor levels in antigen stimulated lymphocytes. *Journal of Immunology, 124*, 2430–2435.

Crawford, J., Eye, M. K., & Cohen, H. J. (1987). Evaluation of monoclonal gammapathies in the well elderly. *American Journal of Medicine, 82*, 39–45.

Cronstein, B. N., Kimmel, S. C., Levin, R. I., Martinuik, F., & Weissmann, G. (1992). A mechanism for the antiinflammatory effects of corticosteroids: The glucocorticoid receptor regulates leukocyte adhesion to endothelial cells and expression of endothelial-leukocyte adhesion module-1 and intercellular adhesion molecule-1. *Proceedings of the National Academy of Sciences USA, 89*, 9991–9995.

Cupps, T. R., & Fauci, A. S. (1982). Corticosteroid-mediated immunoregulation in man. *Immunology Reviews, 65*, 133–155.

Davila, D. R., Edwards, C. K., Arkins, S., Simon, J., & Kelley, K. W. (1990). Interferon-Y–induced priming for secretion of superoxide anion and tumor necrosis factor-α declines in macrophages from aged rats. *FASEB Journal, 4*, 2906–2911.

DeTurck, K. H., & Vogel, W. H. (1980). Factors influencing plasma catecholamine levels in rats during immobilization. *Pharmacology, Biochemistry and Behavior, 13*, 129–131.

Dobbs, C. M., Vasquez, M., Glaser, R., & Sheridan, J. F. (1993). Mechanisms of stress-induced modulation of viral pathogenesis and immunity. *Journal of Neuroimmunology, 48*, 151–160.

Effros, R. B., & Walford, R. L. (1983b). The immune response of aged mice to influenza: Diminished T-cell proliferation, interleukin-2 production and cytotoxicity. *Cellular Immunology, 81*, 298–305.

Effros, R. B., & Walford, R. L. (1983a). Diminished T-cell response to influenza virus in aged mice. *Immunology, 49*, 387–392.

Effros, R. B., & Walford, R. L. (1984). The effect of age on the antigen-presenting mechanism in limiting dilution precursor cell frequency analysis. *Cellular Immunology, 88*, 531–539.

Effros, R. B., & Walford, R. L. (1987). Infection and immunity in relation to aging. In E. A. Goidl (Ed.), *Aging and the immune response. cellular and humoral aspects* (pp. 45–65). New York: Marcel Dekker.

Engwerda, C. R., Handwerger, B. S., & Fox, B. S. (1994). Aged T cells are hyporesponsive to costimulation mediated by CD28. *Journal of Immunology, 152*, 3740–3747.

Felten, D. L., Felten, S. Y., Bellinger, D. L., Carlson, S. L., Ackerman, K. D., Madden, K. S., Olschowka, J. A., & Livnat, S. (1987). Noradrenergic sympathetic neural interactions with the immune system: Structure and function. *Immunology Reviews, 100*, 225–260.

Felten, S. Y., & Felten, D. L. (1991). Innervation of lymphoid tissue. In R. Ader, D. L. Felten, & N. Coehn (Eds.), *Psychoneuroimmunology* (pp. 27–69). San Diego: Academic Press.

Felten, S. Y., & Olschowka, J. A. (1987). Noradrenergic sympathetic innervation of the spleen. II. Tyrosine hydroxylase(TH)–positive nerve terminals form synaptic-like contacts on lymphocytes in splenic white pulp. *Journal of Neuroscience Research, 18*, 37–48.

Feng, N. (1992). *Restraint stress-induced alterations of the pathogenesis and immune response to influenza virus infection in mice*. doctoral dissertation, The Ohio State University, Columbus.

Feng, N., Pagniano, R., Tovar, C. A., Bonneau, R. H., & Sheridan, J. F. (1991). The effect of restraint stress on the kinetics, magnitude, and isotype of the humoral immune response to influenza virus infection. *Brain, Behavior and Immunity, 4*, 370–382.

Fuchs, B. A., Albright, J. W., & Albright, J. F. (1988). b-adrenergic receptors on murine lymphocytes: Density varies with cell maturity and lymphocyte subtype and is decreased after antigen administration. *Cellular Immunology, 114*, 231–245.

Fukuchi, H. Y., Ishida, S. K., Ohata, M., Furuse, T., Shu, C., Teramoto, S., Matsuse, T., Sudo, E., & Orimo, H. (1993). The effects of aging on the function of alveolar macrophages in mice. *Mechanisms of Aging and Development, 69*, 207–217.

Gately, M. K., Wolitzky, A. G., Quinn, P. M., & Chizzonite, R. (1992). Regulation of human cytolytic lymphocyte responses by interleukin-12. *Cellular Immunology, 143*, 127–142.

Gillis, S., Kozak, R., & Durante, M. (1981). Immunological studies of aging. Decreased production of and response to T cell growth factors by lymphocytes from aged humans. *Journal of Clinical Investigation, 67*, 937–942.

Goidl, E. A., & Innes, J. B. (1976). Immunological studies of aging: II. Loss of IgG and high avidity plaque forming cells and increased suppressor cell activity in aging mice. *Journal of Experimental Medicine, 144*, 1037–1048.

Goodwin, J. S., Searles, R. P., & Tung, K. S. K. (1982). Immunologic responses of a healthy elderly population. *Clinical and Experimental Immunology, 48*, 403–410.

Grossmann, A., Ledbetter, J. A., & Rabinovitch, P. S. (1990). Aging-related deficiency in intracellular calcium response to anti-CD3 or concanavalin A in murine T-cell subsets. *Journal of Gerontology: Biological Sciences, 45*, B81–B86.

Hayakawa, K., & Hardy, R. R. (1988). Normal, autoimmune, and malignant CD5+ B cells: The Ly-1 lineage? *Annual Review of Immunology, 6*, 197–218.,

Hermann, G., Beck, F. M., & Sheridan, J. F. (1995). Stress-induced glucocorticoid response modulates mononuclear cell trafficking during an experimental influenza viral infection. *Journal of Neuroimmunology, 56*, 179–186.

Hermann, G., Beck, F. M., Tovar, C. A., Malarkey, W. B., Allen C., & Sheridan, J. F. (1994). Stress-induced changes attributable to the sympathetic nervous system during experimental influenza viral infection in DBA/2 inbred mouse strain. *Journal of Neuroimmunology, 53*, 173–180.

Hermann, G., Tovar, C. A., Beck, F. M., Allen, C., & Sheridan, J. F. (1993). Restraint differentially affects the pathogenesis of an experimental influenza viral infection in three inbred strains of mice. *Journal of Neuroimmunology, 47*, 83–94.

Hirokawa, K., & Makinodan, T. (1975). Thymic involution: Effect on T cell differentiation. *Journal of Immunology, 114*, 1659–1664.

Hopkins, J., McConnell, I., & Lachman, P. J. (1981). specific selection of antigen-reactive lymphocytes into antigenically stimulated lymph nodes in sheep. *Journal of Experimental Medicine, 152*, 706–719.

Hu, A., Ehleiter, D., Ben-Yehuda, A., Schwab, R., Russo, C., Szabo, P., & Weksler, M. E. (1993). Effect of age on the expressed B cell repertoire: Role of B cell subsets. *International Immunology, 5*, 1035–1039.

Huneycutt, B. S. (1990). *Functional characterization and distribution of lymphokine secreting cells following influenza virus infection*. Doctoral dissertation, The Ohio State University, .

Kato, K., & Hirokawa, K. (1988). Qualitative and quantitative analysis of autoantibody production in aging mice. *Aging: Immunology and Infectious Disease, 1* (3), 177–190.

Kiecolt-Glaser, J. K., Dura, J. R., Speicher, C. E., Trask, O. J., & Glaser, R. (1987). Spousal caregivers of dementia victims: Longitudinal changes in immunity and health. *Psychosomatic Medicine, 53*, 345–362.

Kiecolt-Glaser, J. K., Glaser, R., Shuttleworth, E. C., Dyer, C. S., Ogrocki, P., & Speicher, C.E. (1987). Chronic stress and immunity in family caregivers of Alzheimer's disease victims. *Psychosomatic Medicine, 49*, 523–535.

Kusnecov, A. V., Grota, L. J., Schmidt, S. G., Bonneau, R. H., Sheridan, J. F., Glaser, R., & Moynihan, J. A. (1992). Decreased herpes simplex viral immunity and enhanced pathogenesis following stressor administration in mice. *Journal of Neuroimmunology, 38*, 129–138.

Lee, R. J., Evans, D. B., Baky, S. H., & Laffan, R. J. (1975). Pharmacology of nadolol (SQ11725), a β-adrenergic antagonist lacking direct myocardial depression. *European Journal of Pharmacology, 33*, 371–382.

Lee, S. W., Tso, A.-P., Chan, H., Thomas, J., Petrie, K., Eugui, E. M., & Allison, A. C. (1988). Glucocorticoids selectively inhibit the transcription of the interleukin-1b gene and decrease the stability of interleukin-1b mRNA. *Proceedings of the National Academy of Sciences USA, 85*, 1204–1208.

Lerner, A., Yamada, T., & Miller, R. A. (1989). PGP-1[hi] T lymphocytes accumulate with age in mice and respond poorly to Concanavalin A. *European Journal of Immunology, 19*, 977–982.

Lewis, V. M., Twomey, J. J., Bealmear, P:., Goldstein, G., & Good, R. A. (1978). Age, thymic involution, and circulating thymic hormone activity. *Journal of Clinical Endocrinology and Metabolism 47*, 145–150.

Lorens, S. A., Hata, N., Handa, R. J., Van de Kar, L. D., Guschwan,, M., Goral, J., Lee, J. M., Hamilton, M. E., Bethea, C. L., & Clancy, J. (1990). Neurochemical, endocrine and immunological responses to stress in young and old Fischer 344 male rates. *Neurobiology of Aging, 11*, 139–150.

Louria, D. B., Sen, P., & Buse, M. (1982). Age-dependent differences in outcome of infections, with special reference to experiments in mice. *Journal of the American Geriatrics Society, 30*, 769–773.

Lynch, F., Doherty, P. C., & Ceredig, R. (1989). Phenotypic and functional analysis of the cellular response in regional lymphoid tissue during an acute virus infection. *Journal of Immunology, 142*, 3592–3598.

Madden, K. S., & Livnat, S. (1991). Catecholamine action and immunologic reactivity. In R. Ader, D. L., Felten, & N. Cohen (Eds.), *Psychoneuroimmunology* (pp. 283–310). San Diego: Academic Press.

Makinodan, T., & Kay, M. M. B. (1980). Age influence on the immune system. *Advances in Immunology, 29*, 287–329.

McCarthy, R., Horwatt, K., & Konarska, M. (1988). Chronic stress and sympathetic–adrenal medullary responsiveness. *Social Science and Medicine, 26*, 333–341.

Mikael, N., Mirza, N. M., Zaharian, B. I., Deulofeut, H., Salazar, M., Yunis, E. J., & Dubey, D. P. (1994). Genetic control of the decline of natural killer cell activity in aging mice. *Growth, Development and Aging, 58*, 3–12.

Miller, R. A. (1989). The cell biology of aging: Immunological models. *Journal of Gerontology: Biological Sciences, 44*, B4–B8.

Miller, R. A., Jacobson, B., Weil, G., & Simons, E. R. (1987). Diminished calcium influx in lectin-stimulated T cells from old mice. *Journal of Cellular Physiology, 132*, 337–342.

Mobley, J. L., & Dailey, M. O. (1992). Regulation of adhesion molecule expression by CD8 T cells *in vivo*. I. Differential regulation of gp90[Mel-14] (LECAM-1), Pgp-1, LFA-1, and VLA-4a during the differentiation of cytotoxic T-lymphocytes induced by allografts. *Journal of Immunology, 148*, 2348–2356.

Moguilewsky, M., & Philibert, D. (1984). RU486: Potent antiglucocorticoid activity correlated with strong binding to the cytosolic glucocorticoid receptor followed by an impaired activation. *Journal of Steroid Biochemistry, 20*, 217–276.

Mosmann, T. R., & Coffman, R. L. (1989). Heterogeneity of cytokine secretion patterns and functions of helper T cells. *Advances in Immunology, 46*, 111–147.

Munck, A., & Guyre, P. M. (1991). Glucocorticoids and immune function. In R. Ader, D. L., Felten, & N. Cohen (Eds.), *Psychoneuroimmunology* (pp. 447–474). San Diego: Academic Press.

Murasko, D. M., Nelson, B. J., & Silver, R. (1986). Immunologic response in an elderly population with a mean age of 85. *American Journal of Medicine, 81*, 612–618.

Nagaki, K., Hiramatsu, S., & Inai, S. (1980). The effect of aging on complement activity (CH50) and complement protein levels. *Journal of Clinical and Laboratory Immunology, 3* (1), 45–50.

Nagel, J. E., Chopra, R. K., & Chrest, F. J. (1988). Decreased proliferation, interleukin-2 synthesis, and interleukin-2 receptor expression are accompanied by decreased mRNA expression in phytohemag-glutinin-stimulated cells from elderly donors. *Journal of Clinical Investigation, 81*, 1096–1102.

Nagel, J.E., Chrest, F.J., & Pyle, R.S. (1983). Monoclonal antibody analysis of T-lymphocyte subsets in young and aged adults. *Immunological Communication 12(2)*, 223-237.

Nordin, A. A., & Proust, J. J. (1987). Signal transduction mechanisms in the immune system. *Endocrinology and Aging, 16*, 919–945.

Perego, C., Vetrugno, G., De Simoni, M. G., & Algeri, S. (1993). Aging prolongs the stress-induced release of noradrenaline in rat hypothalamus. *Neuroscience Letters, 157*, 127–130.

Perussia, B., Chan, S. H., D'Andrea, A., Tsuji, K., Santolui, D., Popisil, M., Young, D., Wolf, S. F., & Trinchieri, G. (1992). Natural killer (NK) cell stimulatory factor or IL-12 has differential effects on the proliferation of TCR-αβ+, TCR-γδ+ T lymphocytes and NK cells. *Journal of Immunology, 149*, 3495–3502.

Proust, J. J., Bender, B. S., & Nagel, J. E. (1989). Developmental biology, senescence, and natural immunity: A review and critical analysis of the literature. In D. S. Nelson (Ed.), *Natural immunity* (pp. 392-418). Orlando, FL: Academic Press.

Rothlein, R., Czajkowski, M., O'Neill, M. M., Marlin, S. D., Mainolfi, E., & Merluzzi, V. J. (1988). Induction of intercellular adhesion molecule 1 on primary and continuous cell lines by pro-inflammatory cytokines. Regulation by pharmacologic agents. *Journal of Immunology, 141*, 1665–1669.

Sadeghi, R., Feldmann, M., & Hawrylowicz, C. (1992). Upregulation of HLA class II, u not intercellular adhesion molecule 1 (ICAM-1) by granulocyte macrophage colony stimulating factor (GM-CSF) or interleukin-3 (IL-3) in synergy with dexamethasone. *European Cytokine Network, 3*, 373–380.

Saltzman, R. L., & Peterson, P. K. (1987). Immunodeficiency of the elderly. *Review of Infectious Diseases, 9*, 1127–1139.

Sheridan, J. F., Feng, N., Bonneau, R. H., Allen, C. M., Huneycutt, B. S., & Glaser, R. (1991). Restraint differentially affects anti-viral cellular and humoral immune responses in mice. *Journal of Neuroimmunology, 31*, 245–255.

Stone, E. A. (1987). Central cyclic-AMP–linked noradenergic receptors: New findings on properties as related to the actions of stress. *Neuroscience & Biobehavioral Reviews, 11*, 391–398.

Sparrow, D., Silbert, J. E., & Rowe, J. W. (1980). The influence of age on peripheral lymphocyte count in men: A cross-sectional and longitudinal study. *Journal of Gerontology, 35* (2), 163–166.

Terpenning, M. S. & Bradley, M. S. (1991). Why aging leads to increased susceptibility to infection. *Geriatrics ,46* (2), 77–80.

Thoman, M. L., & Weigle, W. O. (1989). The cellular and subcellular bases of immunosenescence. *Advances in Immunology, 46*, 221–261.

Utsuyama, M., Varga, Z., Fukami, K., Homma, Y., Takenawa, T., & Hirokawa, K. (1993). Influence of age on signal transduction of T cells in mice. *International Immunology 5* (9), 1177–1182.

Wade, A. W., & Szewczuk, M. R. (1984). Aging, idiotype repertoire shifts and compartmentalization of the mucosal-associated lymphoid system. *Advances in Immunology, 36*, 143–148.

Waldorf, D. S., Wilkens, R. F., & Decker, J. L. (1968). Impaired delayed hypersensitivity in an aging population: Association with antinuclear reactivity and rheumatoid factor. *Journal of the American Medical Association, 203*, 831–834.

Wells, M. A., Albrecht, P., & Ennis, F. (1981). Recovery from a viral respiratory infection. I. Influenza peneumonia in normal and T-deficient mice. *Journal of Immunology, 126*, 1036–1041.

Werb, Z., Foley, R., & Munck, A. (1978). Interaction of glucocorticoids with macrophages-identification of glucocorticoid receptors in monocytes and macrophages. *Journal of Experimental Medicine, 147*, 1684–1694.

Yong-He, Z., & Nai-ki, M. (1986). Nonspecific influx of cytotoxic T cells into influenza virus–infected lungs of mice. *Inflammation, 10*, 9–14.

Zharhary, D., & Klinman, N.R. (1984). B cell repertoire diversity to PRI influenza virus does not decrease with age. *Journal of Immunology, 133*, 2285–2287.

8

Immune Functions, Their Psychological Correlates, and Health

George F. Solomon
Department of Psychiatry and Biobehavioral Sciences
University of California, Los Angeles

Donna Benton
Department of Gerontology
University of Southern California

MENTAL HEALTH AND COURSE OF DISEASE

Both medicine and, to a lesser extent, behavioral and psychosomatic medicine primarily have been concerned with disease, its etiology (nowadays, one hopes, multifactorily considered), pathophysiology, psychophysiology, and treatment. The authors of this chapter and some of their prior collaborators have been interested in psychobiological mechanisms in health and relative health (e.g., prompt recovery from or slow progression of disease). Moos and Solomon related slow progression of, relatively little incapacitation by, and good response to medical treatment in rheumatoid arthritis to relative absence of dysphoric affects and effective coping (Moos & Solomon, 1964, 1965; Solomon & Moos, 1965). We suggested that patients who did less well were experiencing ego disorganization with concomitant increases in anxiety and depression and decreases in ability to continue former modes of psychological adaptation and coping. We compared two groups of physically healthy relatives of patients with rheumatoid arthritis: those whose blood showed the autoantibody associated with rheumatoid arthritis, an anti-IgG autoantibody, rheumatoid factors (FII), known to have some predictive significance for later development of the disease, with those relatives whose sera were FII negative. The FII negative family members ranged from mentally healthy to neurotic or even more seriously mentally disturbed, similar to a distribution curve of psychological–psychiatric disturbance in any random population. On the other hand, the FII *positive* relatives were functioning extremely well; they were psychiatrically asymptomatic and reported satisfaction with relationships and occupations. Thus, it appeared to us that mental well-being might serve as a protective factor in the face of a most likely genetically determined biological predisposition to disease (in this case, as marked by a specific autoantibody).

Continuing with the strategy of studying ill persons who are doing relatively well, a group of collegues and we looked at unusually long-term survivors with AIDS (utilizing different longevity criteria following diagnosis with Kaposi's sarcoma or Pneumocystis carinii pneumonia) before the advent of antiretroviral treatment. We found these people to be quite remarkable psychologically, tending to use 15 highly adaptive coping methods that we were able to identify. Of these attitudes and strategies, prominent ones were: a sense of personal control over the illness course (the reciprocal of hopelessness, helplessness, fatalism, and pessimism), active coping (including nonpassive involvement in medical treatment), a sense of meaningfulness in life, assertiveness, and awareness of an ability to meet one's own needs elements were prominent (Solomon, Temoshok, O'Leary, & Zich, 1988).

Recently we were able to confirm similar characteristics in a relatively small group of clinically rare individuals with AIDS (as now defined by the Centers for Disease Control) who had remained asymptomatic for prolonged periods (more than 6 months, mean < 19) or have never been symptomatic in the face of very low numbers (below $50/mm^3$) of CD4+ T cells (Solomon et al., 1994). We sought possible immunologic factors, on the one hand, and psychological characteristics on the other that might relate to the absence of symptomatic disease. Immunologically, these individuals had normal levels of natural killer (NK) cell cytotoxic activity, very rare in advanced HIV disease (Brenner, Dascal, Margolese, & Weinberg, 1989). Many studies have shown NK activity to be sensitive to a variety of psychosocial and behavioral influences, ranging from naturalistic stress (Moss, Moss, & Peterson, 1989) and experimental stress (Naliboff,

Benton, Solomon, Morley, Bloom, Fahey, & Makinodan, 1991) to depressive illness (Irwin, Locke, & Caldwell, 1992) and exercise (Fiatarone et al., 1989). Psychologically, as stated, the asymptomatic HIV+ persons with very low CD4+ cells were quite similar to the long-term survivors with AIDS previously described. Reconfirmed characteristics were a sense of personal control over one's own health, a future orientation in life, and the ability to withdraw from taxing involvements and "nurture" oneself. Nearly all had close friends. Most were willing to disagree with others openly, could express negative emotions, could assert themselves, and could give priority to their own needs. They could both ask for and refuse favors. They did not feel hopeless, helpless, or powerless in the face of life's difficulties, including illness. These persons, who were unusually well physically in the face of laboratory evidence of significant immune compromise, tended most often to describe themselves as responsible, conscientious, alert, quick, and aggressive and least often as meek, bitter, and guilty. Most had experienced joy, anger, or both within the past week and, thus, were emotionally expressive of both positive and negative feelings.

These findings of positive psychological aspects in those doing relatively well in the face of autoimmune disease and of the acquired immunodeficiency syndrome appear to be particularly relevant to healthy aging because of the increased incidence of autoantbodies (including rheumatoid factor) in the aged (Cammarata, Rodman, & Fennel, 1967) and because of the usual immunodeficiency of aging that bears some resemblance to that of AIDS. (In 1910, Kaposi described the sarcoma that bears his name and is a common manifestation of AIDS in old men, whose immune systems, no doubt, had become deficient.)

IMMUNITY AND
HEALTH IN AGING

Immunosenescence, a subject more fully discussed in chapters by Bruce S. Rabin, may be defined as those immunologic changes that occur in all older individuals (including those of nonhuman mammalian species) that are not the result of immunodeficiencies caused by genetic defects, malnutrition, infection, toxins, or malignancies. The increased incidence of cancer, infections, autoimmune disorders, monoclonal gammapathies, and amyloidosis in elderly people is felt to be linked with this decline in immunocompetence (Axelson, Bachman, & Hallen, 1966; Gruys, 1979;

Makinodan, James, Imamizu, & Chang, 1984; Pazmino & Yuhas, 1973). Interventions that increase longevity (e.g., dietary restriction, administration of growth hormone) also enhance immunity (Goya, Gagnerault, DeMorales, Savino, & Dardenner, 1992; Weindruch, Gottesman, & Walford, 1982). Declines in immunity, such as impaired curtaneous hypersensitivity, have been correlated with increased mortality in the aged (Roberts-Thompson, Youngchiazud, Whittingham, & Mackay, 1974). Immunosenescence is complex and highly variable among individuals of the same age. Indeed, different components of the immune system are not uniformly affected by aging. The most significant decrements occur in cellular immunity, a functional defect because cell numbers are little decreased with age (Dybaker, Lauritzen, & Krakauer, 1981). Helper (CD4+) T cell functional decline is reflected in low production of IL-2 (Thoman & Weigle, 1981). B cell function is decreased in relation to primary, not secondary antibody response to antigen (Ruben, Nagel, & Fireman, 1973). Thus, recent rather than long-term memory tends to decline with aging of both the central nervous system and the immune system. Aged people have a higher percentage of "memory" or "committed" lymphocytes and a lower percentage of "naive" cells that can respond to novel antigens. More efficient frontal lobe learning tends to be replaced by less efficient occipital lobe activity during short-term memory acquisition in elderly people, as determined by positron emission tomography (PET) scanning.

Natural killer (NK) cells (non-B, non-T lymphocytes) are capable of cell lysis without prior sensitization or major histocompatibility complex restriction. In rodents, as is most likely the case in humans, they have been found to play a major role in prevention of metastic spread of cancer, to lyse viral-infected cells, and to play a role in longevity. The data on NK cell function in human aging is confusing, as NK activity has been reported to be maintained, increased, or decreased in the elderly. A prior review of ours cited six papers reporting increased activity, two reporting no change, five reporting decreased activity, and three, which measured only cells with NK-associated surface markers, reporting increased numbers (Solomon, Fiatarone, 1988). A study of 23 healthy centenarians (age 100 to 106) found diminished response to a T cell mitogen, phytohemagglutinin (PHA), but higher NK activity than in middle aged persons and, in some cases, than in young controls (Sansoni et al., 1993). It was also observed that these centenarians remained active and future oriented and were psychologically resilient following inevitable losses of close former contemporaries.

A PSYCHOIMMUNOLOGIC
PROSPECTIVE STUDY
OF HEALTHY ELDERLY

We initially looked at immunologic and psychological measures in a sample of young control ($N = 38$, mean age 29) and old ($N = 58$, mean age 73) physically healthy, community-dwelling women. In the first year of the study, measures of immunity (NK cytoxic activity, numbers of lymphocytes bearing markers associated with NK cell activity [CD16+ and CD56+], and T cell function determined by PHA-induced mitogenesis) were done every 3 months (Solomon, Fiatarone, et al., 1988). These healthy older adults had higher NK activity than did the younger adults in the sample; whereas, mitogenic response to PHA was not significantly different between the two age groups, an unusual finding in the elderly. After the initial year, measures were taken yearly for 30 of the healthy older subjects. For all time periods measured (1986–1992), there were no significant changes in NK activity or T cell mitogenesis as compared to baseline (1986, average of three measures). This immunological stability of functional measures over time in healthy elderly is of interest in view of the generally high variability of measures of immunity in the elderly. In the older subjects, numbers of CD16+ and CD56+ cells significantly increased as compared to baseline (1986, average of three measures). Psychological measures of anxiety, depression, anger, and hopelessness were also assessed over time (1986–1992) for the older subjects. All were within normal limits. Except for anxiety, which decreased from baseline, measures of psychological distress did not significantly change. Thus, both immunologically and psychologically the older adults in our sample have not shown significant changes from baseline, strongly suggesting but not proving a link between mental and physical health in older persons. These healthy elderly have maintained measures on NK cell numbers and activity and T cell function within normal limits (as standardized in a younger population).

It is important to note that during the period of follow-up there have been only one major health change (herpes zoster) and three deaths (two myocardial infarctions and one cancer). When we looked at psychological–immune relationships, we found that in older people there was a significant relationship between feelings of anger and NK activity during the first year of the study. However, no such relationship has emerged in subsequent years. It is interesting that those healthy older people who subjectively perceived themselves (nonverbally by placement of a mark along a "life-line") as nearer the end of life than would be "realistic"

showed lower NK activity (Grohr, Solomon, & Benton, 1994). The antic-
ipation of experiencing a significant life event farther in the future predicted lowered NK activity 2 years later than was the case in those persons who looked forward to a more immediate significant event. Our aim
had been to determine prospectively whether life stress, relative failure of
coping, and consequent psychological distress precede immunologic
changes, which, in turn, precede illness and death. We could come to no
conclusions in this regard because our cohort of healthy elderly, in general, remained so.

In most studies, healthy elderly have shown significantly, but variably,
depressed T cell mitogen (PHA) responses as compared to younger people (Murasko, Nelson, Matour, Goonewardene, & Kaye, 1991; Thompson
et al., 1984). Yet, others, like us, have found no such change in mitogen
response to PHA. Our findings likely differ from most others because of
methodological factors. Our results are based on thrice-repeated samples
averaged over 12 months with annual follow-ups for 6 years; whereas,
previous studies looked at a single sample only. Also, differences may be
related to sample selection in that our subjects were screened for excellent health, medication use, and independent living.

A subsample of our healthy elderly population performed maximal
bicycle ergometry exercise (Fiatarone et al., 1989). Their response in
increased NK activity and numbers did not differ from those of young
control subjects. It was subsequently found that the increase in NK activity, but not numbers, was opioid mediated (Fiatarone et al., 1988).
However, an experimental mental stress (time-pressured mental arithmetic) led to increased NK activity in young, not old, subjects; both
showed increased numbers of NK cells (CD56+, CD16+) (Naliboff et al.,
1991). In contrast to aerobic exercise, that increase in NK cell activity in
the young subjects by mental stress was not opioid mediated (Naliboff,
Solomon, Benton, Fahey, & Gilmore, 1995).

CONCLUSIONS

Immunosenescence, usually considered to occur inevitably with aging, is
not found in very healthy elderly persons who live independently. In particular, deep into old age in such persons, natural killer (NK) cell numbers and cytotoxic activity remain equivalent or higher to that in young
persons. However, by the time such people reach 100 years of age, they

do show some decline in T cell function. Even with normal or high baseline levels of T cell and NK cell activity, physically healthy older people may still be more vulnerable to experientially induced down-regulation and less capable of up-regulation than are young persons, in view of our findings in regard to mental stress and NK activity and those of Schleiffer and colleagues that depression-associated reduction in T cell activity is age-related (Schleifer, Keller, Bond, Cohen, & Stein, 1989). There appears to be a very close correlation between physical and psychological well-being in the aged. Even subjective feelings of being older and of not having important events to look forward to in the relatively near future seem to have negative immunologic consequences in the elderly. An implication is that interventions aimed at improving coping, promoting positive anticipations, decreasing psychological distress, and encouraging community residence may help morbidity and even delay mortality in older persons. Depression should be promptly treated. Bereavement, which can be immunosuppressive (Bartrop et al., 1977; Schleifer, Keller, Camerino, Thornton, & Stein, 1983; Irwin, Daniels, Smith, Bloom, & Weiner, 1987), should lead to social support, psychological intervention, or both. Exercise, except in frail elderly for whom we have recently found it to be associated with immunologic and functional decrements (Rincon, Solomon, Benton, & Rubenstein, 1996), should be encouraged.

REFERENCES

Axelson, U., Bachman, R., & Hallen, J. (1966). Frequency of pathological proteins (M components) on 6,995 sera from an adult population. *Acta Medica Scandinavica, 179,* 235–247.

Bartrop, R. W., Luckhurst, E., Lazarus, L., Kiloh, L. G., & Penny, R. (1997). Depressed lymphocyte function after bereavement. *Lancet, 16,* 834–836.

Brenner, G., Dascal, A., Margolese, R., & Weinberg, M. (1989). Natural killer cell function in patients with acquired immune deficiency and related syndromes. *Journal of Leukocyte Biology, 46,* 75–83.

Cammarata, R., Rodman, G., & Fennel, R. (1967). Serum antigamma globulin and antinuclear factors in the aged. *Journal of the American Medical Association, 199,* 456–458.

Dybaker, R., Lauritzen, M., & Krakauer, R. (1981). Relative reference values for clinical, chemical, and hematological quantities for healthy elderly people. *Acta Medica Scandinavica, 209,* 1–9.

Fiatorone, M., Morley, J., Bloom, E., Benton, D., Makinodan, T., & Solomon, G. (1988). Endogenous opioids and the exercise-induced augmentation of natural killer cell activity. *Journal of Laboratory and Clinical Medicine, 112,* 544–552.

Fiatarone, M., Morley, J., Bloom, E., Benton, D., Solomon, G., & Makinodan, T. (1989). The effect of exercise on natural killer cell activity in young and old subjects. *Journal of Gerontology, 44,* M37–M45.

Goya, R., Gagnerault, M., DeMorales, M., Savino, W., & Dardenner, A. (1992). In vivo effects of growth hormone on thymus function in aging mice. *Brain, Behavior, and Immunity, 6,* 341–354.

Grohr, P., Solomon, G., & Benton, D. (1994, November). Immunological and psychological correlates of perceived place in lifespan in elderly women. *Research Perspectives in
Psychoneuroimmunology*, 16–20. Key Biscayne, FL. A conference, which at that time did not
publish abstracts in a journal. Availiable from PsychoNeuroImmunology Research Society, 212
Edward R. Madigan Lab. 1201 W. Gregory Dr., Urbana, IL 61801

Gruys, E. (1979). A comparative approach to amyloidosis: Minireview. *Developmental and
Comparative Immunology, 3*, 23–36.

Irwin, M., Daniels, M., Smith, T., Bloom, E., & Weiner, H. (1987). Impaired natural killer cell activity during bereavement. *Brain, Behavior, and Immunity, 1*, 98–104.

Irwin, M., Locke, U., & Caldwell, C. (1992). Depression and reduced natural killer cell cytotoxicity:
A longitudinal study of depressed patients and controls. *Psychological Medicine, 22*, 1045–1050.

Makinodan, T., James, S., Inamizu, T., & Chang, M. (1984). Immunologic basis for susceptibility to
infection in the aged. *Gerontology, 30*, 279–284.

Moos, R., & Solomon, G. (1964). Personality correlates of the rapidity of progression of rheumatoid
arthritis. *Journal of Psychosomatic Research, 8*, 17–28.

Moos, R,. & Solomon, G. (1965). Personality correlates of the degree of functional incapacity of
patients with physical disease. *Journal of Psychiatric Research, 3*, 1–10.

Moss, R., Moss, H., & Peterson, R. (1989). Microstress, mood, and natural killer cell activity.
Psychosomatics, 30, 279–283.

Murasko, D., Nelson, B., Matour, D., Goonewardene, I., & Kaye, D. (1991). Heterogeneity of
changes in lymphoproliferative ability with increasing age. Annals of the New York Academy of
Sciences. *Academy of Sciences, 521*, 43–58.

Naliboff, B., Benton, D., Solomon, G., Morley, J., Bloom, E., Fahey, J., & Makinodan, T. (1991).
Psychological, psychophysiological, and immunological changes in young and old subjects during brief laboratory stress. *Psychosomatic Medicine, 53*, 121–132.

Naliboff, B., Solomon, G., Benton, D., Fahey, J., & Gilmore, S. (1995) Experimental mental stress-
induced increases in natural killer cell activity are not opioid-mediated. *Journal of Psychosomatic
Research, 39*, 345–359.

Pazmino, N., & Yuhas, J., (1973). Senescent loss of resistance to murine sarcoma virus (Maloney) in
the mouse. *Cancer Research, 33*, 2668–2672.

Rincon, H., Solomon, G., Benton, D., & Rubenstein, L., (1996). Exercise in frail elderly men
decreases natural killer cell activity. *Aging, 8*, 109–112.

Roberts-Thomson, I., Youngchiazud, U., Whittingham, S., & Mackay, I. (1974). Aging, immune
response, and mortality. *Lancet, 2*, 368–370.

Ruben, F., Nagel, J., & Fireman, P. (1973). Antitoxin responses in the elderly to tetanus-diphtheria
(Td) immunization. *American Journal of Epidemiology, 103*, 145–149.

Sansoni, P., Cossarizza, A., Brianti, V., Fagnoni, F., Snelli, G., Monti, D., Marcoto, A., Passeri, G.,
Ortolani, C., Forti, E., Fagiolo, U., Passeri, M., & Francheschi, C. Lymphocyte subsets and natural killer cell activity in healthy old people and centenarians. *Blood, 82*, 2767–2773.

Schleifer, S., Keller, S., Camerino, M., Thornton, J., & Stein, M. (1983). Suppression of lymphocyte
stimulation following bereavement. *Journal of the American Medical Association, 250*, 374–377.

Schleiffer, S. J., Keller, S. E., Bond, R. N., Cohen, J., & Stein, M. (1989). Major depressive disorder
and immunity. *Archives of General Psychiatry, 46*, 81–87.

Solomon, G., & Moos R. (1965). Psychologic aspects of response to treatment in rheumatoid arthritis. *General Practice, 32*, 113–119.

Solomon, G., Fiatarone, M., Benton, D., Morley, J., Bloom, E., & Makinodan, T. (1968).
Psychoimmunologic and endorphin function in the aged. *Annals of the New York Academy of
Sciences, 521*, 43–57.

Solomon, G., Temoshok, L., O'Leary, A., & Zich, J. (1988). An intensive psychoimmunologic study
of long-surviving persons with AIDS: Pilot work, background studies, hypothesis, and methods.
Annals of the New York Academy of Sciences, 521, 43–58.

Solomon, G., Benton, D., Harker, J., Bonavida, B., & Fletcher M. (1994). Prolonged asymptomatic states in HIV seropositive persons with fewer than 50 CD4+ T-cells/mm3. Psychoimmunologic findings. Annals of the New York Academy of Sciences. *Academy of Science, 41*, 185-191.

Thoman, M., & Weigle, W. (1981). Lymphokines and aging: Interleukin-2 production and activity in aged animals. *Journal of Immunology, 127*, 2102–2106.

Thompson, J., Wekstein, D., Rhodes, J., Kirpatrick, C., Brown, S., Roszman, T., Straus, R., & Tietz, N. (1984). The immune status of healthy centenarians. *Journal of the American Geriatric Society, 32*, 274–281.

Weindruch, R., Gottesman, R., & Walford, R. (1982). Modification of age-related immune decline in mice dietarily restricted from or after midadulthood. *Proceedings from the National Academy of Science, 79*, 898–902.

9

Negative Affect and the Disablement Process in Late Life: A Life-Span Control Theory Approach

Richard Schulz
University of Pittsburgh

Jutta Heckhausen
Max Planck Institute for Human Development and Education, Berlin, Germany

Alison O'Brien
University of Pittsburgh

CONTROL AND THE DISABLEMENT PROCESS IN THE ELDERLY

Disability in the elderly is typically measured in terms of their ability to perform basic and instrumental activities of daily living (ADLs and IADLs) such as eating, toileting, dressing, bathing, preparing meals, shopping, using a telephone, and doing housework. It is estimated that approximately 35% of individuals 65 years of age and older have difficulty with one or more ADLs or IADLs. With increasing age, the rates of disability increase dramatically. For individuals age 85 years and over, about 62% fall into this category (Prohaska, Mermelstein, Miller, & Jack, 1993). The long-standing interest in disability in the elderly is based on several factors, including the fact that disability serves as a key indicator of an older person's ability to remain independent in the community, quality of life, and life expectancy. Although many researchers have focused in recent years on issues of measurement and on the prevalence, correlates, and causes of disability, little attention has been paid to psychological factors that characterize the disabling process in the elderly.

To date, much of the psychological research has been limited to documenting the relation between disability in the elderly and outcomes such as depressive symptomatology, clinical depression, and suicide (Kennedy, Kelman, & Thomas, 1990; Williamson & Schulz, 1992a, 1992b). This association has been observed in diverse populations, including individuals with spinal cord injury (Frank, Elliott, Corcoran, & Wonderlich, 1987), rheumatoid arthritis (Katz & Yelin, 1993), multiple sclerosis (Garland & Zis, 1991), Parkinson's disease (Cummings, 1992), and stroke (Robinson & Starkstein, 1990; Spencer, Tompkins, & Schulz, 1997; Thompson, Sobolew-Shubin, Graham, & Janigian, 1989). Attempts to explain these associations fall into two general categories: those describing conditions with acute onset such as spinal cord injury (SCI), and those of progressively debilitating disorders such as rheumatoid arthritis (RA).

The acute onset of disability caused by a condition such as SCI requires an individual to confront significant loss all at once. Theoretical models in this area typically focus on the affective stages individuals go through as they adjust to acute loss (e.g., Bracken & Shepard, 1980; Livneh & Antonak, 1991). Although models vary in content, they are similar in that they propose a time-ordered series of stages (Friedland & McColl, 1992). The individual responds to injury initially with shock, often accompanied by anxiety and denial. This in turn is followed by negative affect, including depression, as well as hostility and anger. During this period the individual grieves the losses owing to injury. Over time, most individuals are able to accept and adjust to their disability (Kerr & Thompson, 1972), particularly those who have high levels of social support and high levels of perceived control (Schulz & Decker, 1985; Thompson & Spacapan, 1991). In this type of framework, time since injury along with a broad range of psychological factors such as perceived control, finding meaning, and making appropriate social comparisons are typically found to be important predictors of an affective state (Thompson & Spacapan, 1991).

In contrast to the abrupt onset of disability in SCI, disorders such as RA are characterized by a progressively degenerative decline, with periods of remission and exacerbation. Significant associations between functional limitations and depression are consistently found in this research area (Katz & Yelin, 1993). Existing models identify a wide range of psychological factors thought to affect the relationship between disability and depression. In particular, constructs such as helplessness (Nicassio, Wallston, Callahan, Herbert, & Pincus, 1984), stressful life events (Hurwicz & Berkanovic, 1993), loss of social roles (Fifield, Reisine, & Grady, 1991) coping styles (Beckham, Keefe, Caldwell & Roodman, 1991), personality variables (Affleck, Tenne, Urrows, & Higgins, 1992), self-efficacy (Lorig, Chastain, Ung, Shoor, & Holman, 1989), and social support (Creed & Ash, 1992) have been found to account for significant variance in depression in RA patients beyond illness characteristics and functional limitations.

A central theme in virtually all models of adjustment to disability is the importance of perceived control as a mediator of affective outcomes, although the role of control is typically described in only general terms. Our goal for this chapter is to articulate a more specific control-process framework that can be applied to understanding adjustment to diverse disabling conditions. This model builds on and elaborates on recent developments in control theory (Heckhausen & Schulz, 1995). Specifically, we propose that threats to or actual losses in individuals' ability to actively control important outcomes in their lives initiate behavioral and intrapsychic control maintenance strategies to buffer that threat. Negative affect emerges when control maintenance strategies are unable to compensate for this threat. Initial threats to control are experienced as heightened anxiety, and as this threat evolves into permanent losses such as chronic disability, depression ensues. The duration and intensity of the affective response to loss in control depend on (a) the importance of the threatened domains to the individual, and (b) the availability of intrapsychic strategies to attenuate the impact of loss on global levels of control.

Although our perspective can be applied to individuals of all ages, it is most relevant to the elderly. Threats to control are generally more prevalent in late life and frequently impact critical functional domains. Consequently, the emotional response to declines in control during late life can be of an intensity and duration to result in significant affective outcomes such as depression. This argument is developed by noting distinctions between primary and secondary control, describing life-course development in terms of control processes, and examining the role of control in the disablement process.

Primary and Secondary Control

A fundamental characteristic of human beings is the desire to produce behavior-event contingencies and thus exert primary control over the environment around them. The developmental origin of activities directed at controlling external events and acquiring generalized expectations about control can be traced to the very beginning of life. The striving for behavior-event contingencies or primary control has been shown to be part of the evolutionary determined make-up of newborn infants, an important marker of subsequent development and a universal feature of human behavior that is invariant across culture and historical time (Heckhausen & Schulz, 1993, 1995, 1999; Schulz & Heckhausen, 1999).

An important innovation in the development of control theory was the work of Rothbaum, Weisz, and Snyder (1982), in which they conceived of control as a two-process construct consisting of primary and secondary control. Primary control targets the external world and attempts to achieve effects in the immediate environment external to the individual, whereas secondary control targets the self and attempts to achieve changes directly within the individual. Both primary and secondary control may involve cognition and action; however, primary control is almost always characterized in terms of behavior engaging the external world. In contrast, secondary control is predominantly characterized in terms of cognitive processes localized within the individual, such as setting goals, adjusting expectancies and making causal attributions.

Our view of primary and secondary control (Heckhausen & Schulz, 1995) differs from that of Rothbaum et al. (1982) and emphasizes the functional primacy of primary over secondary control. Because primary control is directed outward, it enables individuals to explore and shape their environment to fit their particular needs and optimize their developmental potentials. Without engaging the external world, the developmental potential of the organism cannot be realized. As a result, primary control is preferred by and has greater adaptive value to the individual. A related and complementary assumption of this view is that human beings abhor losses in their ability to exercise desired behavior-event contingencies and are vulnerable to anxiety and depression when faced with anticipated or actual losses in primary control. The major function of secondary control is to minimize losses in, maintain, and expand existing levels of primary control. An important ancillary function of secondary control is to protect the individual from experiencing negative affect when attempts at primary control fail (Heckhausen & Schulz, 1998).

The Life-Course Trajectory of Control

The development of primary and secondary control over the life course is illustrated in Fig. 9.1. As can be seen from the figure, early development is characterized by an increasing ability to exert primary control over the environment. The action-outcome experiences of the child provide the basis for the development of self-competence, including generalized and exaggerated expectancies of control and perceptions of self-efficacy. Children between the ages of 3 and 4 are able to experience appropriate emotional reactions to failure and therefore require compensating mechanisms to counteract this threat to their motivational resources. During childhood and adolescence a broad range of secondary control strategies develop, including changing aspiration levels, denial, egotistic attributions, and reinterpretation of action goals. Perceptions of control are highly exaggerated early in life, showing little correspondence to actual primary control. This delusional sense of control is adaptive in that it provides the motivation to engage the environment at a time when the organism is rapidly developing.

Early adulthood is characterized by increasing levels of primary and secondary control as well as increasing selectivity with respect to the domain specificity of control. To maximize developmental potential,

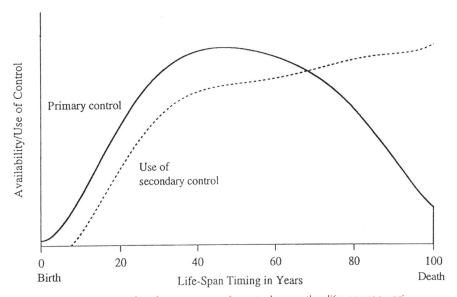

FIG. 9.1. Levels of two types of control over the life course: primary control and secondary control

selectivity in the investment of time and energy increase throughout adulthood. Because of the limited capacity of the individual and external constraints, the increased selectivity at older ages has to be compensated for with decreased diversity in the domains to which resources are devoted. The trade-off between diversity and selectivity in the range of activities in which individuals participate in a hallmark of development in late middle age and old age.

During late middle age and old age, increasing age-related biological and social challenges to primary control put a premium on secondary control strategies as a means of maintaining perceptions of primary control. As the ratio of gains to losses in primary control becomes less and less favorable during late life, individuals increasingly rely on secondary control processes in order to maintain the potential for primary control in the face of situations such as physical difficulties, bereavement, cognitive declines, or financial limitations. Attempts to enhance or maintain primary control under such constraints may incur high costs in frustration, wasted effort, and failure. Thus, secondary control is not an end in itself but rather a means for preserving overall levels of primary control. Particularly in late life, global feelings of control depend on the capacity of secondary control processes to compensate for threatened losses in primary control (Heckhausen & Schulz, 1995; Schulz & Heckhausen, 1996).

Control and the Disablement Process

In order to characterize disability in terms of control-related processes and show how disability engenders negative emotional response, we first describe the sociomedical model of the disabling process by Verbrugge and Jette (1994). The model of the disabling process (Fig. 9.2) describes a progression from left to right that begins with pathology and ultimately results in disability. We argue that this progression also characterizes increasing threats to primary control as the disablement process unfolds. In response to this threat, individuals initially engage in primary control measures to reinforce a global sense of control. To the extent that primary control is not restored through action alone, secondary control mechanisms attempt to compensate for the loss. As impairments increase and lead to functional limitations, the ability to exercise primary control is severely curtailed. Reliance on secondary control processes is increasingly necessary to maintain global levels of control as decline progresses; however, compensatory processes may falter when the loss is central to an individual's self-concept.

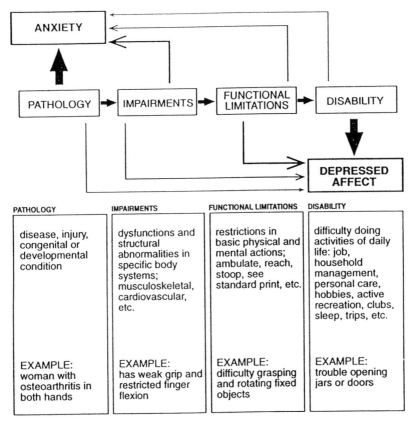

FIG. 9.2. Proposed model of the association between negative affect and increasing threats to primary control posed by the disablement process. Based on "The disablement process," by L. M. Verbrugge and A.M. Jette, 1994, *Social Science and Medicine.*

Anxiety is predicted to be more intense early in the disablement process when pathology is detected, but its long-term consequences remain undefined. As the effects of pathology increasingly manifest themselves as disability, anxiety declines and depressive affect becomes the dominant psychological response. Thus, it is likely that most individuals can effectively cope with the threats of pathology and even impairment in old age because they do not seriously impede their ability to interact with the environment. However, when impairment progresses to functional limitations and disability, the capacity to cope is severely compromised as the ability to exert primary control is reduced. The individual responds emotionally to these acute threats to primary control by becoming demoralized and depressed. These affective consequences are likely to be further aggravated to the extent that the specific domains of functioning threatened are central to the individual's sense of self.

Partial support for this model is found in the empirical literature showing that depression is associated with disability in the elderly, after controlling for physical illness (Williamson & Schulz, 1992a, 1992b). Additional support is derived from studies reporting increases in depression to be associated with changes in functional status in older adults (Parmalee, Katz, & Lawton, 1992; Turner & Noh, 1988), individuals with Parkinson's disease (Cummings, 1992), and individuals with rheumatoid arthritis (Creed & Ash, 1992). The well-documented relationship between depression and measures indicative of global control such as mastery (Pearlin & Schooler, 1978) lends further support to our model. Specifically, lower levels of depression are found to be associated with higher levels of mastery (Turner & Noh, 1988), self-efficacy (Lorig et al., 1989), perceived ability to cope with illness (Hurwicz & Berkanovic, 1993), and perceived ability to meet personal goals (Elliott, Witty, Herrick, & Hoffman, 1991). Helplessness, which can be conceptualized as a lack of primary control, is highly related to depression in individuals with rheumatoid arthritis (Smith, Peck & Ward, 1990).

In our model, anxiety engendered by a threatened loss of primary control serves as the motivational source for restoring prior levels of primary control. Perceiving a threat implies the arousal of anxiety; and to the extent that anxiety facilitates appropriate action, it serves as a positive motivator for direct and intrapsychic action. At extreme levels, anxiety can be debilitating and result in an inappropriate response or no action. In general, two strategies can be used to deal with the threat to primary control and reduce the anxiety engendered by that threat: behavioral action on the environment aimed maintaining or restoring primary control in the threatened domain, or intrapsychic action (secondary control) aimed at preserving global levels of primary control.

Examples of Direct Action (Primary Control). A variety of behaviors can reduce the restrictions or difficulties individuals experience in late life, with the consequence of restoring prior levels of primary control. Individuals can obtain medical care or rehabilitation, take medications or follow other therapeutic regimens, obtain special equipment and devices, modify the physical environment, or change their lifestyle or behavior. The common feature of these responses to threatened loss is that they involve direct action on the environment; although engaging in these behaviors acknowledges the threat, the behavior itself is aimed at maintaining functioning and preventing or minimizing the threat of disability. To the extent that these strategies succeed, individual self-esteem and affect should remain intact, but anxiety and depression should be minimized.

Examples of Intrapsychic Action (Secondary Control). If the probability of success of an action sequence is judged to be high, the reaction to an impending loss of primary control is to increase efforts to maintain it. If, however, maintenance of primary control through direct action appears unlikely, the individual can resort to secondary control by adjusting goals, interpretations, or causal attributions. For severely disabling conditions experienced by older adults, attempts at primary control may often be futile, leaving only secondary control processes to preserve a sense of primary control. Under conditions of threat, secondary control processes provide a rich array of options designed to maintain the existing potential for primary control. Individuals can adjust to anticipated losses by invoking strategies such as defensive pessimism ("I expected the worst"; Norem & Cantor, 1986), predictive control ("I've known it all along"; Rothbaum et al., 1982), or self-handicapping by avoiding effort so an anticipated failure can be attributed to lack of effort rather than one's own diminished ability (Pyszczynski & Greenberg, 1983).

Failure to reclaim primary control can be dealt with by adjusting one's aspiration level (Schulz & Decker, 1985; Taylor, Wood, & Lichtman, 1984) or restructuring one's goal hierarchy (e.g., sour grapes—"It wasn't important to me"; Easter, 1983). An example of the use of this type of strategy was demonstrated in a study of rheumatoid arthritis patients in which cognitive restructuring (e.g., adjusting goals) was inversely related with depression and helplessness (Parker et al., 1988). Individuals can also ascribe control to a beneficent powerful other such as God and gain vicarious control through identification with this power.

Secondary control after failure can be achieved through social comparison processes such as downward social comparison. That is, individuals make themselves feel better about a given performance or state of affairs by comparing themselves with those who are worse off (Taylor & Lobel, 1989; Thompson, 1985; Wills, 1981). Downward comparison can be an especially effective mechanism for impaired older adults who have friends or family with more severe disability. Another variation of downward comparison processes is to contrast one's own functioning with age stereotypes that portray the elderly as sickly and weak, thereby minimizing the perception of one's own degree of disability. Finally, both primary and secondary control strategies can operate together, as would be the case when an individual seeks social support that facilities downward social comparisons.

These strategies are ubiquitous in everyday life and enable the individual to maintain relatively stable or increasing levels of global primary control throughout the adult life course. An important psychological consequence of using these strategies is that they reduce anxiety, help maintain positive affect, and serve as a motivational resource to keep individuals engaged in important life activities. However, it should be noted that these strategies can fail. Direct action such as taking medication or following a treatment regimen may not alleviate a problem. In the face of life stresses in addition to disability, secondary control mechanisms can be strained and increase vulnerability to negative affect (Frank & Elliott, 1897; Turner & Noh, 1988). Ultimately, backup secondary control strategies, such as restructuring one's goal hierarchy, may not be viable because the threatened disability is a fundamental aspect of everyday life. For example, it would be difficult to convince oneself that the ability to eat or toilet independently is not an important defining characteristic of everyday life.

Both primary and secondary control strategies can be maladaptive in that they undermine the future potential for primary control. Thus, taking a narcotic medication to alleviate pain may address the acute discomfort caused by pain but can also undermine functioning in the future by causing delirium and other dementia-like symptoms, as well as falls. Similarly, secondary control strategies such as self-handicapping or downward social comparison may inhibit the motivational resources needed to maintain physical functioning through direct action on the environment. In addition, when effective secondary control strategies are not available, individuals may render themselves more vulnerable to depression by engaging in maladaptive cognitions such as catastrophizing, self-blaming, or wish fulfilling through fantasy (Affleck et al., 1992; Beckham et al., 1991; Parker et al., 1988). Some evidence suggests that disabled individuals exhibiting high levels of neuroticism may be particularly vulnerable to maladaptive cognitions and depression (Affleck et al., 1992; Morris, Robinson, Raphael, Samuels, & Molloy, 1992).

Failure of Control and Emergence of Depressive Affect

When both primary and secondary control strategies fail to redress losses in primary control, the individual is likely to become demoralized and depressed. We have focused on the disabling process in the elderly because it represents areas of functioning in which direct action alternatives and cognitive intrapsychic processes in conjunction are ultimately unable to protect the individual from fundamental losses in primary control. To the extent that these losses are gradual and anticipated, the individual may be able to muster the cognitive strategies needed to both maintain a constant perception of control and decrease vulnerability to the affective consequences of a loss. For example, older adults affected by progressively declining conditions, such as arthritis, may initially be able to modify their behavior to adapt to the condition and use secondary control strategies, such as downward comparison, to maintain high global levels of control. The individual is vulnerable to heightened anxiety early in the disablement process as the capacity for primary control begins to recede; however, most individuals compensate for these initial losses through intrapsychic mechanisms, preserving global levels of control and buffering negative affect. Ultimately, the condition deteriorates to the point at which independent functioning is no longer possible. It is at this point that we would expect the majority of disabled individuals to experience demoralization and depression, because it is unlikely that secondary control mechanisms are powerful enough to compensate for the inability to perform activities in important life domains. We would describe this state as helplessness, a state in which secondary control mechanisms have failed to compensate for losses in the ability to exercise primary control. It is the point at which levels of mastery and self-efficacy bottom out, the impact of secondary control strategies are negligible, and the risk for clinical depression is greatest.

Sudden and substantial threats to primary control may not allow individuals adequate time to adapt and compensate through secondary control processes. For instance, when an individual experiences disability following a stroke, his or her resources are likely to be inadequate to meet these immediate threats to primary control. Anxiety, and later depression, are likely to be outcomes of events such as this, which are sudden in onset, disrupt an individual's typical experience of primary control, and may have permanent effects. But even in these cases, control beliefs can be developed and elaborated. For instance, a stroke victim can engage in primary control by obtaining rehabilitation and, over time, can adapt to the disability through internal processes such as adjusting goal hierarchies.

Clinical Implications

Most individuals develop a broad repertoire of primary and secondary control strategies by the time they reach adulthood. These strategies facilitate effective coping with the inevitable biological and sociocultural constraints that characterize middle age and old age. The ultimate challenges faced by most individuals in late life are personal losses and the breakdown of fundamental abilities to carry on the daily activities of life.

Clearly, these types of losses have direct relevance to and importance for most individuals' sense of self, a fact to which the design of any intervention must be sensitive. Another point to consider for clinical intervention is whether a loss of primary control is of gradual or abrupt onset. As discussed earlier, gradual decline allows for the concurrent implementation of secondary control strategies, whereas a sudden loss of primary control limits the repertoire of secondary control strategies to those that can be used after the fact.

Intervention efforts for individuals facing physical decline focus primary on a variety of strategies aimed at preventing or limiting the effects of the disablement process. It is possible to implement interventions at any stage in the model of disability presented earlier in this chapter (Verbrugge & Jette, 1994). Thus, primary prevention is aimed at averting the onset of pathology. Secondary prevention is aimed at managing pathology and preventing impairment, and tertiary prevention is designed to reduce disease impact that may be manifested in impairment, functional limitation, or disability. In terms of the primary and secondary control model described here, these strategies typically involve direct actions that help to maintain or expand primary control. In this regard, primary prevention strategies are likely to be most effective in maximizing primary control because of their long-term positive impact, followed by secondary and tertiary prevention strategies.

Relatively little attention has been paid to the role of intrapsychic secondary control strategies in maximizing functioning. In our view, maximal positive effects are likely to be achieve when action-oriented and cognitive strategies work hand in glove. Secondary control strategies provide both motivational resources and direction to primary control efforts. It therefore become important to understand which intrapsychic strategies an individual uses and, if necessary, change them through therapeutic interventions or add new ones to the individual's repertoire of strategies.

Finally, it is important to recognize that all efforts at preventing or ameliorating disability, and depression associated with disability, may ultimately fail as the individual succumbs to decline and death. Coming to grips with this eventuality imposes an immense challenge to individuals with disability and their families, as well as to clinicians and health care providers. Developing effective intervention strategies that preserve positive affect and protect against demoralization and depression, under circumstances in which both primary and secondary control mechanisms may fail, is one of the greatest challenges facing the therapeutic community.

ACKNOWLEDGMENTS

Preparation of this chapter was in part supported by grant MH46015 from the National Institute of Mental Health and by a grant from the AARP Andrus Foundation. An earlier version of this manuscript was presented at the 46th Annual Scientific Meeting of the Gerontological Society of America, Nov. 21, 1993, New Orleans, LA.

REFERENCES

Affleck, G., Tennen, H., Urrows, S., & Higgins, P. (1992). Neuroticism and the pain–mood relation in rheumatoid arthritis. Insights from a prospective daily study. *Journal of Consulting and Clinical Psychology, 60,* 119–126.

Becken, J. C., Keefe, F. J., Caldwell, D. S., & Roodman, A. A. (1991). Pain coping strategies in rheumatoid arthritis: Relationships to pain, disability, depression, and daily hassles. *Behavior Therapy, 22,* 113–124.

Bracken, M. B., & Shepard, M. J. (1980). coping and adaptation following acute spinal cord injury. A theoretical analysis. *Paraplegia, 18,* 74–85.

Creed, F., & Ash, G. (1992). Depression in rheumatoid arthritis. Aetiology and treatment. *International Review of Psychiatry, 4,* 23–24.

Cummings, J. L. (1992). Depression and Parkinson's disease. A review. *American Journal of Psychiatry, 149,* 443–454.

Easter, J. (1983). *Sour grapes: Studies in the subversion of rationality.* Cambridge: Cambridge University press.

Elliott, T. R., Witty, T. E., Herrick, S. E., & Hoffman, J. T. (1991). Negotiating reality after physical loss: Hope, depression, and disability. *Journal of Personality and Social Psychology, 61,* 603–613.

Fifield, J., Reisine, S. T., & Grady, K. (1991). Work disability and the experience of pain and depression in rheumatoid arthritis. *Social Science and Medicine, 33,* 579–585.

Frank, R. G., & Elliott, T. R. (1987). Life stress and psychologic adjustment following spinal cord injury. *Archives of Physical Medicine and Rehabilitation, 68,* 344–347.

Frank, R. G., Elliott, T. R., Corcoran, J. R., & Wonderlich, S. A. (1987). Depression after spinal cord injury. Is it necessary? *Clinical Psychology Review, 7,* 611–630.

Friedland, J., & McColl, M. (1992). Disability and depression: Some etiological considerations. *Social Science and Medicine, 34,* 395–403.

Garland, E. J., & Zis, A. P. (1991). Multiple sclerosis and affective disorders. *Canadian Journal of Psychiatry, 36,* 112–117.

Heckhausen, J., & Schulz, R. (1993). Optimization by selection and compensation. Balancing primary and secondary control in life span development. International *Journal of Behavioral Development, 16,* 287–303.

Heckhausen, J., & Schulz, R. (1995). A life-span theory of control. *Psychological Review, 102,* 284–304.

Heckhausen, J., & Schulz, R. (1999). The primary of primary control in a human universal: A reply to Gould's (1999) critique of the life-span theory of control. *Psychological Review, 106,* 605–609.

Hurwicz, M., & Berkanovic, E. (1993). The stress process in rheumatoid arthritis. *Journal of Rheumatology, 20,* 1836–1844.

Katz, P. P., & Yelin, E. H. (1993). Prevalence and correlates of depressive symptoms among persons with rheumatoid arthritis. *Journal of Rheumatology, 20,* 790–796.

Kennedy, G. J., Kelman, J. R., & Thomas, C. (1990). The emergence of depressive symptoms in late life. The importance of declining health and increasing disability. *Journal of Community Health, 15,* 93–104.

Kerr, W. G., & Thompson, M. A. (1972). Acceptance of disability of sudden onset in paraplegia. *Paraplegia, 10,* 94–102.

Livneh, H., & Antonak, R. F. (1991). Temporal structure of adaptation to disability. *Rehabilitation Counseling Bulletin, 34,* 298–319.

Lorig, K., Chastain, R. L., Ung, E., Shoor, S., & Holman, H. R. (1989). Development and evaluation of a scale to measure perceived self-efficacy in people with arthritis. *Arthritis and Rheumatism, 32,* 37–44.

Morris, P. L. P., Robinson, R. G., Raphael, B., Samuels, J., & Molloy, P. (1992). The relationship between risk factors for affective disorder and poststroke depression in hospitalized stroke patients. *Australian and New Zealand Journal of Psychiatry, 26,* 208–217.

Nicassio, P. M., Wallston, K. A., Callahan, L. F., Herbert, M., & Pincus, T. (1984). The measurement of helplessness in rheumatoid arthritis: The development of the Arthritis Helplessness Index. *Journal of Rheumatology, 12,* 462–467.

Norem, J. K., & Cantor, N. (1986). Defensive pessimism: Harnessing anxiety as motivation. *Journal of personality and Social Psychology, 51,* 1208–1217.

Parker, J., McRae, C., Smarr, K., Beck, N., Frank, R., Anderson, S., & Walker, S. (1988). Coping strategies in rheumatoid arthritis. *Journal of Rheumatology, 15,* 1376–1383.

Parmalee, P. A., Katz, I. R., & Lawton, M. P. (1992). Incidence of depression in long-term care settings. Journal of Gerontology: *Medical Sciences, 47,* M189–M196.

Pearlin, L. I., & Schooler, C. (1978). The structure of coping. *Journal of Health and Social Behavior, 19,* 2–21.

Prohaska, T., Mermelstein, R., Miller, B., & Jack, S. (1993). Functional status and living arrangements. In J. F. Van Nostrand, S. E. Furner, & R. Suzman (Eds.), *Health data on older Americans: United States, 1992* (DHHS Publication No. PHS 93-1411, pp. 23–41). Washington, DC: U.S. Government Printing Office.

Pyszczynski, T., & Greenberg, J. (1983). Determinants of reduction in intended effort as a strategy for coping with anticipated failure. *Journal of Research in Personality, 17*(4), 412–422.

Robinson, R. G., & Starkstein, S. E. (1990). Current research in affective disorders following stroke. *Journal of Neuropsychiatry, 2,* 1–14.

Rothbaum, F., Weisz, J. R., & Snyder, S. S. (1982). Changing the world and changing the self: A two-process model of perceived control. *Journal of Personality and Social Psychology, 42,* 5–37.

Schulz, R., & Decker, S. (1985). Long-term adjustment to physical disability. The role of social support, perceived control, and self-blame. *Journal of Personality and Social Psychology, 48,* 1162–1172.

Schulz, R., & Heckhausen, J. (1996). A life span model of successful aging. *American Psychologist, 51,* 702–714.

Schulz, R., & Heckhausen, J. (1998). Emotion and control: A life span perspective. In K. W. Schaie & M. P. Lawton (Eds.), *Annual review of gerontology and geriatrics,* (Vol 17, pp. 185–205). New York: Springer.

Schulz, R., & Heckhausen, J. (1999). Aging, culture, and control: Setting a new research agenda. *Journal of Gerontology, 54,* 139–145.

Smith, T. W., Peck, J. R., & Ward, J. R. (1990). Helplessness and depression in rheumatoid arthritis. *Health Psychology, 9,* 377–389.

Spencer, K. A., Tompkins, C. A., & Schulz, R. (1997). Assessing depression in persons with brain pathology: The case of stroke. *Psychological Bulletin, 122,* 132–152.

Taylor, S. E., & Lobel, M. (1989). Social comparison activity under threat: Downward evaluation and upward contracts. *Psychological Review, 96,* 569–575.

Taylor, S. E., Wood, J. V., & Lichtman, R. R. (1984). Attributions, beliefs about control, and adjustment to breast cancer. *Journal of Personality and Social Psychology, 46,* 489–502.

Thompson, S. C. (1985). Finding positive meaning in a stressful event and coping. *Basic and Applied Social Psychology, 6,* 279–295.

Thompson, S.C., Sobolew-Shubin, A., Graham, M. A., & Janigian, A. S. (1989). Psychosocial adjustment following a stroke. *Social Science and Medicine, 28,* 239–247.

Thompson, S. C., & Spacapan, S. (1991). Perceptions of control in vulnerable populations. *Journal of Social Issues, 47*(4), 1–21.

Turner, R. J., & Noh, S. (1988). Physical disability and depression: A longitudinal analysis. *Journal of Health and Social Behavior, 29,* 23–37.

Verbrugge, L. M., & Jette, A. M. (1994). The disablement process. *Social Science and Medicine, 38,* 1–14.

Williamson, G. M., & Schulz, R. (1992a). Pain, activity restriction and symptoms of depression among community-residing elderly adults. *Journal of Gerontology: Psychological Sciences, 47,* 367–372.

Williamson, G. M., & Schulz, R. (1992b). Physical illness and symptoms of depression among elderly outpatients. *Psychology and Aging, 7,* 343–351.

Wills, T. (1981). Downward comparison principles in social psychology. *Psychological Bulletin, 90,* 245–271.

10

Psychological Factors, Health, and Disease: The Impact of Aging and the Life Cycle

Redford B. Williams
Duke University

Behavioral medicine research over the past several years has identified a number of psychosocial characteristics that affect the development and course of a wide range of life-threatening illnesses (for review, see Williams, 1994, 1995). Included among these psychosocial risk factors are hostility, depression, social isolation, high job strain, and low socioeconomic status (SES). The specific mechanisms whereby these factors influence the pathogenesis and prognosis of major causes of death such as coronary heart disease (CHD) and cancer have not been identified yet, but considerable research points to accompanying health behaviors (smoking, dietary habits, and alcohol consumption) and biological characteristics (altered functions of the sympathetic and parasympathetic nervous systems [SNS, PNS], of the hypothalamic-pituitary-adrenal [HPA] axis, and of the immune system) as likely mediators. Finally, research evaluating interventions targeting psychosocial risk factors in groups of patients with CHD and cancer offer considerable promise that secondary prevention will be shown to have an important place in the treatment and rehabilitation of major chronic diseases.

I have reviewed elsewhere (Williams, 1994, 1995) the research supporting the general points made in the preceding paragraph, and it is not my purpose to cover the same ground in this chapter. Rather, my main focus here is on the differential impact of these psychosocial risk factors, biobehavioral mechanisms of pathogenesis, and interventions on the development and course of illness across the adult life cycle. How do psychosocial risk factors exert their influence on health across the adult life cycle, and is their impact the same in older as in younger persons? I also consider, briefly, the impact of antecedent forces acting at the opposite end of the life cycle, childhood, on the subsequent development in adulthood of psychosocial risk factors.

AGE AND THE IMPACT OF PSYCHOSOCIAL RISK FACTORS

First, it has already been shown that the impact of "physical" risk factors on CHD incidence varies as a function of age. The Pooling Project Research Group (1978) reported that the risk ratio for CHD increases with age for blood pressure but decreases for serum cholesterol and smoking. The stronger impact of blood pressure on CHD risk with increasing age probably reflects the greater vulnerability to the continuing enhanced work load imposed by elevated blood pressure in a cardiovascular system that has been weakened by the accumulation of damage owing to that increased wear and tear over the preceding years. In contrast, the diminishing impact of smoking and hyperlipidemia with increasing age have been attributed to "survival" effects. That is, some individuals may have biological characteristics that make them particularly vulnerable to the pathogenic effects of smoking and hyperlipidemia. If they are removed by death or early development of disease, then the older persons remaining in the population at risk would, lacking such biological vulnerability factors, be biologically hardier and hence resistant to the effects of smoking and hyperlipidemia, thereby accounting for these factors' weakening impact with increasing age.

A considerable body of research shows that psychosocial risk factors' impact on health also varies as a function of age, and this differential impact with increasing age appears similar to that of hyperlipidemia and smoking, rather than hypertension. In a cross-sectional study of correlates of coronary atherosclerosis (CAD) among 2,289 patients undergoing coronary angiography, Williams et al. (1988) found that both smoking and hyperlipidemia showed the same diminution in effect size with increasing age as noted previously in prospective studies. The same trend was noted for Type A behavior assessed by structured interviews (SI), but to an even more pronounced degree. Whereas the odds ratio for the relation of smoking and hyperlipidemia to CAD severity only decreased with increasing age in both men and women, this study found an actual reversal of the relationship between Type A and CAD. As shown in Fig. 10.1, among the younger patients the Type A's were more likely ($p = 0.005$) to have a significant luminal diameter occlusion of 75% or more; among those age 46 to 55, there was no difference between A's and B's; and among those older than 55, it was the Type Bs who were more likely ($p = 0.02$) to have more severe CAD.

Because there is now a consensus (Smith, 1992) that increased CHD risk owing to Type A behavior is primarily a function of the "toxic" hostility component, my colleagues and I reanalyzed data from a previous study (Dembroski, MacDougall, Williams, Haney, & Blumenthal, 1985) in which "potential for hostility" ratings performed on structured interviews had been found to correlate strongly with CAD severity in a subset of the Duke angiographic patient sample. We (Williams et al., 1988) found a strong age X potential for hostility interaction ($p = 0.002$), such that the effect size relating potential for hostility to CAD severity was much

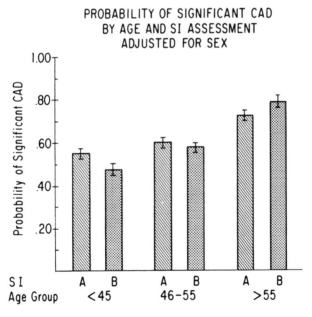

FIG. 10.1.   Association between Type A behavior pattern and CAD severity as a function of age. Adapted from data in "Type A behavior and angiographically documented coronary atherosclerosis in a sample of 2,289 patients," by R. B. Barefoot et al., 1988, "Psychosomatic Medicine, 50, p. NA.

stronger among the younger patients, diminishing to nonsignificance among the older patients. In this respect, potential for hostility behaved in its relationship to CAD severity more similarly to smoking and hyperlipidemia than to Type A behavior. In contrast to Type A behavior, which showed an actual crossover—significantly positively related to CAD severity in younger patients, but significantly negatively related in older patients—in its relationship to CAD, potential for hostility showed a larger effect size, comparable to that for smoking and hyperlipidemia, among the younger patients and did not cross over among the older patients. Siegman, Dembroski, and Ringel (1987) also found a self-report measure of hostility, "nonneurotic hostility" scores derived from a factor analysis of the Buss–Durkee Hostility Inventory, to correlate with CAD severity in another angiographic sample, but again only among the younger patients.

Confirmation of the differential impact with increasing age of hostility of CHD and all-cause mortality comes from several prospective studies. In their analysis of structured interview-based ratings of potential for hostility from the Multiple Risk Factor Intervention Trial study, Dembroski, MacDougall, Costa, and Grandits (1989) found that hostility ratings were significant predictors of CHD events, even after controlling for physical risk factors—but only among the subjects age 47 or younger; among the older subjects, hostility did not predict increased risk.

Another measure of hostility—the Cook-Medley Ho scale from the MMPI—that had been found to correlate with CAD severity in the Duke angiographic sample (Williams et al., 1980) had also been found to have a diminishing impact on health with increasing age. Among the 1,877 middle aged male participants in the Western Electric Study (Shekelle, Gale, Ostfeld, & Paul, 1983), those with higher Ho scores at age 45 were about 1.5 times more likely to die from all causes over the ensuing 20-year period than were those with low scores—an effect size remarkably similar to the cross-sectional association between Ho scores and CAD severity in the Williams et al. (1980) study of middle aged angiographic patients. In contrast, as shown in Fig. 10.2, among a sample of physicians who were followed up from age 25 to age 50 by Barefoot, Dahlstrom, and Williams (1983) the all-cause mortality among those with higher Ho scores was nearly seven times higher than that of those with low Ho scores by the end of the 25-year follow-up period.

From the foregoing discussion it is clear that hostility, whether measured by a self-report instrument like the Cook–Medley Ho scale or behavioral assessments based on the Type A structured interview, does predict increased risk of dying, but with a smaller impact as age increases. As

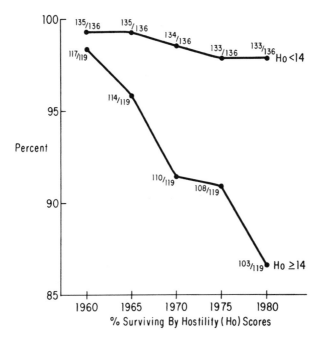

FIG. 10.2.   Impact of Cook–Medley Ho scores on mortality during a
25-year follow-up period. From "Hostility, CHD incidence, and total
mortality: A 25-year follow-up study of 255 physicians," by J. C.
Barefoot, W. G. Dahlstrom, and R. B. Williams, 1983, Psychosomatic
Medicine, 45, p. 61. Reprinted with permission.

noted, the diminishing impact with increasing age of physical risk factors
such as smoking and hyperlipidemia has been explained as an example of
survival effects—the more vulnerable persons having dropped out as the
population ages, the risk factor becomes a weaker predictor among older
groups. Inspection of Fig. 10.2 shows how such a survival effect could be
achieved for Cook–Medley Ho scores. If, instead of when they were age
25, the doctors' initial Ho scores in the Barefoot, Dahlstrom, and Williams,
(1983) study had been obtained at a comparable age—45—to those of the
subjects in the Western Electric Study (Shekelle et al., 1983), it would not
have been until the 1975–1980 period shown on the abscissa of Fig. 10.2.
By that time, 11 of the 16 deaths during the 25-year follow-up period would
have already occurred—most likely among those most vulnerable to the
pathogenic effects of hostility. It is also likely that the doctors with high Ho
scores remaining in the sample at 1980 would be hardier than those who
died earlier, making them less vulnerable to the health-damaging effects of
high hostility. If this is true, the impact of hostility on mortality should be
weaker in a subsequent follow-up of this sample than in the first 25 years.

There is some indication that the health-damaging effects of other psychosocial risk factors also diminish with increasing age. Thus, Kasl and Berkman (1981) cite evidence that both low SES and reduced social support are associated with smaller standardized mortality ratios in older as compared to younger groups. Although evidence is sparse regarding aging effects on the impact of other psychosocial risk factors such as depression and high strain jobs, there is little reason to expect they would not show a similar diminution in effect with increasing age. However, only more research can determine this.

Whatever further research reveals in this regard, one should not assume that the diminishing impact of psychosocial risk factors with increasing age means that psychosocial risk factors have no clinically important impact on health among the elderly, nor that one need not be concerned with developing interventions aimed at ameliorating such impacts. First, despite the smaller impact of psychosocial factors on health among the elderly, psychosocial factors have been abundantly shown to still have an adverse impact among elderly samples. Thus, a measure of hostility—factor L ("suspiciousness") on the Catell 16 PF—was an independent predictor of increased mortality in a sample of 500 men and women age 58.9 years at intake who were followed up over 15 years (Barefoot et al., 1987). Similarly, social isolation has been shown in several studies (for review, see Rowe & Kahn, 1987) to predict higher mortality rates among elderly samples.

The continuing impact of psychosocial risk factors on both CHD and all-cause mortality among older persons is highlighted by a series of recent reports from the Glostrup, Denmark, study by Barefoot and colleagues. Approximately 800 men and women who were born in Glostrup in 1914 were enrolled in this study of CHD risk factors, including the MMPI, when they were 50 years old in 1964. Independently of physical risk factors, both hostility (Barefoot, Larsen, Leith, & Schroll, 1995) and depression (Barefoot & Schroll, 1996) predicted increased CHD incidence as well as all-cause mortality over a follow-up period of nearly 30 years after intake. Of particular importance in the Glostrup data, the combination of high hostility and depression scores predicted by higher mortality than did either of these psychosocial risk factors alone, but only in the low SES group (Barefoot, Williams, Siegler, & Schroll, 1995).

Even given the decreasing relative risk associated with psychosocial risk factors as age increases, their continuing significant impact on CHD and all-cause mortality among the elderly means that in terms of absolute numbers of deaths the psychosocial risk factors probably account for more deaths among the elderly than among younger groups. The impact of psychosocial risk factors appears to be enhanced when combinations of factors are present in certain individuals or groups (e.g., low SES). Therefore, it continues to be important to identify the biobehavioral mechanisms whereby psychosocial factors influence health and disease among the elderly, and to use such knowledge to aid in developing interventions that might ameliorate the health-damaging effects.

BIOBEHAVIORAL MECHANISMS OF PSYCHOSOCIAL RISK FACTORS ACROSS THE ADULT LIFE CYCLE

A characteristic set of biobehavioral characteristics—increased SNS and HPA axis function, decreased PNS function, increased caloric intake and body mass index, increased smoking, and increased alcohol consumption—with the potential to damage health has been found (see Williams, 1994, 1995) to be associated with both hostility and depression (and, with less extensive evidence, associated with social isolation, high job strain, and lower SES). These associations appear to vary as a function of age and across the adult life cycle.

First, however, one should note that the psychosocial risk factors themselves show age-related changes. Barefoot et al. (1991) found a curvilinear association between age and scores on the Cook-Medley Ho scale in a national survey of 2,536 adults. Ho scores were highest in the late teens and twenties, fell to lower levels between age 30 and 60, and rose again, though not as high as during early adulthood, after age 60. The increase after age 60 was largely accounted for by increasing scores on the cynicism subset of items. Rowe and Kahn (1987) noted the occurrence of several transitions such as bereavement and relocation among the elderly that would be expected to contribute to increased levels of depression, as well as decreased social support and sense of control, in late life. As noted, although their impact decreases with age, the psychosocial risk factors continue to predict increased CHD risk and all-cause mortality in older age groups. Therefore, the increased prevalence of psychosocial risk factors among the elderly could be responsible for a potentially preventable increase in health problems.

Via what pathways do psychosocial risk factors influence pathogenesis across the adult life cycle? The most extensive evidence exists for hostility. In the UNC Alumni Heart Study cohort of over 4,000 men and women who had completed the MMPI as college freshmen in the mid-1960s, Siegler, Peterson, Barefoot, and Williams (1992) found that higher Ho scores in late adolescence predicted increased body mass index, smoking, alcohol use, and lipid ratio (Total cholesterol/HDL cholesterol) at age 43. The increased body mass index and lipid ratio at age 43 among those with high Ho scores could be owing in part to increased eating behavior between age 19 and 43: In the CARDIA study of young adults (Scherwitz et al., 1992), those with high Ho scores consumed an average of 600 more calories per day than did those with low Ho scores. In the UNC Alumni Heart Study cohort (Lipkus, Barefoot, Williams, & Siegler, 1994), high Ho scores in young adulthood predicted not only the prevalence of smoking at midlife but also the initiation of smoking among those who were not smokers when they completed the MMPI in college and failure to quit smoking over the ensuing 20-plus years of follow-up.

In addition to the just noted increased levels of physical risk factors, increased levels of SNS and HPA axis activity are also likely contributors to pathogenic processes among persons with high hostility levels. It has long been known that basal levels of plasma norepinephrine (NE; Ziegler, Lake, & Kopin, 1976) and NE responses to mental stress (Barnes, Raskind, Gumbrecht, & Halter, 1982) increase with age. Partially balancing (or perhaps even contributing to it) this increased release of NE from SNS nerve endings with increasing age is a decreased beta-adrenergic receptor number with increasing age (Weiss, Greenberg, & Cantor, 1979), which probably accounts for decreasing responses of some adrenergically mediated cardiovascular responses with increasing age (Lakatta, 1980).

Of note, whereas beta-receptor mediated tachycardia and forearm vasodilator responses to beta agonists are diminished in older humans, the dilator response to alpha-receptor blockade with phentolamine does not differ between young and old subjects, suggesting that although beta receptors can down-regulate with age, alpha receptors may not (Buhler et al., 1980). An increasing dominance of peripheral vasoconstrictor over vasodilator responses with age could contribute to the development of hypertension and associated cardiovascular responses with age could contribute to the development of hypertension and associated cardiovascular health problems among persons with high hostility. Although Ho scores at age 19 among the UNC Alumni Heart Study subjects did not predict hypertension at age 43, those who had higher hostility scores at age 43 were more likely to be hypertensive (Siegler, Peterson, Barefoot, & Williams, 1992), suggesting that a failure to show the usual decrease in hostility from the teenage years to midlife may be associated with development of hypertension. This interpretation is supported by the finding in the doctors followed up by Barefoot, Dahlstrom, and Williams (1983), who were 25 years old when they completed the MMPI in medical school, that higher Ho scores did predict increased incidence of clinical hypertension by age 50. Because the high Ho scores observed in teenagers appear to stabilize at lower levels by age 25 (Barefoot et al., 1991), the prediction of subsequent hypertension by Ho scores at age 25 but not age 19 is consistent with a casual role of high hostility levels in the development of hypertension.

A biological mechanism that might account for such an etiological role could begin with the already documented increase in SNS activity among younger high hostile subjects. This increased SNS function is reflected in increased urinary epinephrine excretion during daytime (Suarez, Williams, Harlan, et al., 1991) as well as in decreased lymphocyte beta-receptor number (Shiller, Suarez, Kuhn, Schanberg, & Williams, 1994) among high Ho subjects. Interestingly, in the latter study, although beta-receptor number was decreased in high Ho subjects, their forskolin-stimulated cyclic-AMP formation was increased, indicating increased adenyl cyclase function. This latter adjustment could account for the observation in these subjects that isoproterenol-stimulated cyclic-AMP—which depends on both beta-receptor number and adenyl cyclase—was similar in high and low Ho subjects. If with increasing age high Ho persons continue to maintain a decrease in beta-receptor number but not the increase in adenyl cyclase function, the resultant down-regulation in overall beta receptor function could leave them as they age with a diminished beta-receptor mediated vasodilator response capability. This, combined with the failure to down-regulate alpha-receptor mediated vasoconstrictor responses with increasing age as posited by Buhler et al. (1980), is one mechanism at the cellular–molecular level whereby hostility could contribute to the development of hypertension across the adult life cycle. More research—specifically focusing on SNS and receptor functions in high vs. low Ho subjects—is required, however, to confirm the importance of such a mechanism.

In contrast to the increased SNS function among high Ho subjects, there is evidence that PNS function is decreased in persons with high hostility, though only among those under 45 years of age (Sloan et al., 1994). Ho scores were not associated with PNS function among subjects older than 45, perhaps owing to the known age-associated decrease in PNS function.

In addition to the foregoing potential mechanism involving increased SNS activity and associated changes in adrenergic receptor function across the adult life cycle, other research points to another potential pathogenic mechanism whereby hostility could contribute to the development of CHD: a differential relationship in high vs. low Ho subjects between SNS reactivity to mental stress and blood lipid levels. In a study of middle aged men, Suarez, Williams, Kuhn, Zimmerman, and Schanberg (1991) found that higher total serum cholesterol levels were associated with larger plasma

catecholamine responses to a mental arithmetic in high Ho subjects; in low
Ho men, however, those with higher cholesterol levels had smaller catecholamine responses to the task. Other analyses showed that it was the low
density lipoprotein component of the total cholesterol that was responsible
for these differential lipid–catecholamine relationships in high vs. low Ho
subjects. Suarez, Williams, Kuhn, et al. (1991) postulated that this pattern
of relationships could result from effects of higher cholesterol levels to upregulate adrenergic receptors, thereby leading to a compensatory decrease
in catecholamine responses to stress in lower Ho subjects with higher cholesterol levels. In contrast, among high Ho subjects, this cholesterol-
induced up-regulation of adrenergic receptors is prevented from occurring
by the effect of their increased SNS reactivity to down-regulate beta receptors (Shiller et al., 1994). This, combined with the known effects of catecholamines to mobilize lipids and thereby increase cholesterol levels, could
explain the higher cholesterol levels as a function of larger catecholamine
responses to stress in high Ho subjects. Weaker interactions between hostility and cholesterol levels in predicting catecholamine reactivity to mental stress in younger subjects (Suarez, Harralson, Bates, Tyrey, & McNeir,
1995) suggest that this differential pattern of associations between lipids
and SNS reactivity in high versus low HO persons becomes more prominent—presumably the result of interactions among blood lipids, catecholamines, and adrenergic receptors postulated by Suarez, Williams,
Harlan, et al. (1991)—during the passage from young adulthood to midlife.

It is important that one be aware that characteristics such as increased
catecholamine reactivity, higher cholesterol levels, and smoking that tend
to co-occur in persons (and groups) with increased psychosocial risk factors do not, in and of themselves, lead directly to the life-threatening illnesses that are predicted by psychosocial risk factors. These biobehavioral characteristics can only act via effects on the cellular and molecular
processes that are proximately responsible for disease processes like
atherogenesis and tumorigenesis. Given the emerging consensus that oxidized LDL plays a critical role in atherogenesis (Ross, 1993), and noting
that stimulation of beta receptors on macrophages mimics the effects of
oxidized LDL (Thai, Lewis, Williams, Johnson, & Adams, 1995) on
macrophage cytokine gene expression, Adams (1994) has proposed that
the increased levels of smoking and cholesterol (which would increase
oxidized LDL levels) and catecholamines in persons with high Ho levels
could be contributing to pathogenesis via effects on cellular–molecular
functions of the monocyte–macrophage system.

Preliminary findings that anger has different effects on expression of
interleukin-1 on monocytes of high vs low HO women (Suarez, Sasaki,

Lewis, Williams, & Adams, 1996) suggest that application of the techniques of cellular–molecular biology has much to offer as researchers extend the search for pathogenic mechanisms whereby psychosocial risk factors contribute to ill health. As noted, psychosocial risk factors appear to affect biobehavioral characteristics in ways that vary across the adult life span. It is likely, therefore, that we shall be able to find accompanying changes in the relationship between psychosocial risk factors and the cellular–molecular biology of the monocyte–macrophage system across the adult life cycle. Therefore, as with other approaches to increasing our understanding of the role of psychosocial factors in health and disease, application of the tools of cellular–molecular biology will also benefit from a life-span, aging perspective.

Although I have concentrated on hostility in the foregoing discussion of biobehavioral mechanisms whereby psychosocial factors participate in pathogenesis, a similar case could be made for depression, which, like hostility, is associated with increased smoking (Glassman et al., 1990) and alcohol use (Hartka et al., 1991), as well as increased SNS (Vieth et al., 1994) and HPA axis function (Holsboer, van Bardeleben, Gerken, Stalla, & Muller, 1984). Riegle (1973) proposed that chronic enhanced HPA reactivity to stress leads to decreased sensitivity of feedback inhibition of adrenocortical responses to stress with increasing age. Everitt (1973) proposed that the higher levels of adrenocortical hormones with increasing age, which should be even more pronounced among persons with psychosocial risk factors, will accelerate aging and shorten life. More recent research (see Sapolsky, 1994) confirms the pathogenic potential of chronically increased HPA axis function.

INTERVENTIONS TO AMELIORATE THE HEALTH-DAMAGING EFFECTS OF PSYCHOSOCIAL RISK FACTORS IN LATE LIFE

Ultimately, the purpose of understanding how psychosocial risk factors contribute to accelerated aging and shortening of the life span is to guide us in developing interventions that can slow aging and prolong both the quantity and quality of life. There is already encouraging evidence from secondary prevention trials that psychosocial interventions that provide social support and teach patients coping skills to manage stress have a real potential to improve prognosis in middle aged and elderly patients with CHD (Frasure-Smith & Prince, 1985; Friedman et al., 1986) and cancer (Fawzy et al., 1993; Spiegel, Bloom, Kraemer, & Gottheil, 1989). Rodin (1986) cites several studies in which providing elderly nursing home residents with increased control over their living situations and training in coping skills was associated with long-lasting decreases in cortisol levels as well as decreased mortality rates over an 18-month follow-up period.

Although these results are encouraging, they have been limited in scope and sample sizes, and much more research is required before one can be confident that psychosocial interventions can improve the quality and quantity of life among older persons. Rodin (1986) noted that increased control over one's living situation and medical treatment benefits some individuals more than others, with some experiencing efforts to give them more control and personal responsibility as aversive. This latter state of affairs could lead to physiological costs that harm health, rather than improve it. It is important, therefore, that in any trials of psychosocial interventions we include sufficient numbers of older persons of both sexes to allow us to detect not only beneficial effects but harmful effects as well. Monitoring of biobehavioral factors that mediate pathogenic effects of psychosocial risk factors should be done to allow for an "early warning" of potentially harmful effects within specific subgroups—for example, elderly women.

CHILDHOOD ANTECEDENTS OF PSYCHOSOCIAL RISK FACTORS AND BIOBEHAVIORAL MECHANISMS

Before closing, I want to shift my focus briefly from the end of life to the beginning, when the psychosocial risk factors and accompanying biobehavioral mechanisms of disease have their origins. Although it cannot be doubted that genetic influences play an important role, it is also very clear that adverse early experiences have the potential to increase levels of psychosocial and biobehavioral characteristics that can damage health. For example, a preponderance of negative over positive parent–child interactions have been shown to predict both lower intelligence and school performance (Hart & Risley, 1995) and increased hostility (Matthews, Woodall, Kenyon, & Jacob, 1995) later on. Danish studies have found increased obesity in young adulthood among those who as children lived in poor quality housing (Lissau-Lund-Sorensen & Sorensen, 1992) or experienced parental neglect (Lissau & Sorensen, 1994).

Reduced brain serotonin might account for the clustering of psychosocial factors such as hostility and depression and accompanying health-damaging biobehavioral factors such as smoking, increased alcohol use, and increased SNS function in the same individuals and groups. Although no research has focused on low brain serotonin as a precursor of this constellation of psychosocial and biobehavioral risk factors, there is evidence linking low serotonin to each one individually. For example, reduced brain serotonin turnover, indexed by lower CSF 5HIAA levels, has been found in men and women with high "acting out hostility" scores (Roy, Adinoff, & Linnoila, 1994) or alcoholism (Ballenger, Goodwin, Major, et al., 1979). Stimulation of CNS 5HT1A receptors causes decreased SNS and increased PNS outflow (Saxena & Villalon, 1990), thus setting the stage for increased SNS and decreased PNS outflow when serotonin is not available. Based on such evidence as this, along with other evidence linking reduced brain serotonin function with depression, smoking, and altered eating behaviors, I have hypothesized (Williams, 1994) that reduced brain serotonin function might be a major factor in causing the psychosocial and biobehavioral risk discussed in this chapter to cluster in the same individuals and groups.

It becomes very interesting, therefore, to not that the same sorts of adverse early experiences just noted to predict increased psychosocial and biobehavioral risk characteristics also have the capacity to lead to reduced brain serotonergic function. Thus, compared to mother-reared monkeys, monkeys separated from their mothers at birth and raised with age-matched peers show reduced brain serotonin turnover, as indexed by cerebrospinal fluid (CSF) levels of 5HIAA, at 6 months of age (Higley, Suomi, & Linnoila, 1992). By 5 years of age, the peer-reared monkeys' CSF 5HIAA levels are more profoundly decreased relative to those of mother-reared monkeys, and their behavior is characterized by increased aggression, increased HPA axis reactivity, decreased affiliative acts, and increased alcohol consumption (Higley, Suomi, Mehlman, et al., 1995).

Much further research is required before we can fully understand the origins of psychosocial and biobehavioral characteristics that act across the adult life cycle to accelerate aging and shorten the life span. confirmation of the harmful impact of early harsh environments, and the neurobiological pathways for that impact (e.g., reduced brain serotonergic function), should ultimately lead us to the most effective and efficient preventive interventions.

SUMMARY AND CONCLUSIONS

- Psychosocial risk factors such as hostility, depression, social isolation, job strain, and lower SES contribute to the development of a broad range of life-threatening illnesses across the life span. Although the relative impact of these factors decreases with increasing age, they still contribute to excess and premature mortality among the older segment of the population.
- Biobehavioral mechanisms—decreased PNS function, increased SNS and HPA axis function, increased smoking and alcohol use— have been identified that have the potential to impact cellular–molecular mechanisms of pathogenesis. The action of these mechanisms appears to vary across the life cycle. The tools of cellular–molecular biology should be applied in future research to understand how psychosocial risk factors cause major illnesses such as CHD and cancer.
- It is likely that interventions targeting psychosocial risk factors and accompanying biobehavioral mechanisms will prove effective in enhancing both the quantity and quality of life among the elderly. We should not assume this, however, but should be careful to evaluate subgroups among the elderly who may be adversely affected by certain types of intervention.
- Finally, although we should work hard to understand how psychosocial risk factors damage health once they are present in adulthood, it will probably prove ultimately more beneficial to the health of the population to identify the childhood antecedents—and mediating neurobiologic mechanisms—of psychosocial risk factors and to use this knowledge to guide us in devising effective measures to prevent the development of health-damaging psychosocial and biobehavioral characteristics in the first place.

ACKNOWLEDGMENTS

Preparation of this manuscript was supported in part by grants P01-HL36587 and R01-HL44998 from the National Heart, Lung and Blood Institute; K05-MH70482 from the National Institute of Mental Health; 5P60-AG11268 and P02-AG12058 from the National Institute of Aging; and grants from the Nathan Cummings Foundation, the Fetzer Institute, and the John D. and Catherine T. MacArthur Foundation.

REFERENCES

Adams, D. O. (1994). Molecular biology of macrophage activation: A pathway whereby psychosocial factors can potentially influence health. *Psychosomatic Medicine, 56*, 316–327.

Ballenger, J., Goodwin, F. K., Major, L. F., Brown, G. L. (1979). Alcohol and central serotonin metabolism in man. Archives of *General Psychiatry, 36*, 224–227.

Barefoot, J. C., Peterson, B. L., Dahlstrom, W. G., Siegler, I. C., Anderson, N. B., & Williams, R. B. (1991). Hostility patterns and health implications: Correlates of Cook–Medley hostility scale scores in a national survey. *Health Psychology, 10*, 18–24.

Barefoot, J. C., Larsen, S., Lieth, L., & Schroll, M. (1995). Hostility, incidence of acute myocardial infarction, and mortality in a sample of older Danish men and women. *American Journal of Epidemiology, 142*, 477–484.

Barefoot, J. C., & Schroll, M. (1996). Symptoms of depression, acute myocardial infarction, and total mortality in a community sample. *Circulation, 93*, 1976–1980.

Barefoot, J. C., Siegler, I. C., Nowlin, J., Haney, T. L., Peterson, B. L., & Williams, R. B. (1987). Suspiciousness, health, and mortality: A follow-up study of 500 older adults. *Psychosomatic Medicine, 49*, 450–457.

Barefoot, J. C., Dahlstrom, W. G., & Williams, R. B. (1983). Hostility, CHD incidence, and total mortality: A 25-year follow-up study of 255 physicians. *Psychosomatic Medicine, 45*, 59–63.

Barefoot, J. C., Williams, R. B., Siegler, I. C., & Schroll, M. (1995). Depressive affect, hostility and socioeconomic status (SES): Interrelationships and joint effects on health. *Psychosomatic Medicine, 57*, 66.

Barnes, R. F., Raskind, M., Gumbrecht, G., & Halter, J. B. (1982). the effects of age on the plasma catecholamine response to mental stress in man. *Journal of Clinical Endocrinology and Metabolism, 54*, 64–69.

Buhler, F. R., Kiowski, W., van Brummelen, P., Amann, F. W., Bertel, O., Landmann, R., Lutold, B. E., & Bolli, P. (1980). Plasma catecholamines and cardiac, renal and peripheral vascular adrenoreceptor-mediated responses in different age groups of normal and hypertensive subjects. *Clinical and Experimental Hypertension, 2*, 409–426.

Dembroski, T. M., MacDougall, J. M., Costa, P. T., & Grandits, G. A. (1989). Components of hostility as predictors of sudden death and myocardial infarction in the Multiple Risk Factor Intervention Trial. *Psychosomatic Medicine, 51*, 514–522.

Dembroski, T. M., MacDougall, J. M., Williams, R. B., Haney, T. L., & Blumenthal, J. A. (1985). Components of Type A, hostility, and anger-in: Relationship to angiographic findings. *Psychosomatic Medicine, 47*, 219–233.

Everitt, A.V. (1973). The hypothalamic-pituitary control of aging and age-related pathology. *Experimental Gerontology, 8*, 265–277.

Fawzy, F. I., N. W., Hyun, C. S., Elashoff, R., Gutherie, D., Fahey, J. L., & Morton, D. L. 91993). Malignant melanoma: Effects of an early structured psychiatric intervention, coping and affective state on recurrence and survival six years later. *Archives of General Psychiatry, 50*, 681–689.

Frasure-Smith, N., & Prince, R. (1985). The Ischemic Heart Disease Life Stress Monitoring Program: Impact on mortality. *Psychosomatic Medicine, 47*, 431–445.

Friedman, M., Thoresen, C. E., Gill, J. J., Ulmer, D., Powell, L. H., Price, V. A., Brown, B., Thompson, L., Rabin, D. D., Breall, W. S., Bourg, E., Levy, R., Dixon, T. (1986). Alteration of Type A behavior and its effect on cardiac recurrences in post myocardial infarction patients: Summary results of the Recurrent Coronary Prevention Project. *American Heart Journal, 112*, 653–665.

Glassman, A. H., Helzer, J. E., Covey, L. S., Cottler, L. B., Stetner, F., Tipp, J. E., & Johnson, J. (1990). Smoking, smoking cessation, and major depression. *Journal of the American Medical Association, 264*, 1546–1549.

Hart, T., & Risley, T. R. (1995). *Meaningful differences in the everyday experience of young American children.* Baltimore: Paul H. Brookes.

Hartka, E., Johnstone, B., Leino, E. V., Motoyoshi, M., Temple, M. G., & Fillmore, K. M. (1991). A meta-analysis of depressive symptomatology and alcohol consumption over time. *British Journal of Addiction, 86*, 1283–1298.

Higley, J. D., Suomi, S. J., & Linnoila, M. (1992). A longitudinal assessment of CSF monoamine metabolites and plasma cortisol concentrations in young rhesus monkeys. *Biological Psychiatry, 32*, 127–145.

Higley, J. D., Suomi, S. J., Mehlman, P., Linnoila, M. (1995). *A nonhuman primate model of Type I & II excessive alcohol consumption.* Paper presented at the annual meeting of the American College of Neuropsychopharmacology, San Juan, Puerto Rico.

Holsboer, F., van Bardeleben, U., Gerken, A., Stalla, G. K., & Muller, O. A. (1984). Blunted corticotrophin and normal response to human corticotrophin-releasing factor in depression. *New England Journal of Medicine, 311*, 1127–1130.

Kasl, S. V., & Beckman, L. F. (1981). Some psychosocial influences on the health status of the elderly: The perspective of social epidemiology. In J. L. McGaugh, S. B. Kiesler, & J. G. March (Eds.), *Aging: Biology and behavior* (pp. 345–385). New York: Academic Press.

Lakatta, E. G. (1980). Age-related alterations in the cardiovascular response to adrenergic mediated stress. *Federation Proceedings, 39*, 3173–3177.

Lipkus, I. M., Barefoot, J. C., Williams, R. B., & Siegler, I. C. (1994). Personality measures as predictors of smoking initiation and cessation in the UNC Alumni Heart Study. *Health Psychology, 13*, 149–155.

Lissau, I., & Sorensen, T. I. A. (1994). Parental neglect during childhood and increased risk of obesity in young adulthood. *Lancet, 343*, 324–327.

Lissau-Lund-Sorensen, I., & Sorensen, T. I. A. (1992). Prospective study of the influence of social factors in childhood on risk of overweight in young adulthood. *International Journal of Obesity, 16*, 169–175.

Matthews, K. L., Wodall, K. L., Kenyon, K., & Jacob, T. (1995). Negative family environment as a predictor of boys' future status on measures of hostile attitudes, interview behavior, and anger expression. *Health Psychology, 15*, 30–37.

Pooling Project Research Group (1978). Relationship of blood pressure, serum cholesterol, smoking habit, relative weight, and ECG abnormalities to incidence of major coronary events: Final reports of the Pooling Project. *Journal of Chronic Disease, 31*, 201–306.

Riegle, G. D. (1973). Chronic stress effects on adrenocortical responsiveness in young and aged rats. *Neuroendocrinology, 11*, 1–10.

Rodin, J. (1986). Aging and health: Effects of the sense of control. *Science, 233*, 1271–1276.

Ross, R. (1993). The pathogenesis of atherosclerosis: A perspective for the 1990s. *Nature, 362*, 801–805.

Rowe, J. W., & Kahn, R. L. (1987). Human aging: Usual and successful. *Science, 237*, 143–149.

Roy, A., Adinoff, B., & Linnoila, M. (1994). Acting out hostility in normal volunteers: Negative correlation with levels of 5HIAA in cerebrospinal fluid. *Psychiatric Research, 24*, 187.

Sapolsky, R. M. (1994). *Why zebras don't get ulcers: A guide to stress, stress-related diseases, and coping.* New York: W. H. Freeman.

Saxena, P. R., & Villalon, C. M. (1990). Cardiovascular effects of serotonin agonists and antagonists. *Journal of Cardiovascular Pharmacology, 7*, S17–S34.

Scherwitz, L. W., Perkins, L. L., Chesney, M. A., Hughes, G. H., Sidney, S., & Manolio, T. A. (1992). Hostility and health behaviors in young adults: The CARDIA study. *American Journal of Epidemiology, 136*, 136–145.

Shekelle, R. B., Gale, M., Ostfeld, A. M., & Paul, O. (1983). Hostility, risk of coronary heart disease, and mortality. *Psychosomatic Medicine, 45*, 109–114.

Shiller, A. D., Suarez, E. C., Kuhn, C. M., Schanberg, S. M., Williams, R. B. (1994). Hostility is associated with lymphoctye beta-2 adrenergic receptor/adenylate cyclase activity. *Psychosomatic Medicine, 56*, 174.

Siegler, I. C., Peterson, B. L., Barefoot, J. C., & Williams, R. (1992). Hostility during late adolescence predicts coronary risk factors at mid-life. *American Journal of Epidemiology, 136*, 146–154.

Siegman, A. W., Dembroski, T. M., & Ringel, N. (1987). Components of hostility and the severity of coronary artery disease. *Psychosomatic Medicine, 49,* 127–135.

Sloan, R. P., Shapiro, P. A., Bigger, J. T., Jr., Bagiella, E. Steinman, R. C., & Gorman, J. M. (1994). Cardiac autonomic control and hostility in healthy subjects. *American Journal of Cardiology, 74,* 298–300.

Smith, T. W. (1992). Hostility and health: current status of a psychosomatic hypothesis, *Health Psychology, 11,* 139–150.

Spiegel, D., Bloom, J. R., Kraemer, H. C., & Gottheil, E. (1989). Effect of psychosocial treatment on survival of patients with metastatic breast cancer. *Lancet, 2,* 888–890.

Suarez, E. C., Harralson, T. L., Bates, M. P., Tyrey, M., & McNeer, T. C. C. (1995). *Neuroendocrine responses are associated with lipids in hostile women.* Paper presented at the annual meting of the American Psychosomatic Society, New Orleans, LA.

Suarez, E. C., Sasaki, M., Lewis, J. G., Williams, R. B., & Adams, D. O. (1996). Anger increases expression of interleukin-1 on monocytes in hostile women. *Psychosomatic Medicine, 58,* 87.

Suarez, E. C., Williams, R. B., Harlan, E. S., Peoples, M. C., Kuhn, C. M., & Schanberg, S. M. (1991). Hostility-related differences in urinary excretion rates of catecholamines. *Psychophysiology, 28,* S54.

Suarez, E. C., Williams, R. B., Kuhn, C. M., Zimmermann, E. H., & Schanberg, S. M. (1991). Biobehavioral basis of coronary-prone behavior in middle-aged men. Part II: Serum cholesterol, the Type A behavior pattern, and hostility as interactive modulators of physiological reactivity. *Psychosomatic Medicine, 53,* 528–537.

Thai, S. F., Lewis, J. G., Williams, R. B., Johnson, S. P., & Adams, D. O. (1995). Effects of oxidized LDL on mononuclear phagocytes: Inhibition of induction of four inflammatory, cytokine gene RNAs, release of NO, and cytolysis of tumor cells. *Journal of Leukocyte Biology, 57,* 427–433.

Vieth, R. C., Lewis, N., Linares, O. A., Barnes, R. F., Rashkind, M. A. Villacres, E. C., Murburg, M. M., Ashleigh, E. A., Castillo, S., Peskind, E. R., Pascualy, M., & Halter, J. B. (1994). Sympathetic nervous system activity in major depression: Basal and desipramine-induced alterations in plasma nonepinephrine kinetics. *Archives of General Psychiatry, 51,* 411–422.

Weiss, B., Greenberg, L., & Cantor, E. (1979). Age-related alterations in the development of adrenergic denervation supersensitivity. *Federation Proceedings, 38,* 1915–1921.

Williams, R. B. (1994). Neurobiology, cellular and molecular biology, and psychosomatic medicine. *Psychosomatic Medicine, 56,* 308–315.

Williams, R. B. (1995). Psychosocial factors in health and disease: What do we know, what can be do? In *Proceedings of the National Symposium on Networks and Health* (pp. 138–157). Copenhagen: Danish Ministry of Health.

Williams, R. B., Barefoot, J. C., Haney, T. L., Harell, R. E., Blumenthal, J. A., Pryor, D. B., & Peterson, B. (1988). Type A behavior and angiographically documented coronary atherosclerosis in a sample of 2,289 patients. *Psychosomatic Medicine, 50,* 139–152.

Williams, R. B., Haney, T. L., Lee, K. L., Kong, Y., Blumenthal, J. A., & Whalen, R. E. (1980). Type A behavior, hostility, and coronary atherosclerosis. *Psychosomatic Medicine, 42,* 539–549.

Ziegler, M. G., Lake, C. R., & Kopin, I. J. (1976). Plasma nonadrenaline increases with age. *Nature, 261,* 333–335.

11

Coping with Chronic Illness Among the Elderly: Maintaining Self-Esteem

Vicki S. Helgeson
Carnegie Mellon University

Kristin Mickelson
Kent University

During the 20th century, the leading cause of death in the United States shifted from infectious disease to chronic disease. This shift led to a longer life span. The latter portion of the life span, however, is often characterized by disability from chronic illness. In this chapter we examine how people cope with chronic illness, with a particular focus on the elderly because they are the ones most likely to be afflicted. First, we briefly describe the adjustment issues the chronically ill face and then the adjustment issues the elderly face. The coping task that both the chronically ill and the elderly face is maintaining their sense of self in the face of physical, social, and mental declines. Research shows that neither the chronically ill nor the elderly suffer lasting damage to self-esteem. Thus, in this chapter we focus on strategies that the chronically ill use to maintain self-esteem. These strategies apply to all age groups, but we emphasize their utility among the elderly.

ADJUSTMENT TO
CHRONIC ILLNESS

Chronic illness can be construed as a victimization experience. According to Janoff-Bulman and Frieze (1983), victimization involves the shattering of basic assumption about the world and oneself, including assumptions that one is invulnerable, that the world is a meaningful and comprehensible place, and that the self is worthy and good. It is challenges to this latter assumption that we believe hold particular significance for chronic illness. According to Cohen and Lazarus (1979), one of the primary tasks the chronically ill face is maintaining a positive self-image. Thus, we address the damage to self-worth and the restoration of self-esteem following chronic illness.

People generally operate under the assumption that they are worthy, good, and decent—an assumption that maintains high self-esteem (Janoff-Bulman & Frieze, 1983). Victimization leads one to question this assumption. It is difficult to reconcile a negative experience such as victimization with the belief that one is a good person (Thompson & Janigian, 1988). Victimization activates negative self-images. A weak, needy, dependent, injured self now exists. Janoff-Bulman (1989) conducted a study of victims and nonvictims and compared them on eight assumptions about the world and the self. The one that most reliably discriminated between victims and nonvictims was perceived self-worth. Victims had lower perceived self-worth than did nonvictims.

Chronic illness is a victimization experience that poses particular threats to self-esteem because it brings about lasting changes in the physical self. The physical effects of chronic illness may alter one's body image, interfere with daily activities, and restrict social activities (Wood, Taylor, & Lichtman, 1985). Physical appearance, physical capabilities, vocational and recreational interests, and relationships are all defining aspects of one's identify. Charmaz (1991) describes the threat to self-esteem that chronic illness poses as a "loss of the self." She says that society acknowledges the physical suffering that results from chronic illness, but that there is a kind of suffering that society neglects—the loss of self, or the loss of the self that existed prior to illness. Chronic illness undermines former self-images. Adjustment difficulties occur when new, equally valued self-images do not replace the old ones.

Despite the threat to self-esteem that chronic illness poses, it does not appear that chronically ill people remain distressed. Kruse and Lehr (1989) compared the developmental processes of chronically ill and healthy elderly persons as they aged over an 18-year period. They found that aging tended to be a growth process—a time for "new potentials" for both groups. Both groups showed success in coping with the challenges and new restrictions of age. In a study of five chronically ill populations, Cassileth et al. (1984) found that patients did not significantly differ from the general public on measures of psychological well-being. They did note, however, that the more recently diagnosed patients scored lower on psychological well-being than did those who had been diagnosed for longer periods. We argue that there are ways for chronically ill individuals to restore self-esteem and that the more recently diagnosed may be still struggling with these strategies.

ADJUSTMENT TO AGING

As people move into their late adult years, they begin to experience a variety of losses—physical, mental, and social. These losses pose a threat to the aging person's self-concept, or in other words, self-esteem. Researchers in the past have theorized that old age is related to a decline in self-esteem and well-being as well as an increase in helplessness and depression. More recently, however, empirical studies have failed to confirm these hypotheses. Although the elderly certainly do experience losses in a variety of domains, recent studies have shown that the aging person actually demonstrates a remarkable stability in self-esteem (Brandtstadter & Greve, 1994; Brandtstadter, Wentura, & Greve, 1993; Chene, 1991).

What accounts for the stability of self-esteem in the face of social and physical declines? There are several theories of successful aging (Baltes & Baltes, 1990; Brandtstadter & Greve, 1994). Each emphasizes the distinction between objective and subjective indexes of well-being. Traditional definitions of health rely on objective well-being; that is, the absence of disease. This definition may not be useful when studying the elderly because over 85% of the elderly suffer from at least one chronic disease (Minkler, 1985; Schienle & Eiler, 1984). Despite wide differences in objective well-being, the majority of the elderly report good subjective well-being. For example, in one study of those age 62 and over, 67% of respondents rated their health as good or excellent (Suls, Marco, & Tobin, 1991). Objective indicators of well-being account for only a small portion of the variance in the elderly's subjective reports of well-being (Suls et al., 1991).

The current consensus is that aging is not related to a decrease in self-esteem but rather a reassessment of goals and standards that results in a stabilizing of one's self-concept. Aging may limit domains of functioning, but successful aging involves prioritizing and emphasizing remaining domains of functioning (Baltes & Baltes, 1990). Aging is not only accompanied by decline and restriction but presents new opportunities for growth (Kruse & Lehr, 1989). According to Schulz, Heckhausen, and O'Brien (1994), aging is associated with negative affect only when the individual suffers a loss of control over important outcomes. Although aging is associated with a loss of primary control (i.e., changing the world to fit one's own desires; Rothbaum, Weitz, & Snyder, 1982), secondary control strategies (i.e., changing one's internal processes to fit the changing world; Rothbaum et al., 1982) can compensate (Schulz et al., 1994). We argue that these secondary control strategies are aimed at restoring self-esteem.

The elderly individual who faces the onset of chronic illness must cope with a particularly severe assault on self-esteem. Chronic illness signifies old age, raises issues of mortality, and is accompanied by physical, mental, and social decline. Yet the chronically ill elderly, on average, are not severely distressed. In this chapter, we discuss three primary mechanisms by which the individual afflicted with chronic illness can restore self-esteem: (a) social comparison, (b) denial, and (c) deriving meaning from the experience. We discuss the first mechanism in grater depth than the other two because there is a larger literature base on social comparison and greater advances have been made in understanding its role in restoration of self-esteem. For each of the three mechanisms, we include findings from other researchers and present data of our own.

We present data from two studies of cardiac patients. The first study consisted of 60 patients attending a cardiac rehabilitation program (46 men, 14 women). Ages ranged from 45 to 82, with a mean of 65. Patients were eligible to participate in the study if they had attended the program for less than 18 months. There are two phases to cardiac rehabilitation. Patients enter the first phase, the monitored program, shortly after hospital discharge. It is a 13-week program in which the patient's blood pressure and heart rate are monitored during exercise. On completion of the monitored program, patients advance to the unmonitored phase, which lasts indefinitely. There were 27 patients in the monitored program and 33 patients in the unmonitored program. Two thirds of the sample (67%) had a history of myocardial infarction, 57% had a history of angioplasty, and 60% had a history of coronary bypass surgery. Portions of these data are presented in Helgeson and Taylor (1993). The data are cross-sectional.

The second study consisted of 50 patients (35 men, 15 women) who had sustained a first coronary event (myocardial infarction or unstable angina), had no prior history of heart disease, and had no history of other major chronic illnesses (e.g., cancer). Thus, this sample represents a group of people who are adjusting to the onset of chronic illness. Ages range from 37 to 75, with a mean of 60 and median of 64. These patients were interviewed in the hospital (Time 1: T1) and in their homes six months following discharge (Time 2: T2). In both studies, self-esteem was measured with the Rosenberg (1965) Self-Esteem Scale and psychological distress was measured with the Brief Symptom Inventory (Anxiety, Hostility, Depression, Somatization subscales; Derogatis & Spencer, 1982).

First, we discuss the association of age to self-esteem, psychological well-being, and adjustment to chronic illness. Second, we discuss the role of self-esteem in adjustment to chronic illness. Third, we discuss each of the three mechanisms by which self-esteem may be restored following chronic illness. We conclude by outlining other strategies that may increase self-esteem and suggesting future directions for research.

RELATION OF AGE
TO WELL-BEING

Presumably, increased age is associated with deteriorating physical health. Yet research typically has not found a relation between age and self-esteem or life satisfaction (see Baltes & Baltes, 1990, for a review). When relations are found, age appears to have positive effects. For example, in a cross-sectional study of adults, increased age was associated with increased self-esteem and increased life satisfaction, when income, education, and race were statistically controlled (Gove, Ortega, & Style, 1989).

Both of the studies we conducted showed that age was not associated with self-esteem. As expected, age was associated with worse physical health but better subjective well-being. In Study 1, increased age was associated with working at a lower physical capacity at the rehabilitation program, $r = -.48$, $p < .05$, yet better mental health, $r = .28$, $p < .05$. In Study 2, increased age was associated with a greater number of other health problems, $r = .43$, $p < .01$, yet better subjective well-being: less psychological distress at T1 and T2 ($r = -.48$, $p < .001$; $r = -.56$, $p < .001$), greater life satisfaction at T1 and T2 ($r = .25$, $p = .09$; $r = .44$, $p < .01$), and better adjustment to the illness ($r = .26$, $p = .09$). Increased age also was associated with better subjective well-being at T2 when controls for T1 were implemented, suggesting that age led to better psychological recovery from the initial cardiac event.

RELATION OF SELF-ESTEEM
TO ADJUSTMENT TO
CHRONIC ILLNESS

Although the chronically ill do not appear to be more psychologically distressed than healthy populations, we do not know of any studies that have compared self-esteem, per se, of chronically ill individuals to that of healthy individuals. There is evidence, however, that the severity of chronic illness is related to self-esteem. In two studies of patients with rheumatoid arthritis, those with greater disability from the disease had lower self-esteem (Affleck & Tennen, 1991; DeVellis et al., 1990).

What is the relation of self-esteem to adjustment to chronic illness? Does high self-esteem lead to more successful adjustment, or does distress associated with chronic illness lower self-esteem? Both studies that we conducted reveal an inverse relation between self-esteem and psychological distress. In Study 1, self-esteem was associated with decreased distress, $r = -.37, p < .01$. In Study 2, similar cross-sectional associations of self-esteem and distress emerged (T1: $r = -.39, p < .05$; T2: $r = -.59, p < .001$). To determine the casual relation (i.e., whether high self-esteem buffers one from the adverse effects of chronic illness, or whether greater distress from chronic illness leads to lower perceived worth), the longitudinal relations of self-esteem and distress were examined in Study 2. T1 self-esteem was associated with decreased distress at T2 ($r = -.39, p < .05$) but not when controls for T1 distress were implemented. Thus, there is no evidence that high self-esteem leads to a decrease in distress following chronic illness. T1 distress, however, was associated with decreased self-esteem at T2 ($r = -.49, p < .001$), even with controls for T1 self-esteem ($r = -.35, p < .05$). It appears that there is some evidence for a reciprocal relation between self-esteem and distress, but there is more evidence for the position that distress following chronic illness reduces self-esteem than for the position that self-esteem buffers one from distress following chronic illness. In the next section of this chapter we describe several ways that self-esteem following chronic illness can be restored and lasting psychological distress minimized.

SOCIAL COMPARISONS

In his original statement of social comparison theory, Festinger (1954) said that human beings are driven to evaluate their opinions and abilities and that when objective standards are absent, we compare ourselves to other people. He also identified two conditions that increase the drive for social comparison: ambiguous situations, and opinions or abilities that are particularly relevant to the self. Thus, social comparison should be especially likely to occur following chronic illness because all the conditions that Festinger said lead to social comparison exist. An objective standard for adjustment to chronic illness does not exist, the future course of chronic illness is ambiguous, and physical health is highly self-relevant.

Social comparison also has been postulated to be one of the strategies of "successful aging." One contributor to the elderly's perceptions of good health is information gained from social comparison (Blalock, DeVellis, DeVellis, & Sauter, 1988). The elderly can retain high self-esteem and high life satisfaction in the face of multiple losses by comparing themselves to other elderly confronting similar losses (Baltes & Baltes, 1990; Heidrich & Ryff, 1993a, 1993b). In other words, the elderly's standard of health changes. When the majority of elderly rate their health as good, they are likely comparing themselves to other elderly rather than to younger age groups. In fact, the elderly who compare their present health to their past health (temporal comparison) report less favorable health perceptions (Suls et al., 1991).

The study of social comparison processes has become increasingly complex since Festinger first outlined his theory in 1954 (see volume edited by Suls & Wills in 1991). We make the following distinctions in examining the implications of social comparison for restoration of self-esteem following chronic illness. We examine the effects of (a) engaging in social comparison (i.e., frequency of making social comparison), (b) the comparison target (i.e., with whom one compares oneself), and (c) the affect (positive or negative) derived from a particular comparison.

Making Social Comparisons

Although social comparison provides an opportunity to increase self-esteem, the extent to which someone engages in social comparison actually may represent greater psychological distress. Social comparison can be a response to threat, and greater threat leads to more psychological distress. Research has supported this hypothesis. In a study of elderly men and women, those who mentioned comparing themselves with another person evidenced more concerns about their health (Suls et al., 1991). In a study of elderly women, more frequent social comparisons were associated with increased distress (Heidrich & Ryff, 1993b). In that same study, more frequent social comparisons also were associated with worse physical health.

Our studies support these findings. In Study 1, the frequency of making social comparisons was marginally associated with increased distress, $r = .23$, $p = .08$, and in Study 2, more frequently comparing the self to others was significantly associated with increased distress, $r = .31$, $p < .05$, and lower self-esteem, $r = -.32$, $p < .05$. Thus, it is not simply the process of engaging in social comparison that restores self-esteem.

Comparison Target

Festinger (1954) suggested that there was a particular group of people with whom we would compare ourselves—similar others. Given a group of people who vary on the dimension of interest (Wheeler, Shaver, Jones, Goethals, & Cooper, 1969), similar others were thought to provide the most accurate information. According to Festinger, the underlying motive for social comparison was accurate, unbiased self-evaluation.

Researchers soon realized that the goal of social comparison was not always unbiased self-evaluation. In 1981, Wills proposed a different motive for social comparison—self-enhancement. When faced with threat, Wills suggested, people may attempt to enhance their self-esteem by comparing themselves with less fortunate others, that is, by engaging in downward comparison.

Because chronic illness poses a threat to self-esteem, downward comparison should be especially likely. Downward comparison has been documented to be a pervasive response to the onset of chronic illness when spontaneous comparisons have been recorded during interviews of people with cancer (Wood et al., 1985), rheumatoid arthritis (DeVellis et al., 1990; Affleck, Tennen, Pfeiffer, et al., 1987), and heart disease (Helgeson & Taylor, 1993).

One way in which downward comparison has been measured is by having patients rate themselves and similar others on dimensions of physical and psychological health. When patients rate their own illness as less severe than that of others and their own adjustment as superior to that of others, they are engaging in a kind of downward comparison we call downward evaluation. Downward evaluation (i.e., rate self as better off than others) has been documented among AIDS patients (Taylor, Kemeny, Reed, & Aspinwall, 1991), breast cancer patients (Wood et al., 1985), mothers of infants with severe perinatal problems (Affleck, Tennen, Pfeiffer, et al., 1987), and rheumatoid arthritis patients (Affleck, Tennen, Pfeiffer, et al., 1987; DeVellis et al., 1990). Downward evaluation also has been observed among the elderly; they perceive their health to be better than that of same-age peers (Levkoff, Cleary, & Wetle, 1987).

In both studies that we conducted, cardiac patients were asked to rate themselves and other patients on a number of dimensions (Study 1: physical health, psychological health, and coping resources; Study 2; physical health, emotional health). To the extent that patients rate themselves above others, they are engaging in downward evaluation. In both studies, the majority of patients rated themselves as faring better than others.

How can the majority of chronically ill individuals perceive that their physical or emotional health is better than that of others? We have two answers to this question. First, the comparison referent may be hypothetical rather than real. Taylor, Wood, and Lichtman (1983) found that women with breast cancer manufactured hypothetical downward comparison referents. Suls et al. (1991) suggested that the elderly's positive health evaluations are based on comparisons to a cognitively constructed other, specifically a frail and ill elderly person. They suggest that the majority of the elderly do not fit this comparison referent. The frail and ill elderly person may be created by the media but exaggerated by the person's own motive to enhance self-esteem. One way to enhance self-esteem is to overestimate the number of others who share a negative attribute.

Second, patients can focus on one of a number of dimensions when engaging in social comparison—physical symptoms, age, financial resources, social resources, severity of illness. People are likely to select dimensions on which they are doing favorably as compared to others. For example, among patients who sustained a first heart attack, Cowie (1976) noted that patients compared themselves favorably to others who were worse off or at greater risk for another cardiac event, for example, those who were older, who had more severe symptoms, who had more risk factors, or who had died. Taylor (1983) found in her study of women with breast cancer that patients compared on dimensions on which they were doing favorably as compared to others. For example, women with lumpectomies were relieved that they did not have to have the entire breast removed, whereas women with mastectomies were relieved that the cancer had not metasticized.

Is downward comparison adaptive? In the laboratory, those who are randomly assigned to downward comparison evidence an increase in self-esteem (Reis, Gerrard, & Gibbons, 1993). In the field, those who spontaneously engage in downward comparison are rated as better adjusted than those who do not (Affleck, Tennen, Pfeiffer, et al., 1987).

In the field, where the comparison target is not as easily manipulated, the possibility exists that downward evaluations are accurate; that is, those who perceive themselves to be better off than others are actually doing better than others. In a study of rheumatoid arthritis patients, there was some degree of accuracy in patients' social comparisons (i.e., patients who rated their own illness as less severe actually had less severe disease), but the relation of downward evaluation to good adjustment remained significant when disease severity was statistically controlled (Affleck, Tennen, Pfeiffer, et al., 1987). Thus, downward comparisons appear to be beneficial for people who span the range of objective conditions.

In Study 1, downward evaluation was related to higher self-esteem ($r = .48$, $p < .001$) and reduced stress ($r = -.27$, $p < .05$). These relations held even when number of weeks enrolled in the rehabilitation program was statistically controlled, suggesting that this ability to perceive oneself as far better than others is psychologically helpful across a variety of objective conditions. In Study 2, downward evaluation was only measured at T2 because patients did not have sufficient opportunity to compare their situation to that of similar others at T1 during hospitalization. At T2, downward evaluation was cross-sectionally associated with higher self-esteem ($r = .34$, $p < .05$), reduced psychological distress ($r = -.45$, $p < .01$), fewer physical symptoms from disease ($r = -.40$, $p < .05$), and better adjustment to illness ($r = -.42$, $p < .01$). When T1 statistical controls for these variables were implemented, the associations with downward evaluation remained significant. Thus, downward evaluation was associated with smaller decreases in self-esteem and smaller increases in distress following the coronary event. The association of downward evaluation to better health outcomes remained significant when disease severity was statistically controlled.

These data leave unanswered the question of whether self-esteem is the causal variable that leads to downward evaluation, which then reduces distress, or whether downward evaluation leads to increased self-esteem, which then reduces stress. To address this issue, we conducted a series of partial correlational analyses. In Study 1, we found that the relation of self-esteem to reduced distress did not change when downward evaluation was statistically controlled. The relation of downward evaluation to reduced distress ($r = -.27$, $p < .05$) disappeared, however, when self-esteem was statistically controlled ($r = -.11$, $n.s.$). Study 2 revealed a similar pattern of findings. The relation of self-esteem to reduced distress did not change when controlling for downward evaluation. The relation of downward evaluation to reduced distress ($r = -.31$, $p < .05$) was no longer statistically significant when self-esteem was controlled ($r = -20$, $n.s.$). These results are compatible with the interpretation that downward evaluation (perceiving own situation as favorable as compared to that of others) restored self-esteem, which then reduced distress (Fig. 11.1).

FIG. 11.1.   Self-esteem mediates the relation of downward evaluation to decreased psychological distress.

Wills (1981) suggested that downward comparison was evoked by threat. Wood et al. (1985) found in their study of women with breast cancer that downward comparison was more common among women who were in an earlier phase of the illness—presumably, when the threat was more severe. Downward comparison also was more common among more recently diagnosed rheumatoid arthritis patients (Affleck, Tennen, Pfeiffer, et al., 1987), presumably because the threat was more severe. In that study, one might expect that those more recently diagnosed had less severe disease and that their downward comparisons were accurate. However, disease severity was not related to time since diagnosis. In our studies, we considered the possibility that downward comparison would be more adaptive under conditions of greater threat.

In Study 1, patients were divided into two groups, those in the monitored phase of the program and those in the unmonitored phase of the program. We reasoned that the threat of another coronary event would be greater for patients in the monitored than the unmonitored phase of the program. As expected, patients' physical capacities (i.e., level at which they exercised, number of minutes exercised) were lower during the monitored phase than the unmonitored phase. The association of downward evaluation to reduced distress was significant among those in the monitored phase ($r = -.35$, $p < .05$) but was not significant among those in the unmonitored phase ($r = -.15$, $n.s.$).

In Study 2, more and less severe groups were computed in two ways. First, patients could be divided into groups based on admission diagnosis (myocardial infarction vs. unstable angina). The relation of downward evaluation to distress was significant for myocardial infarction patients ($r = -.46$, $p < .05$) but not for unstable angina patients ($r = -.31$, $n.s.$). Second, patients could be divided into more and less severe groups based on the number of diseased vessels documented by angiography. The relation of downward evaluation to reduce distress was significant for patients with multivessel disease ($r = -.35$, $p < .05$) but not single vessel disease ($r = -.15$, n.s.). Thus, in both studies, downward evaluation seemed to provide greater benefits to patients facing more severe threat.

Forced Comparisons

We have examined patients' social comparison preferences, but patients do not always have the opportunity to choose those with whom they will compare themselves. For example, friends and family may present the patient with social comparisons by telling stories about other people with the same illness. In Study 1, we asked patients to describe the stories others had told them. After each story, the patient rated it as positive or negative and as being helpful, unhelpful, or having no effect. The interviewer classified the story as an upward comparison or a downward comparison according to whether the patient described the comparison as worse off or better off than him- or herself. About half the stories were positive (e.g., another patient doing well, coming through the tragedy) and half the stories were negative (e.g., another patient having difficulties or engaging in poor health behavior). The valence of the story was closely tied to comparison direction, $X2(1) = 24.04$, $p < .001$. Almost all the upward comparison stories were positive, and all the downward comparison stories were negative. In addition, the upward comparison stories were more likely to be perceived as helpful, whereas the downward comparison stories were more likely to be perceived as having no effect (patients rarely reported a story had a negative effect on them), $X2(2) = 5.70$, $p = .06$. The lack of effectiveness for downward comparison stories is in sharp contrast to the findings on the benefits of downward evaluation. These results suggest that the comparison target alone does not determine which social comparison will be beneficial.

Comparison Affect

Researchers have suggested that it is not the direction of comparison that influences adjustment but the affect derived from the comparison (Buunk, Collins, Taylor, VanYperen, & Dakof, 1990). Downward comparisons may make one feel lucky in comparison or may remind one of the potential for deterioration. When patients have the opportunity to select comparison targets, they may choose hypothetical downward comparison targets that will make them feel lucky in comparison but with whom they will not have to interact. To the extent that forced downward comparisons represent people whom the patient knows or has contact with, the potential for deterioration may be more salient. Thus, forced downward comparisons may be more likely than selected downward comparisons to lead to negative affect. The affect derived from upward comparison also can be positive or negative. Upward comparisons may lead to frustration that one is not doing as well as one could be or may provide inspiration and models for self-improvement.

The affect derived from a comparison determines its impact on subjective well-being. Heidrich and Ryff (1993b) found that how social comparisons made a group of elderly women feel was more predictive of distress than the mere frequency of engaging in social comparison. Positive consequences of social comparison (comparison led to feeling good about self) were associated with reduced distress (Heidrich & Ryff, 1993a, 1993b). Consistent with the threat severity hypothesis advanced above, positive consequences from social comparisons were more strongly related to mental health among the women in the worst physical health.

In both studies that we conducted, patients were asked to rate the extent to which they derived positive and negative feelings from both downward and upward comparisons. In Study 1, patients responded to four questions, each reflecting the frequency of experiencing the particular feeling: lucky when comparing downward, fearful when comparing downward, inspired when comparing upward, frustrated when comparing upward. None of these ratings were related to self-esteem. The affect derived from the comparison was related to psychological distress, however. Feeling lucky when comparing downward was associated with reduced distress ($r = -.26$, p < .05), and feeling threatened when comparing downward was associated with increased distress ($r = .34$, p < .01). Feelings regarding upward comparisons were not related to adjustment. Upward comparisons may not have had as much impact as downward comparisons because they were more easily discounted. Many patients reported that upward comparison others were better off because they had been attending the program for a longer period.

In Study 2, patients responded to four 4-item scales, reflecting more reliable indexes of positive and negative affect from upward and downward comparison. Self-esteem was related to less negative affect from downward comparison, $r = -.42$, $p < .01$, and less negative affect from upward comparison, $r = -.43$, $p < .01$, consistent with the findings from Buunk et al.'s (1990) study of cancer patients. Affect from both upward and downward comparison was related to distress. Negative affect from downward comparison was associated with greater distress, $r = .30$, $p < .05$, negative affect from upward comparison was associated with greater distress, $r = .45$, $p < .05$, and positive affect from upward comparison was marginally related to reduced distress, $r = -.37$, $p < .10$. Although the two studies do not provide converging evidence on the most important comparison target, both suggest that it is the affect derived from comparison rather than the comparison target that is important.

Summary

One way to restore self-esteem following chronic illness is to compare one's own situation to that of others, in particular to worse-off others. Despite the adverse effects of chronic illness on the physical, social, and mental self, those who perceive their own situation to be better than that of others—those who engage in downward evaluation—suffer less psychological distress. It also appears that downward evaluation is of greater benefit to those who face more severe threat. That is, those who are worse off than others benefit the most from perceiving themselves to be better off than others. Downward comparison and upward comparison have the potential to lead to both positive and negative affect. Taken collectively, research suggests that downward comparisons involving hypothetical others or some "average" other enhance mood by making one feel lucky, whereas downward comparisons that involve interactions with real others may arouse fear and anxiety. Indeed, the implication of social comparison processes for adjustment to chronic illness is complex. It is not simply a matter of with whom you compare or whether you compare that determines adjustment, but the affect derived from the comparison.

The case for the relevance of social comparison to adjustment to chronic illness is further complicated by the fact that a substantial number of patients report they do not engage in social comparison. Although patients from both studies made many spontaneous social comparisons during the interview, when confronted with the question about how often patients compare themselves to others, many patients said that they did not engage in social comparison. In Study 1, 40% of patients said that they never compared themselves to other patients. In Study 2, 45% of patients said that they never compared themselves to other patients. This occurred despite the fact that social comparison was presented as a normal and socially desirable behavior. Although some patients in Study 2 said that they did not know anyone else with a heart problem, we knew this was not the case in Study 1, which took place in a cardiac rehabilitation program. Rather than compare themselves with others, many patients emphasized their progress and the unique aspects of themselves (e.g., great deal of family resources) or their situation (e.g., had a lot of stress). Often these remarks reflected social comparisons (e.g., "I don't compare myself to others because my heart attack was less severe than others"). Many raised concerns about the effect their conclusion would have on the soundness of the research—concerns that they would skew the data. Other research has found that some people reject social comparison in favor of uniqueness perceptions (e.g., Affleck, Tennen, Pfeiffer, et al., 1987). In Studies 1 and 2, the failure to report making social comparisons was correlated with denial.

DENIAL

Denial also may serve to maintain self-esteem. One way to reduce the threat to self-esteem that chronic illness poses, and one way to cope with the uncertain future of chronic illness, is to deny it. The anxiety-reducing features of denial may be quite helpful under these circumstances. Janis (1958) has said that denial increases under conditions of ambiguity and that intellectual denial or minimization can be nonpathological when the threat is ambiguous. The future of heart disease is likely to be perceived as ambiguous for the cardiac patient (Christman et al., 1988).

Previous research has shown denial to be a common response to the onset of coronary heart disease (Croog & Levine, 1977). The effects of denial, however, are controversial. On the positive side, denial has been associated with reduced psychological distress (Levine et al., 1987), resumption of sexual activity, return to work, better medical outcomes during hospitalization, and less mortality in the coronary care unit (Croog, Shapiro, & Levine, 1971; Granger, 1974; Hackett, Cassem, & Wishnie, 1968; Levenson, Mishra, Hamer, & Hastillo, 1989; Stern, Pascale, & McLoone, 1975). On the negative side, denial has been associated with noncompliance (e.g., smoking in the hospital, failure to follow prescribed medical regimen in and out of the hospital; Croog, & Levine, 1977; Granger, 1974; Stern et al., 1975).

Dimensions of Denial

One explanation for the diverse findings on the health consequences of denial is that the construct has been measured in quite different ways. Measurement of denial ranges from a lengthy interview protocol to single questions asking patients whether they had a heart attack or whether they felt tense or apprehensive during hospitalization. When these single questions are used, the relation of denial to psychological distress outcomes is inherently confounded. Previous researchers assumed that denial is unidimensional (Hackett & Cassem, 1974), but Havik and Maeland (1986) demonstrated that there are multiple facets of denial. Specifically, they distinguish between denial of illness (i.e., denying one is ill and needs treatment) and denial of impact (i.e., admitting one is ill but minimizing the severity of the problem). We suggest that denial of illness may be unhealthy because patients would reject or fail to attend to information necessary for good health care, whereas denial of impact may be healthy because it would reduce anxiety, help patients to resume a normal life, and restore self-esteem. We used Havik and Maeland's measures of denial of illness and denial of impact to test these hypotheses in both studies.

In Study 1 and Study 2, denial of illness was not related to self-esteem or psychological distress. Denial of impact, however, was related to both self-esteem and psychological distress. In Study 1, denial of impact was related to higher self-esteem ($r = .25$, $p < .05$) and reduced distress ($r = -.27$,

$p < .05$). In Study 2, cross-sectional associations of denial of impact to self-esteem appeared at T1 ($r = .25, p < .10$) and T2 ($r = .47, p < .01$). T1 denial of impact also was related to T2 self-esteem, when T1 self-esteem was statistically controlled ($r = .37, p < .05$), suggesting that denial of impact helped to restore self-esteem. Denial of impact was cross-sectionally associated with reduced distress (T1: $r = .37, p < .01$; T2: $r = -.46, p < .01$). T2 denial of impact (but not T1) was associated with less distress at T2, even when T1 distress was statistically controlled ($r = -.41, p < .01$).

Causality

Next, we asked whether high self-esteem led to denial of impact, which then reduced distress, or whether denial of impact increased self-esteem, which then reduced stress. Partial correlational analyses were conducted to address this issue. Both studies suggested that denial of impact leads to a restoration of self-esteem, which then reduces distress (Fig. 11.2). In Study 1, the relation of self-esteem to reduced distress did not change when controlling for denial of impact. The relation of denial of impact to reduced distress ($r = -.27, p < .05$), however, was reduced to nonsignificance when self-esteem was statistically controlled ($r = -.19, n.s.$). In Study 2, the relation of self-esteem to reduced distress did not change when controlling for denial of impact. The relation of denial of impact to reduced distress at T2 ($r = -.46, p < .01$) is reduced to nonsignificance when controlling for self-esteem ($r = -.25, n.s.$).

Denial Versus Social Comparison

Social comparison and denial are two very different ways of restoring self-esteem. With social comparisons, individuals are seeking out others with whom they can compare themselves. With denial, individuals are not aligning themselves with others but differentiating themselves from others. Thus, it seems unlikely that someone could engage in denial and social comparison simultaneously. In Study 1 (but not Study 2), denial of impact was negatively correlated with the frequency of social comparison

FIG. 11.2.   Self-esteem mediates the relation of denial of impact to decreased psychological distress.

($r = -.33$, $p < .05$). Denial is not inconsistent with downward evaluation, however. Downward evaluation, in a sense, requires that one differentiate the self from others. In Study 1, denial of impact was associated with downward evaluation, $r = .44$, $p < .001$, but denial of illness was not. In Study 2, T1 and T2 denial of impact were associated with downward evaluation ($r = 27$, $p > .09$; $r = .51$, $p < .001$, respectively), whereas denial of illness was not. In both studies, patients were asked whether they perceived their situation as more similar to or more different from those of other cardiac patients. Denial of impact was associated with perceiving one's situation as different from those of other cardiac patients (Study 1: $r = .40$, $p < .05$; Study 2: $r = .27$, $p = .09$).

Summary

Previous research has revealed contradictory findings on the health consequences of denial. One reason for the confusion is that denial has been measured in quite different ways, with each set of researchers assuming that they are measuring the same construct. There are multiple aspects of denial. We distinguish denial of illness (refusing to admit one has a health problem) from denial of impact (admitting one is ill but minimizing the severity of its consequences). Our research shows that denial of impact leads to restoration of self-esteem and reduced psychological distress, whereas denial of illness does not. Future research should continue to explore the distinction between denial of illness and denial of impact, for example, by examining whether denial of illness alone leads to poor health care and noncompliance.

DERIVING MEANING

At the beginning of this chapter, we said that victimization in general and chronic illness specifically calls into question one's belief in the world as meaningful and sensible and the self as worthy or good. One way to resolve these issues is to make sense of or derive some kind of meaning from the experience. There are two ways to find meaning from the onset of chronic illness. First, one can try to understand why the event happened, that is, identify the cause. Second, one can derive something positive from the experience. These different ways of finding meaning have been referred to as secondary control strategies; that is, ways of accommodating the self to the aversive event (Affleck, Tenne, & Gersham, 1985). As shown in the following discussion, the search for causes is not beneficial unless a cause is identified, whereas deriving something positive from the experience helps to restore self-esteem and improve adjustment.

Causes

To address the issue of causality, one can search for causal attributions ("What caused the heart attack?") or selective incidence attributions ("Why me?"). Lowery, Jacobsen, and McCauley (1987) found that asking "Why me?" was associated with increased anxiety, increased depression, reports of decreased subjective well-being, and decreased optimism about the future among a group of chronically ill people (heart disease, diabetes, arthritis).

In Study 2, patients were asked at T1 and T2 how frequently they make causal attributions and selective incidence attributions. Asking "Why me?" at T1 and T2 was cross-sectionally associated with decreased self-esteem (T1: $r = -.43$, $p < .01$; T2: $r = -.33$, $p < .05$). "Why me?" at T1 also was associated with increased distress at T2 with and without controls for T1 distress (with controls, $r = .27$, $p < .10$; without controls, $r = .36$, $p < .05$). The relations of causal attributions to self-esteem and psychological distress were in the same direction, but the associations were not as strong.

Thus, consistent with previous research, searching for causes was related to worse adjustment. Researchers have distinguished between the search for meaning and the finding of meaning, realizing that the search for meaning is only adaptive when meaning is found (Silver, Boon, & Stones, 1983; Thompson, 1991). We asked patients if they had found answers to their causal searches. The majority had not. The continued search may reflect continued distress or rumination about the event. Not only does an endless search for meaning fail to help, but continued attempts to search for meaning can be maladaptive (Silver et al., 1983).

Patients who find meaning in chronic illness by locating a cause for the illness seem to be better adjusted. Taylor et al. (1983) found that the mere finding of a cause was beneficial to women with breast cancer. No one particular cause, however, was associated with better adjustment. Cowie (1976) inquired about patients' understanding of their heart attacks and found that patients reconstructed the event so that it seemed more intelligible and expected than it really was. Having had the heart attack, patients reinterpreted past events as warning signs and perceived their heart attacks as inevitable outcomes.

Positive Contributions

Finding meaning in chronic illness involves much more than understanding the cause of the event. Meaning has been conceptualized by Thompson and Janigian (1988) as a sense of order and purpose: "An event is meaningful when we understand how it follows in an orderly fashion from our view and beliefs and when it has a purpose whose value we recognize" (p. 263). Meaning can be found by either changing one's perception of the event (emphasize the positive aspects) or changing one's life to incorporate the event (personal priorities, view of the world; Thompson & Janigian, 1988). There is some evidence that patients do both.

Researchers often focus on the aversive effects of chronic illness and neglect the potential benefits. In fact, many instruments used to assess adjustment to chronic illness do not provide for positive changes to have occurred. For example, the Psychosocial Adjustment to Illness Scale (Derogatis & Lopez, 1983) is used to assess adjustment to illness across a wide variety of domains (e.g., vocational adjustment, sexual adjustment). For each domain of functioning, patients indicate the degree to which the illness has negatively affected functioning. Researchers now realize, however, that positive changes do occur as a result of victimization in general and chronic illness in particular. By emphasizing the positive attributes of a victimizing experience, one can continue to believe that one is a worthwhile person (Janoff-Bulman, 1989).

Several studies have shown that patients report benefits from chronic illness. In a study of patients who were 3 to 5 months post-MI (myocardial infarction), one third reported that their lives had improved as a result of the heart attack (Laerum, Johnsen, Smith, & Larsen, 1987). In a study of middle aged and elderly spinal cord injury victims, many felt that they had benefited from the victimization (Schulz & Decker, 1985). In Study 2, three fourths of patients said something positive had come from the experience.

What are the benefits of chronic illness? People perceive positive effects from chronic illness by observing changes in life domains that have an overall positive effect on quality of life. For example, women with breast cancer reported that the illness led them to reappraise their lives, reorder their priorities, and make positive changes in themselves (Taylor, 1983). Several studies of chronic illness have examined positive and negative changes in six life domains: daily activities, future, plans, view of self, view of world, relationships, personal priorities. Cancer patients reported mostly positive changes in the domains of daily activities and relationships (Collins, Taylor, & Skokan, 1990), whereas AIDS patients reported mostly positive changes in their view of themselves and in their relationships (Taylor et al., 1991).

In Study 2, patients were asked to describe the implications the illness has had for these same six life domains. Patients reported more positive than negative changes in the domains of relationships and daily activities and an equal number of positive and negative changes in their view of themselves. The most common relationship changes were increased closeness and a greater concern with relationships. The most common changes in daily activities were improved health behavior (e.g., exercise) and increased relaxation. Changes in the self included developing better interpersonal qualities (e.g., more patient, considerate, understanding) and a more negative self-image (e.g., lack self-confidence).

Does deriving something positive from a negative experience improve adjustment? Affleck, Tennen, Croog, and Levine (1987) found that men who derived benefits from their myocardial infarction 7 weeks later had decreased morbidity 8 years later. Mothers of infants with severe perinatal problems evidenced better psychological adjustment if they were able to find something positive in the experience (Affleck et al., 1985). Successful adjustment has been related to the perception of positive changes in life domains by cancer patients (Collins et al., 1990) but to the perception of a mixture of positive and negative changes by AIDS patients (Taylor et al., 1991). In Study 2, an index of positive changes and an index of negative changes was computed for each life domain. The strongest association to adjustment involved the view of self domain. Positive changes in the self were associated with better adjustment to illness ($r = -38$, $p < .05$) and higher scores on well-being ($r = .30$, $p < .05$), whereas negative changes in the self were associated with lower self-esteem ($r = -.45$, $p < .01$), increased psychological distress ($r = .40$, $p < .01$), and lower scores on well-being ($r = -.30$, $p < .05$).

In Study 2, patients also completed an inventory of possible benefits from the illness. The items were adapted from Behr, Murphy, and Summers' (1991) Positive Contribution scale used with parents of children with disabilities. The index of positive contributions was not related to T1 or T2 self-esteem but was related to an increase in self-esteem between T1 and T2 ($r = .31$, $p < .05$). Positive contributions also were related to T2 distress with and without controls for T1 distress ($r = -.30$, $p < .05$; $r = -.41$, $p < .01$; respectively). There was a trend for positive contributions to be associated with age, $r = .27$, $p = .08$. Thus, the elderly may be more likely to derive something positive from chronic illness, and positive contributions appear to be another way to restore self-esteem and reduce distress.

Summary

The onset of chronic illness shatters one's assumption that the world is a meaningful and comprehensible place. One way to restore this assumption following chronic illness is to find meaning in the experience. Patients can find meaning by either understanding the cause of the event or deriving something positive from the event. Those who continue to search for causes or meaning are more psychologically distressed, but those who find meaning are less distressed. Previous researchers have focused on the negative consequences of chronic illness and overlooked the possibility that positive consequences may occur. One way of coping with chronic illness that minimizes the assault of self-esteem is to perceive that one's life has benefited from the experience.

OTHER WAYS TO INCREASE
SELF-ESTEEM

We have examined three ways by which chronically ill patients may restore self-esteem. There are undoubtedly other ways that have been studied less. We briefly describe one other strategy that future research should explore.

One loss suffered by those who are chronically ill, especially the elderly, is the lost opportunity to help others. Physical limitations may make it difficult to help others. Patients spend more time in the role of support recipient and less time in the role of support provider. There are costs to self-esteem associated with receiving help and benefits to self-esteem in providing assistance. Social psychologists have shown that helping others has the potential to improve mood (Williamson & Clark, 1989). Helping others can increase self-esteem by instilling a sense of self-efficacy (Spiegel, Bloom, & Yalom, 1981). The "helper-therapy" principle (i.e., the idea that it is therapeutic to help others) is said to be a key principle of support groups (DeVita, Hellman, & Rosenberg, 1989). In fact, a common motivation for joining support groups is to help others. Contributing to another's well-being may be another way to increase one's own sense of self-worth in the face of chronic illness.

CONCLUSION

We began this chapter by pointing out a paradox: Despite the physical disability, restriction of activities, and assault on self-esteem that accompanies chronic illness, the chronically ill report similar levels of subjective well-being to those of healthy populations. Research on the elderly reveals a similar finding: Despite the physical, social, and mental declines that accompany old age, the elderly report similar levels, if not higher levels, of subjective well-being as compared to younger populations. In this chapter we described multiple strategies that the elderly can use to restore self-esteem and facilitate adjustment to chronic illness.

Comparing oneself to others can elevate self-esteem. It is not the mere process of social comparison that enhances self-esteem, however. In fact, actively seeking social comparisons seems to be an indicator of continued distress. In response to threat, an effective strategy to enhance self-esteem is to engage in downward comparison; that is, to compare oneself with worse-off others. A subtle form of downward comparison involves evaluating one's own condition as superior to that of others, or downward evaluation. Downward evaluation seems to be common among the chronically ill and is associated with good adjustment. Yet the direction of comparison or comparison target does not determine adjustment alone. It is the affect derived from social comparison that determines its effect on subjective well-being. We conclude that downward evaluation is more likely to lead to positive affect because the downward comparisons represent a hypothetical, cognitively constructed group of worse-off others who do not pose a realistic threat. Forced downward comparisons, by contrast, represent actual others and may be more likely to induce negative affect.

A second way to restore self-esteem following chronic illness is to deny it. The health consequences of denial are not consistent in previous research. We reconcile this contradictory literature by distinguishing among the different components of denial. Specifically, we distinguish between denial of impact, which reduces the threat, and denial of illness, which removes the threat. Findings from our research show that it is only denial of impact that restores self-esteem and reduces psychological distress. Denial of illness does not appear to be related to subjective well-being. We speculate that denial of illness will be related to poor health behavior and noncompliance. Future research should continue to explore whether denial of illness and denial of impact have distinct health consequences.

Denial of impact is not inconsistent with social comparison. In fact, denial of impact is negatively related to seeking social comparisons and positively related to downward evaluation. Both of these strategies—denial of impact and downward evaluation—reduce the threat of chronic illness, possibly enabling the individual to more effectively cope with it. The third way of restoring self-esteem following chronic illness involves deriving meaning from the experience. This strategy does not directly alter the threat of chronic illness but instead alters the self to fit the experience. In that sense, finding meaning is more of a secondary control strategy. The process of trying to find meaning (i.e., asking "Why me?") is not related to good adjustment and reflects continued distress. But those who construe benefits from the experience—for example, by observing positive changes in relationships or in one's self—are better adjusted and maintain high self-esteem. In our research, age is associated with perceiving benefits from the illness, which fits with the finding that the elderly increasingly rely on secondary control strategies. Research has emphasized the difficulties encountered during chronic illness and overlooked the potential for positive effects. The benefits from chronic illness constitute a promising path for future research.

Future research should examine whether particular people are more likely than others to use one of these strategies to restore self-esteem. For example, are the elderly more likely to use one or all of these strategies? It is not clear whether particular strategies are linked to personality characteristics or whether they reflect strategies that most people are able to use. If it is the latter, interventions can be developed to restore self-esteem in those who have suffered a "loss of self."

ACKNOWLEDGMENTS

The authors are grateful to Pamela Blair-Tuma for her technical assistance with this chapter.

Preparation of this chapter was supported in part by a FIRST Award from the National Institute of Health (5R29 MH48662) to the first author.

REFERENCES

Affleck, G., & Tennen, H. (1991). Social comparison and coping with major medical problems. In J. M. Suls & T. A. Wills (Eds.), *Social comparison: Contemporary theory and research* (pp. 369–393). Hillsdale, NJ: Lawrence Erlbaum Associates.

Affleck, G., Tennen, H., Croog, S., & Levine, S. (1987). Causal attribution, perceived benefits and morbidity after a heart attack: An 8-year-study. *Journal of Consulting and Clinical Psychology, 55,* 29–35.

Affleck, G., Tennen, H., & Gershman, K. (1985). Cognitive adaptations to high-risk infants: The search for mastery, meaning, and protection from future harm. *American Journal of Mental Deficiency, 89*, 653–656.

Affleck, G., Tennen, H., Pfeiffer, C., Fifield, J., & Rowe, J. (1987). Downward comparison and coping with serious medical problems. *American Journal of Orthopsychiatry, 57*, 570–578.

Baltes, P., & Baltes, M. (1990). *Successful aging: Perspectives from the behavioral sciences.* Cambridge, MA: Cambridge University Press.

Behr, S. K., Murphy, D. L., & Summers, J. A. (1991). *Kansas Inventory of Parental Perceptions.* Lawrence: University of Kansas.

Blalock, S., DeVellis, B., DeVellis, R., & Sauter, S. (1988). Self-evaluation processes and adjustment to rheumatoid arthritis. *Arthritis and Rheumatism, 31*, 1245–1251.

Brandtstadter, J., & Greve, W. (1994). The aging self: Stabilizing and protective processes. *Developmental Review, 14*, 52–80.

Brandtstadter, J., Wentura, D., & Greve, W. (1993). Adaptive resources of the aging self: Outlines of an emergent perspective. *International Journal of Behavioral Development, 16*, 323–349.

Buunk, B. P., Collins, R. L., Taylor, S. E., Van Yperen, N. W., & Dakof, G. A. (1990). The affective consequences of social comparison: Either direction has its ups and downs. *Journal of Personality and Social Psychology, 59*, 1238–1249.

Cassileth, B. R., Lusk, E. J., Strouse, T. B., Miller, D. S., Brown, L. L., Cross, P. A., & Tenaglia, B. S. (1984). Psychosocial status in chronic illness: A comparative analysis of six diagnostic groups. *The New England Journal of Medicine, 311*, 506–511.

Charmaz, K. (1991). *Good days, bad days: The self in chronic illness and time.* New Brunswick, NJ: Rutgers University Press.

Chene, A. (1991). Self-esteem of the elderly and education. *Educational Gerontology, 17*, 343–353.

Christman, N. J., McConnell, E. A., Pfeiffer, C., Webster, K. K., Schmitt, M., & Reiss, J., (1988). Uncertainty, coping, and distress following myocardial infarction: Transition from hospital to home. *Research in Nursing and Health, 11*, 71–82.

Cohen, F., & Lazarus, R. (1979). Coping with the stresses of illness. In G. C. Stone, F. Cohen, & N. E. Adler (Eds.), *Health psychology: A handbook* (pp. 77–112). San Francisco: Jossey-Bass.

Collins, R., Taylor, S. E., & Skokan, L. A. (1990). A better world or a shattered vision?: Changes in life perspectives following victimization. *Social Cognition, 8*, 263–285.

Cowie, B. (1976). The cardiac patient's perception of his heart attack. *Social Science and Medicine, 10*, 87–96.

Croog, S. H., & Levine, S. (1977). *The heart patient recovers.* New York: Human Sciences Press.

Croog, S. H., Shapiro, D. S., & Levine, S. (1971). Denial among male heart patients. *Psychosomatic Medicine, 33*, 385–397.

Derogatis, L. R., & Lopez, M. C. (1983). *The Psychosocial Adjustment to Illness Scale: Administration, scoring and procedures manual–I.* Baltimore, MD: John Hopkins University Press.

Derogatis, L. R., & Spencer, P. M. (1982). *The Brief Symptom Inventory (CPI): Administration, scoring, and procedures manual–I.* Baltimore, MD: Johns Hopkins University School of Medicine.

DeVellis, R., Holt, K., Renner, B., Blalock, S., Blanchard, L., Cook, H., Klotz, M. L., Mikow, V., & Harring, K. (1990). The relationship of social comparison to rheumatoid arthritis symptoms and affect. *Basic and Applied Social Psychology, 11*, 1–18.

DeVita, Jr., V. T., Hellman, S., & Rosenberg, S. A. (Eds.). (1989). *Cancer: Principles & practice of oncology* (3rd ed., Vol. 1). Philadelphia: J. P. Lippincott.

Festinger, L. (1954). A theory of social comparison processes. *Human Relations, 7*, 117–140.

Gove, W., Ortega, S., & Style, C. (1989). The maturational and role perspectives on aging and self through the adult years: An empirical evaluation. *American Journal of Sociology, 94*, 1111–1145.

Granger, J. W. (1974). Full recovery from myocardial infarction: Psychosocial factors. *Heart and Lung, 3*, 600–609.

Hackett, T. P., & Cassem, N. H. (1974). Development of a quantitative rating scale to assess denial. *Journal of Psychosomatic Research, 18*, 93–100.

Hackett, T. P., Cassem, N. H., & Wishnie, H. A. (1968). The coronary care unit: An appraisal of its psychological hazards. *New England Journal of Medicine, 279*, 1365–1370.

Havik, O. E., & Maeland, J. G. (1986). Dimensions of verbal denial in myocardial infarction. *Scandinavian Journal of Psychology, 27*, 326–339.

Heidrich, S., & Ryff, C. (1993a). Physical and mental health in later life: The self-system as mediator. *Psychology and Aging, 8*, 327–338.

Heidrich, S., & Ryff, C. (1993b). The role of social comparison processes in the psychological adaptation of elderly adults. *Journal of Gerontology, 48*, 127–136.

Helgeson, V. S., & Taylor, S. E. (1993). Social comparisons and adjustment among cardiac patients. *Journal of Applied Social Psychology, 23*, 1171–1195.

Janis, I. L. (1958). *Psychological stress: Psychoanalytic and behavioral studies of surgical patients.* New York: Academic Press.

Janoff-Bulman, R., & Frieze, I. H. (1983). A theoretical perspective for understanding reactions to victimization. *Journal of Social Issues, 39*, 1–17.

Kruse, A., & Lehr, U. (1989). Longitudinal analysis of the developmental process in chronically ill and healthy persons—Empirical findings from the Bonn Longitudinal Study of Aging (BOLSA). *International Psychogeriatrics, 1*, 73–85.

Laerum, E., Johnsen, N., Smith, P., & Larsen, S. (1987). Can myocardial infarction induce positive changes in family relationships? *Family Practice, 4*, 302–305.

Levenson, J. L., Mishra, A., Hamer, R. M., & Hastillo, A. (1989). Denial and medical outcome in unstable angina. *Psychosomatic Medicine, 51*, 27–35.

Levine, J., Warrenburg, S., Kerns, R., Schwartz, G., Delaney, R., Fontana, A., Gradman, A., Smith, S., Allen, S., & Cascione, R. (1987). The role of denial in recovery from coronary heart disease. *Psychosomatic Medicine, 49*, 109–117.

Levkoff, S. E., Cleary, P. D., & Wetle, T. (1987). Differences in the appraisal of health between aged and middle-aged adults. *Journal of Gerontology, 42*, 114–120.

Lowery, B. J., Jacobsen, B. S., & McCauley, K. (1987). On the prevalence of causal search in illness situations. *Nursing Research 36*, 88–93.

Minkler, M. (1985). Social support and health of the elderly. In S. Cohen, & S. L. Syme (Eds.), *Social support and health* (pp. 199–216). Orlando, FL: Academic Press.

Reis, T. J., Gerrard, M., & Gibbons, F. (1993). Social comparison and the pill: Reactions to upward and downward comparison of contraception behavior. *Personality and Social Psychology Bulletin, 19*, 13–20.

Rosenberg, M. (1965). *Society and the adolescent self image.* Princeton, NJ: Princeton University Press.

Rothbaum, F., Weisz, J. R., & Snyder, S. S. (1982). Changing the world and changing the self: A two-process model of perceived control. *Journal of Personality and Social Psychology, 42*, 5–37.

Schienle, D. R., & Eiler, J. M. (1984). Clinical intervention with older adults. In M. G. Eisenberg, L. C. Sutkin, & M. A. Jansen (Eds.), *Chronic illness and disability through the life span: Effects on self and family* (pp. 245–268). New York: Springer.

Schulz, R., & Decker, S. (1985). Long-term adjustment to physical disability. The role of social support, perceived control, and self-blame. *Journal of Personality and Social Psychology, 48*, 1162–1172.

Schulz, R., Heckhausen, J., & O'Brien, A. (1994). Control and the disablement process in the elderly. *Journal of Social Behavior and Personality, 9*, 139–152.

Silver, R. L., Boon, C., & Stones, M. H. (1983). Searching for meaning in misfortune: Making sense of incest. *Journal of Social Issues, 39*, 81–102.

Spiegel, D., Bloom, J., & Yalom, I. (1981). Group support for patients with metastatic cancer—A prospective randomized outcome study. *Archives of General Psychiatry, 38*, 527–533.

Stern, M. J., Pascale, L., & McLoone, J. B. (1975). Psychosocial adaptation following an acute myocardial infarction. *Journal of Chronic Disease, 29*, 513–526.

Suls, J., Marco, C., & Tobin, S. (1991). The role of temporal comparison, social comparison, and direct appraisal in the elderly's self-evaluations of health. *Journal of Applied Social Psychology, 21*, 1125–1144.

Suls, J., & Wills, T. A. (1991). *Social comparison: Contemporary theory and research.* Hillsdale, NJ: Lawrence Erlbaum Associates.

Taylor, S. E. (1983). Adjustment to threatening events: A theory of cognitive adaptation. *American Psychologist, 38,* 1161–1173.

Taylor, S. E., Kemeny, M. E., Reed, G., & Aspinwall, L. (1991). Assault of the self: Positive illusions and adjustment to threatening events. In G. A. Goethals, & J. A. Strauss (Eds.), *The self: An interdisciplinary perspective* (pp. 239-254). New York: Springer-Verlag.

Taylor, S. E., Wood J. V., & Lichtman, R. R. (1983). It could be worse: Selective evaluation as a response to victimization. *Journal of Social Issues, 39,* 19–40.

Thompson, S. C. (1991). The search for meaning following a stroke. *Basic and Applied Social Psychology, 12,* 81–96.

Thompson, S. C., & Janigian, A. S. (1988). Life schemes: A framework for understanding the search for meaning. *Journal of Social and Clinical Psychology, 7,* 260–280.

Wheeler, L., Shaver, K. G., Jones, R. A., Goethals, G. R., & Cooper, J. (1969). Factors determining choice of comparison other. *Journal of Experimental Social Psychology, 5,* 219–232.

Williamson, G. M., & Clark, M. S. (1989). Providing help and desired relationship type as determinants of changes in moods and self-evaluations. *Journal of Personality and Social Psychology, 56,* 722–734.

Wills, T. A. (1981). Downward comparison principles in social psychology. *Psychological Bulletin, 90,* 245–271.

Wood, J. V., Taylor, S. E., & Lichtman, R. R. (1985). Social comparison in adjustment to breast cancer. *Journal of Personality and social Psychology, 49,* 1169–1183.

12

Sex, Psychosocial Stress, and Atherosclerosis: A Monkey Model

Michael R. Adams   Jay R. Kaplan
Steven B. Manuck   Carol A. Shively
J. Koudy Williams

From the Comparative Medicine Clinical Research Center, Wake Forest University, Winston-Salem, North Carolina (J.R.K., M.R.A., J.K.W.) and The Department of Psychology, University of Pittsburgh School of Medicine, Pittsburgh, Pennsylvania (S.B.M.)

Coronary heart disease (CHD) remains the largest single cause of death in the United States; more people die from CHD—nearly 500,000 annually—than from all cancers combined (American Heart Association, 1993). Contemporary, large-scale autopsy studies have established that the incidence of CHD is closely associated with the extent and severity of underlying coronary artery atherosclerosis, a relationship that exists both within and between geographic regions (McGill, 1968). One of the best characterized, but least understood, features of both CHD and atherosclerosis, yet one that has not attracted significant research effort until recently, is the relative sparing of premenopausal women as compared to men (McGill & Stern, 1979). Although this phenomenon is sometimes referred to as "female protection," it is more accurately characterized as a delay in disease onset. Women actually succumb to CHD in larger numbers than do men; however, they do so later in life (Higgins & Thom,

1993). The CHD death rate among 40-year-old men in the U.S. is approximately 40 per 100,000 persons, as compared to 8 per 100,000 persons in women of the same age, a 5:1 advantage for women (Thom, 1987). By 60 years of age, mortality rates increase substantially in both sexes, but the mortality ratio is still more than 2:1 in favor of women (rates: 400 per 100,000 men vs. 175 per 100,000 women; Thom, 1987). International investigations reveal that these general relationships persist, without exception, wherever CHD is a major cause of death. Even in Japan, where there is a relatively low incidence of CHD, the male:female mortality ratio is 3:1 (Godsland, Wynn, Crook, & Miller, 1987).

Although direct evidence to support it is very limited, effect(s) of estrogen are widely believed to account for the sex difference in CHD incidence and atherosclerosis (Manson, 1994). This supposition is supported by the well-known observation that estrogen replacement therapy is associated with a significant reduction in CHD risk among postmenopausal women (relative risk of treated women compared to that of controls ≈ 0.50) and a reduction in angiographically documented coronary artery stenosis (Manson, 1994; Gruchow, Anderson, Barboriak, & Sobocinski, 1988; Stampfer et al., 1991; Sullivan et al., 1988), Further supporting a role of estrogen is the fact that CHD risk is greatly increased among women undergoing oophorectomy or premature natural menopause without subsequent hormone replacement therapy (Bengtsson, 1973; Colditz et al., 1987; Manson, 1994; Oliver, 1974; Stampfer et al., 1991). From 25% to 50% of the cardiovascular benefit associated with estrogen replacement results from its effects on plasma lipids (Matthews et al., 1989; Speroff, 1993), that is, increased high density lipoprotein (HDL) concentrations.

However, the natural history of CHD and atherosclerosis among women may not be solely a function of fluctuations in endogenous estrogen production. First, data from the Nurses Health Study (a cohort of 121,700 women subjected to long-term follow-up) indicate that there is no appreciable increase in CHD risk among nonsmoking women having a natural menopause with no estrogen replacement (Colditz et al., 1987). Furthermore, national and international mortality data show a steady increase in age-related CHD mortality rates among women, with no acceleration following menopause (Colditz et al., 1995, Heller & Jacobs, 1988). The steadily increasing CHD mortality rate in aging women contrasts with the obvious downward shift in the mortality curve associated with breast cancer; this latter outcome reflects the carcinogenic effects of estrogen exposure, which diminish following menopause (MacMahon, Cole & Brown, 1973; Pike, 1987; Trichopolous, MacMahon, & Cole,

1972). A shift in the opposite direction would be expected with respect to CHD mortality if endogenous estrogen alone was responsible for low CHD risk among premenopausal women (Godsland, Wynn, Cook, & Miller, 1987).

The puzzling absence of an obvious association between endogenous estrogen and CHD risk in women may be owing, in part, to the intervening role played by psychosocial factors. Numerous studies of women have shown that emotional distress can result in ovarian dysfunction, affecting the hormonal qualities and perhaps even the timing of menopause (Giles & Berga, 1993; Judd, 1992; Kinch, Plunkett, Smout, & Carr, 1965; Seibel & Taymor, 1982). In fact, ovarian dysfunction that presents a secondary amenorrhea is relatively common, affecting between 5% and 29% of women under age 40 (Aiman & Smentek, 1985; Berga et al., 1991; Prior, Vigna, Schechter, & Burgess, 1990; Russell, Bannatyne, Shearman, Fraser, & Corbett, 1982; Starup & Sele, 1973). The cause is frequently environmental or psychogenic (giving rise to the term *functional hypothalamic amenorrhea* [FHA]; Berga et al., 1991; LaVecchia et al., 1987). These observations suggest that not all premenopausal women have equivalent ("normal") hormonal histories. Women with FHA or other ovarian dysfunctions may be estrogen deficient, thus potentially eliminating their "female protection" from atherosclerosis and placing them on a high-risk trajectory for CHD. Two observational studies have shown that menstrual irregularity is associated with an increased risk of premature CHD (LaVecchia et al., 1987; Oliver, 1974; Palmer, Rosenberg, & Shapiro, 1992). However, although estrogen deficiency may play a significant role, it is also likely that psychosocial factors adversely affecting ovarian function potentiate atherogenesis directly by means of excessive neuroendocrine (e.g., pituitary–adrenocortical or sympatho–adrenomedullary) activity (Blumenthal & Matthews, 1993).

Most studies of psychosocial factors and CHD have been conducted in men (Wenger, 1993), partly because myocardial infarction is infrequent among premenopausal women and because chest pain—although often denoting the presence of angina pectoris in men—frequently is unrelated to CHD in women (Haynes & Czajkowski, 1993). Furthermore, reproductive data rarely are collected in conjunction with psychosocial investigations of atherosclerosis and CHD in women. As a result, there is only a general understanding of how psycosocial factors may relate to CHD risk in women. For example, increased CHD risk is observed in women with low educational levels, and those in low-status occupations (e.g., clerical workers and video display terminal operators) and among individuals with an inability to express or discuss anger (Haynes & Czajkowski, 1993). However, studies with animal models have provided insight into how behavioral factors may influence CHD pathogenesis in young and middle aged women. These studies also have identified important future directions for investigation.

A PRIMATE MODEL FOR INVESTIGATION OF PSYCHOSOCIAL AND SEX HORMONE INFLUENCES ON ATHEROSCLEROSIS

We have utilized cynomolgus macaques (*Macaca fascicularis*) for the investigation of sex-related phenomena in atherosclerosis (Kaplan, Adams, Clarkson, Manuck, & Shively, 1991; Kaplan, Manuck, Clarkson, & Prichard, 1985; MacDonald, 1971; Mahoney, 1970). Monkeys offer numerous advantages for investigations of atherosclerosis, particularly when questions focus on psychosocial factors or sex differences. First, diet-induced lesions develop in nonhuman primates (especially macaques and baboons) that are similar in their location and morphologic characteristics to those seen in human beings. Also relevant is the elaborate social repertoire of these animals, which subsumes behaviors analogous to those prominent in epidemiologic studies of the psychosocial antecedents of CHD (e.g., competitiveness, aggression). Finally, these animals exhibit a 28-day menstrual cycle that is hormonally similar to the cycle in women (Clarkson, Williams, Adams, Wagner, & Klein, 1993; Hamm, Kaplan, Clarkson, & Bullock, 1983).

Effects of Psychosocial Factors and Variability in Endogenous Estrogen on Atherosclerosis in Macaques

In an initial study of sex differences in coronary artery atherosclerosis of cynomolgus monkeys, certain psychosocial factors were identified as significant predictors of lesion extent (Hamm et al., 1983). This study used 16 male and 16 female monkeys living in single-gender groupings of four animals each. For 16 months, the animals consumed an atherogenic diet (45% of calories as fat and provided the human equivalent of 1,140 mg cholesterol (TPC) concentrations averaging 430 mg/dl. During the latter half of the study, we evaluated the "competitiveness" of each animal. Technicians placed grapes in each pen, noting the number of grapes taken by each animal and the order of animals taking the grapes. For each of nine trials, animals in each group were assigned a number from 1 (*most successful*) to 4 (*least successful*). At the conclusion of the study, we made histomorphometric determinations of the percentage of lumen occupied by plaque in each section of coronary artery ("lumen stenosis"). We found that males were significantly more affected with atherosclerosis than females, and that competitive animals, both males and females, were significantly less affected than their noncompetitive (submissive) counterparts (Table 12.1). Variability in plasma lipids was concordant with the differences in atherosclerosis; that is, submissive animals had lower HDL concentrations than did competitive animals, whereas males had lower HDL concentrations than did females. However, an analysis of covariance demonstrated that both of the main effects (sex and "competitiveness") were independent of the concomitant differences in plasma lipids.

We next designed experiments to investigate in more detail the role of psychosocial and reproductive factors in atherogenesis. The first of these was a 24-month study involving 23 females and 15 males (Kaplan, Adams, Clarkson, & Koritnik, 1984). Of the 15 males, 10 lived in two all-male

TABLE 12.1
Atherosclerosis and Plasma Lipids in Male and Female
Monkeys Living in Social Groups

	Atherosclerosis (% lumen stenosis)	TPC (mg/dl)	HDLC (mg/dl)	TPC:HDLC Ratio
Male				
Competitive	23 ± 8	374 ± 45	38 ± 8.8	13.2 ± 2.4
Submissive	44 ± 7	491 ± 29	24 ± 2.1	21.7 ± 1.8
Female				
Competitive	7 ± 3	424 ± 63	48 ± 6.0	10.3 ± 2.1
Submissive	14 ± 7	437 ± 37	28 ± 2.1	16.2 ± 1.7

Note. All values mean ± SEM.
Significant effects: Atherosclerosis: males < females; competitive < submissive
HDLC: males < females; competitive < submissive
TPC:HDLC: Males < females, competitive < submissive
TPC = total plasma cholesterol; HDLC = high density lipoprotein cholesterol.

groups of 5 each. The 5 remaining males were assigned as "harem" males to groups of females. The females were divided into groups of 4 or 5, each containing a vasectomized male to simulate a "normal" heterosexual group composition. Animals were fed an atherogenic diet that derived 40% of calories from fat and provided the human equivalent of 860 mg cholesterol per day. In response, TPC concentrations averaged approximately 300 mg/dl for males and females.

We monitored social behavior using focal sampling techniques and an electronic data collection device (Altmann, 1974). Animals were observed for 15 minutes three times per week for the entire experiment. These data determined the social ranking or dominance status of each animal. For cynomolgus monkeys a series of specific facial expressions, postures, and vocalizations indicate the occurrence of a fight, and an animal's relative social status is based on these. Typically, one animal in a fight signals aggression and the other signals submission. This highly asymmetric pattern allows fight outcomes to be judged in terms of clear winners and losers (Sade, 1967, 1973). The animal in each group that defeats all others (as evidenced by an ability to elicit consistently submissive responses) is designated as the first-ranking monkey. The monkey that defeats all but the first-ranking animal is designated as the second-ranking monkey, and so forth. In general, dominance relationships within small groups are transitive; that is, if monkey one is dominant to monkey two, and monkey two is dominant to monkey three, then monkey one is usually dominant to monkey three also (Kaplan, Adams, Clarkson, & Koritnik, 1984). Social status was stable in this experiment, allowing us to use rank for each monkey aggregated over the entire experiment in all analyses. Animals that on average ranked one or two in their social groups were considered "dominant," and the rest were labeled "subordinate."

In addition to being observed for social behavior, animals were subjected to daily vaginal swabbing to monitor menses. Furthermore, we collected blood samples for the determination of plasma progesterone concentrations 7 days following the onset of menstruation (follicular phase) and at 3-day intervals beginning 12 days following the onset of menstruation (luteal phase). These evaluation provided the basis for judging ovarian function in each animal in relation to social factors and atherosclerosis.

At the end of this experiment and all subsequent investigations, we measured coronary artery atherosclerotic plaque size directly with a computerized image analyzer. We also visually graded the coronary sections as an index of intimal changes with a scale of 0 (*no changes*) to 3 (*plaque formation*). Notably, sex and psychosocial factors again interacted to affect coronary artery atherosclerosis, with female "protection" extended only to the dominant animals (Fig. 12.1).

The data describing ovarian function (Table 12.2) show that the subordinate females have five times as many anovulatory cycles and three times as many cycles characterized by luteal-phase deficiencies (Peak

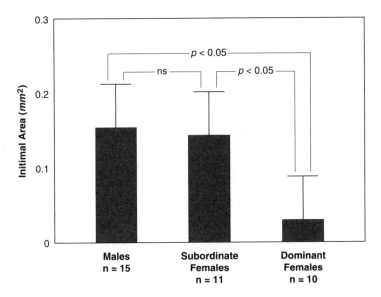

FIG. 12.1.   Coronary artery atherosclerosis extent among socially housed male and female monkeys, where females are divided on the basis of fight winds and losses into dominants (winners) and subordinates (losers). All females are reproductively intact.

TABLE 12.2
Ovarian and Adrenal Function in Dominant and
Subordinate Monkeys

	Dominant	Subordinate	p value[a]
Luteal-phase plasma progesterone (mg/ml)	8.9	4.0	< 0.01
% anovulatory cycles	3.5	16.5	< 0.01
% cycles with luteal-phase deficiencies	8.9	24.3	< 0.01
Adrenal weight (mg/kg body weight)	168	201	< 0.05

Note. All values represent medians.
[a]By Mann-Whitney test.

plasma progesterone concentrations between 2.0 and 4.0 ng/dl) as did their dominant counterparts (Adams, Kaplan, & Koritnik, 1985; Kaplan, Adams, Clarkson, & Koritnik, 1984). Notably, the females with the most extensive coronary artery atherosclerosis were all subordinate, and all had marked ovarian endocrine dysfunction. These data suggest that social subordination may increase coronary artery atherosclerosis risk in females by inducing a relative ovarian endocrine deficiency state similar to that observed in postmenopausal women.

Further evidence of the potential atherogenic significance of impaired ovarian function was provided by the second investigation in this series, a study involving 21 ovariectomized females placed in social groups for the same amount of time and fed the same diet as the 23 intact females described in the earlier discussion (Adams, Kaplan, Koritnik, & Clarkson, 1985). The ovariectomized females as a group had significantly more extensive coronary artery atherosclerosis than did the intact females. The data in Fig. 12.2 suggest that this effect was owing to the loss of protection experienced by the ovariectomized dominant animals as compared to their intact counterparts. The subordinates, intact and

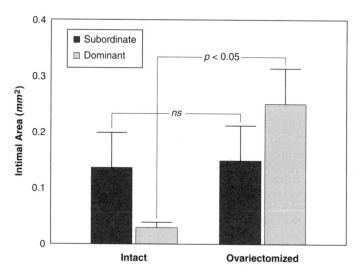

FIG. 12.2. Coronary artery atherosclerosis extent in reproductively intact and overiectomized monkeys, divided into dominant and subordinate subsets. Ovariectomized animals have more atherosclerosis than intacts, an effect owing entirely to the exacerbation of atherosclerosis among dominant ovariectomized monkeys.

ovariectomized, were equally affected with atherosclerosis. This further supports a role for ovarian function in the atherosclerotic effects of low social status.

Mechanisms Mediating Effects of Sex and Psychosocial Factors

Sex and psychosocial factors intact to influence atherosclerosis in monkeys, and perhaps in women as well. The series of experiments reviewed in the previous discussion suggests that such effects are mediated, in part, through nonlipid pathways. One pathway may involve estrogenic interactions with the artery wall (Manson, 1994; Wagner et al., 1991). We have shown, for example, that subcutaneous implantation of 17-β estradiol inhibits the accumulation of LDL degradation products in the coronary arteries of ovariectomized monkeys (Wagner et al., 1991). Others have found that 17-β estradiol prevents the oxidative modification of LDL (Sack, Rader, & Cannon, 1994). Because the oxidation, uptake, and catabolism of plasma LDL appear to be the primary mechanisms by which cholesterol accumulates in the atherosclerotic lesion, estrogen may influence atherosclerosis initiation and progression by modulating these processes.

Estrogenic effects on vascular function also may be relevant to atherogenesis. Numerous studies have demonstrated that atherosclerosis impairs endothelium-dependent dilation of the coronary arteries and augments endothelium-dependent vasoconstriction (Ludmer et al., 1986). These vasomotor abnormalities, in turn, may result in accelerated progression of atherosclerosis, plaque instability or rupture, thrombosis, and myocardial ischemia or infarction (Maseri, L'Abbate, et al., 1978; Maseri, Severi, et al., 1978; Roberts, Durry, & Isner, 1982). We have demonstrated in ovariectomized monkeys that estrogen, administered either acutely or chronically, reverses impairment in vasomotor responsiveness resulting from advanced coronary atherosclerosis (Williams, Adams, Herrington, & Clarkson, 1992; Williams, Adams, & Klopfenstein, 1990; Williams, Honoré, Washburn, & Clarkson, 1994). We also have found that socially dominant, premenopausal monkeys with normal ovarian function exhibit coronary artery dilation in response to acetylcholine infusion, whereas subordinates with poor ovarian function vasoconstrict following the same stimulus (Williams, Shively, & Clarkson, 1994). Furthermore, the dominance-associated variability in endogenous estrogen is itself significantly correlated with the degree of arterial dilation in response to acetylcholine (Williams, Shively, & Clarkson, 1994).

Other effects of estrogens include potential interference in cellular or molecular (or both) processes occurring in the arterial intima. Because locally mediated immune and inflammatory reactions are implicated in the initiation and progression of atherosclerosis, sex hormones may influence atherogenesis through autocrine, paracrine, or endocrine effects on these processes (Ahmed, Penhale, & Talal, 1985; Loy, Loukides, & Polan, 1992; Polan et al., 1989; Schuurs & Verheul, 1990). Furthermore, production of extracellular matrix by the cells of the artery wall is altered in atherosclerosis; this represents yet another process that may be modulated by sex hormones and thus influence atherosclerosis progression.

Although psychosocial factors may indirectly influence atherosclerosis in females through alterations in endogenous estrogen, there is also evidence that nonestrogenic phenomena, such as excessive neuroendocrine stimulation, may be involved. For example, hypercortisolemia is positively associated with extent of angiographically determined coronary artery atherosclerosis (Troxler, Sprague, Albanese, Fuchs, & Thompson, 1977). Furthermore, infusion of physiological concentrations of cortisol causes marked exacerbation of coronary artery atherosclerosis in rhesus monkeys and chickens (Sprague, Troxler, Peterson, Schmidt, & Young, 1980; Stamler, Pick, & Katz, 1956). Among premenopausal monkeys, the adrenal glands of subordinates are larger than those of dominants, and cortisol levels in subordinate monkeys exhibit a greater response to exogenous adrenocorti-cotropic hormone (ACTH) stimulation than do those dominants (Kaplan, Adams, Koritnik, Rose, & Manuck, 1986). Taken together, these results suggest that subordinate social status is a stressor that predictably evokes a potentially atherogenic increase in adrenocortical activity in female monkeys. However, in our studies we have not observed significant associations between atherosclerosis extent and any index of adrenocortical function.

Numerous investigators have proposed that excessive sympathetic activation in response to behavioral stimuli also may be associated with increased atherogenesis (Manuck, Kaplan, & Matthews, 1986; Schneiderman, 1987; Williams, Suarez, Kuhn, Zimmerman, & Schanberg, 1991). Such activation has been linked to endothelial injury (an initial stage of artherogenesis) in both monkeys and rabbits (Kaplan, Petterson, Manuck, & Olsson, 1991; Pettersson, Bejne, Bjork, Strawn, & Bondjers, 1990; Strawn et al., 1991). Current evidence suggests that endothelial injury may be induced via hemodynamic changes (e.g., increases in turbulence and shear stress) that occur as sequelae to the acute alterations in heart rate and blood pressure accompanying sympathetic nervous system activation (Manuck, Kaplan, Muldoon, Adams, & Clarkson, 1991; Schwartz, Gadusek, & Sheldon, 1981). The preferential location of sympathetically induced endothelial damage in the coronary arteries and at aortic bends and bifurcations would seem to support this hemodynamic hypothesis of arterial injury (Manuck, Kaplan, Muldoon, Adams, & Clarkson, 1991). Further evidence for the role of sympathetic activation in atherogenesis is the observation that treatment with a beta-adrenergic blocking agent inhibits the development of behaviorally induced coronary artery atherosclerosis (Kaplan, Manuck, Adams, Weingand, & Clarkson, 1987).

It is significant to note that there is some evidence that ovarian dysfunction in postmenopausal women is accompanied by an increase in sympathetically mediated cardiovascular responsivity to behavioral stimuli (Manuck & Polefrone, 1987; Owens, Stoney, & Matthews, 1993). Such changes may contribute to the increased risk of CHD in older women (Stoney, Davis, & Matthews, 1987). Our studies indicate that premenopausal monkeys with exaggerated heart rate responses to a standardized behavioral challenge had significantly lower luteal-phase plasma progesterone concentrations and a somewhat higher frequency of anovulatory menstrual cycles than did low heart rate responders (Manuck, Kaplan, Adams, & Clarkson, 1989). These individual differences in cardiovascular reactivity to behavioral stress have pathophysiologic consequences, as the monkeys with the largest heart rate responses to challenge had the greatest extent of both coronary and carotid artery atherosclerosis. Furthermore, their hearts were 50% larger than those of low heart rate reactors. If an enhanced cardiovascular responsivity to stress also accompanies chronic ovarian endocrine deficiencies among reproductively intact women, this increased reactivity might account for some of their heightened coronary risk (Stoney, Davis, & Matthews, 1987).

Among female monkeys, social dominance and individual differences in heart rate responsivity to behavioral challenge are not significantly associated (Manuck, Kaplan, Adams, & Clarkson, 1989). Despite this lack of concordance, sympathetic nervous system arousal may mediate the accelerated atherosclerosis reliably observed in subordinate females. Repeated exposure of such females to the aggressive intrusions of dominant animals could trigger excessive and prolonged sympathetic responses. This pattern of environmentally induced, sustained emotional stimulation, in turn, could cause arterial damage similar to that observed in monkeys ("high heart rate reactors") that are intrinsically hyperresponsive to stimulation of any intensity.

Activation of the renin-angiotensin system (RAS) also may have contributed to the accelerated atherogenesis of subordinate, estrogen-deprived female monkeys. Numerous studies show, for example, that renal production of renin is enhanced by sympathetic stimulation and emotional arousal (Hilgers et al., 1994; Reid, Morris, & Ganong, 1978). Reciprocal stimulation of the RAS and sympathetic nervous system occurs in the brain as well as in the kidney and at other peripheral sites (Dorward & Rudd, 1991). Activation of the RAS initiates a cascade (via the activity of renin and angiotensin-converting enzyme [ACE]) that ultimately results in the increased production and circulation of angiotensin II (ANGII), the most potent vasoconstrictor known (Ganong, 1993). Recent research suggests that ANGII accelerates atherosclerosis and does so independently of any pressor effects (Aberg & Ferrer, 1990). This is because ANGII directly affects smooth muscle cell signal tranduction (Rogers & Lokuta, 1994) as well as a number of growth factors (e.g., transforming growth factor-β, platelet-derived growth factor, and basic fibroblast growth factor) that influence smooth muscle proliferation (Mattero, Paxton, Duff, Berk, & Bernstein, 1994). The observation that treatment with an ACE inhibitor prevents the development of atherosclerosis in normotensive monkeys further supports the contention that ANGII is atherogenic (Aberg & Ferrer, 1990) and may constitute part of the mechanism causing excessive lesion development in animals subjected to emotional stress and arousal (e.g., subordinate female monkeys).

Although ANGII is potentially atherogenic, estrogen modulates the RAS in ways that could inhibit lesion formation. For example, unpublished data from Ping and associates suggests that estrogen attenuates the pressor response to ANGII infusion in overiectomized, normotensive and hypertensive rats. In the same model, estrogen suppresses ACE activity, an effect also observed in postmenopausal women receiving hormone replacement therapy (Proudler et al., 1995). The estrogen-induced suppression of ACE activity, in turn, is associated experimentally with a decrease in AGNII and an increase in activity of the vasodilator peptide, angiotension 1-7 (ANG1-7; Brosnihan, Li, & Ferrario, 1995). The stimulatory effects of estrogen on ANG1-7 and inhibitory effects on ACE activity suggest that the increase in renin activity associated with estrogen use (e.g., Proudler et al., 1995) may paradoxically inhibit, rather than accelerate, atherosclerosis. Variability in endogenous estrogen production, such as is observed between dominant and subordinate monkeys, may also influence the balance between ANGII and ANG1-7 production and by this mechanism affect atherogenesis.

SUMMARY AND CONCLUSIONS

Premenopausal women are usually considered to be relatively protected from atherosclerosis and CHD (McGill & Stern, 1979). However, to the extent that the results from our investigations with and their effects on estrogen activity in the premenopausal development of atherfemale monkeys apply also to women, they highlight the potential importance of behavioral stressors osclerosis. In fact, numerous lines of investigation suggest that women and monkeys share a pattern of stress response that may similarly influence premenopausal atherosclerosis risk. As shown in our studies and those of others, socially subordinate female monkeys reliably exhibit adrenocortical hyperactivity and, under both field and laboratory conditions, impaired reproduction (Dittus, 1979; Drickamer, 1974; Sade et al., 1976; Silk, Clark-Wheatley, Rodman, & Samuels, 1981; Walker, Gordon, & Wilson, 1983; Wilson, Gordon, & Bernstein, 1978). Behaviorally, social subordination in captive female monkeys is further accompanied by relative social withdrawal and isolation and generally reduced freedom of movement and expression (Kaplan, Adams, Clarkson, & Koritnik, 1984; Kaplan, Adams, Koritnik, Rose, & Manuck, 1986; Shively, Kaplan & Adams, 1986). These findings indicate that social subordination represents a significant stressor to female monkeys, particularly under conditions of confinement that demand high rates of social interaction.

Among women, the stress-associated syndrome of functional hypothalamic amenorrhea (FHA, also called "psychogenic amenorrhea") similarly involves ovarian dysfunction, adrenal hyperactivity, and behavioral abnormalities (Berga & Girton, 1989; Reifenstein, 1946). Investigators initially observed FHA in women in diverse circumstances who seemed linked by the common denominator of "stress" (Berga & Girton, 1989; Judd, 1992; Nappi et al., 1993; Reifenstein, 1946). Included in these observations were individuals away from home for the first time, those whose husbands were away at war, women threatened with rape, and those interred in prison camps (Judd, 1992; Reifenstein, 1946). The stress-like nature of FHA is underscored by the observation that women with this disorder exhibit hypercortisolism as well as decreased luteinizing hormone pulsatility (Nappi et al., 1993; Suh et al., 1988). women with FHA also exhibit increased cognitive dysfunction and psychiatric morbidity (Giles & Berga, 1993). These observations suggest that FHA may be one of the manifestations of a multifaceted stress disorder, similar in many respects to the syndrome represented by social subordination in monkeys. In both women and monkeys, the excessive adrenocortical response and disrupted gonadotropin-releasing hormone pacemaker activity are presumably potentiated by a stress-related release of corticotropin-releasing factor (Berga et al., 1989; Judd, 1992).

Although there may exist no precise human analogue for subordinate female monkeys, women with FHA appear to share with such animals a profile of neuroendocrine dysfunction that results in a similar propensity for accelerated atherosclerosis and increased risk for CHD. A related observation of potential importance is that in the studies involving monkeys, relatively modest impairment of ovarian function is associated with substantial exacerbation of atherosclerosis (Adams, Kaplan, Koritnik, & Clarkson, 1985; Kaplan et al., in press). Such moderate ovarian abnormalities, in women, probably would be occult (Wu, 1990). If so, the percentage of premenoppausal women at risk of accelerated atherosclerosis may be considerably larger than that indicated by the incidence of (diagnosed) FHA.

ACKNOWLEDGMENTS

The editorial assistance of Karen Klein is gratefully acknowledged, as are the efforts of numerous technicians working in the laboratories of the Comparative Medicine Clinical Research Center of the Wake Forest University School of Medicine. Research in our laboratory was supported by grants from the National Heart, Lung and Blood Institute (HL 45666, R01 HL 38964).

REFERENCES

Aberg, G., & Ferrer P. (1990). Effects of captopril on atherosclerosis in cynomolgus monkeys. *Journal of Cardiovascular Pharmacology, 15* (Suppl. 5), S65–S73.

Adams, M. R., Kaplan, J. R., Koritnik, D. R., & Clarkson, T. B. (1985) Ovariectomy, social status, and atherosclerosis in cynomolgus monkeys. *Arteriosclerosis, 5,* 192–200.

Adams, M. R., Kaplan, J. R., & Koritnik, D. R. (1985). Psychosocial influences on ovarian endocrine and ovulatory function in *Macaca fascicularis. Physiology & Behavior, 35,* 935–940.

Ahmed, S. A., Pendale, W. J., & Talal, N. (1985). Sex hormones, immune responses, and autoimmune diseases: Mechanisms of sex hormone action. *American Journal of Pathology, 121,* 531–551.

Aiman, J., & Smentek, C. (1985). Premature ovarian failure. *Obstetrics & Gynecology, 66,* 9–14.

Altmann, J. (1974). Observational study of behavior: Sampling methods. *Behavior, 48,* 1–41.

American Heart Association. (1993). *1992 heart and stroke facts.* Dallas: Author.

Bergtsson, C. (1973). Ischaemic heart disease in women. *Acta Medica Scandinavica, 549* (Suppl.), 1–128.

Berga, S. L., Girton, L. G. (1989). The psychoneuroendocrinology of functional hypothalamic amenorrhea. *Psychiatric Clinics of North America, 12,* 105–116.

Berga, S. L., Loucks, A. B., Rossmanith, W. G., Kettel, L. M., Laughlin, G. A., & Yen, S. S. C. (1991). Acceleration of luteinizing hormone pulse frequency in functional hypothalamic amenorrhea by dopaminergic blockade. *Journal of Clinical Endocrinology & Metabolism, 72,* 151–156.

Berga, S. L., Mortola, J. F., Girton, L., Suh, B., Laughlin, G., Pham, P., & Yen, S. S. C. (1989). Neuroendocrine aberrations in women with functional hypothalamic amenorrhea. *Journal of Clinical Endocrinology & Metabolism, 68,* 301–308.

Blumenthal, S. J., & Matthews, K. A. (1993). Working group report: Psychosocial aspects of cardiovascular disease in women. In N. K. Wenger, L. Speroff, & B. Packard (Eds.), *Cardiovascular health and disease in women* (pp. 213–216). Greenwich, CT: LeJacq Communications.

Brosnihan, K. B., Li, P., & Ferrario, C. M. (1995). Angiotensin-(1-7) elicits nitric oxide–dependent vasodilation in canine coronary arteries [Abstract]. *Hypertension, 26,* 544.

Clarkson, T. B., Williams, J. K., Adams, M. R., Wagner, J. D., & Klein, K. P. (1993). Experimental effects of estrogens and progestins on the coronary artery wall. In N. K. Wenger, L. Speroff, & D. Packard (Eds.), *Cardiovascular health and disease in women* (pp. 169–174). Greenwich, CT: LeJacq Communications.

Colditz, G.A., Hankinson, S.E., Hunter, D.J., Willett, W.C., Manson, J.E., Stampfer, M.J., Hennekens, C., Rosner, B., & Speizer, F.E. (1995). The use of estrogens and progestins and the risk of breast cancer in postmenopausal women. *New England Journal of Medicine, 332,* 1589-1593.

Colditz, G. A., Willett, W. C., Stampfer, M. J., Rosner, B., Speizer, F. E., & Hennekens, C. H. (1987). Menopause and the risk of coronary heart disease in women. *New England Journal of Medicine, 316,* 1105–1110.

Dittus, W. P. J. (1979). The evolution of behaviors regulating density and age-specific sex ratios in a primate population. *Behaviour, 69,* 265–302.

Dorward, P. K., & Rudd, C. D. (1991). Influence of brain renin–angiotensin system on renal sympathetic and cardiac baroreflexes in conscious rabbits. *American Journal of Physiology, 260,* H770–H778.

Drickamer, L. C. (1974). A ten-year summary of reproductive data for free-ranging *Macaca mulatta. Folia Primatologica (Basel), 21,* 61–80.

Ganong, W. F. (1993). *Review of medical physiology* (17th ed.). Norwalk, CT: Appleton & Lange.

Giles, D. E., & Berga, S. L. (1993). Cognitive and psychiatric correlates of functional hypothalamic amenorrhea: A controlled comparison. *Fertility & Sterility, 60,* 486–492.

Godsland, I. F., Wynn, V., Crook, D., & Miller, N. E. (1987). Sex, plasma lipoproteins, and atherosclerosis: Prevailing assumptions and outstanding questions. *American Heart Journal, 114,* 1467–1503.

Gruchow, H. W., Anderson, A. J., Barboriak, J. J., & Sobocinski, K. A. (1988). Postmenopausal use of estrogen and occlusion of coronary arteries. *American Heart Journal, 115,* 954–963.

Hamm, T. E., Jr., Kaplan, J. R., Clarkson, T. B., & Bullock, B. C. (1983). Effects of gender and social behavior on the development of coronary artery atherosclerosis in cynomolgus macaques, *Atherosclerosis, 48,* 221–233.

Haynes, S. G., & Czajkowski, S. M. (1993). Psychosocial and environmental correlates of heart disease. In P. S. Douglas (Ed.), *Cardiovascular health and disease in women* (pp. 269–282). Philadelphia: W. B. Saunders.

Heller, R. F., & Jacobs, H. S. (1978). Coronary heart disease in relation to age, sex, and the menopause. *British Medical Journal, 1,* 472–474.

Higgins, M., & Thom, T. (1993). Cardiovascular disease in women as a public health problem. In N. K. Wenger, L. Speroff, & B. Packard (Eds.), *Cardiovascular health and disease in women* (pp. 15–19). Greenwich, CT: LeJacq Communications.

Hilgers, K. F., Veelken, R., Kreppner, I., Ganten, D., Luft, F. C., Geiger, H., & Mann, J. F. E. (1994). Vascular angiotensin and the sympathetic nervous system: Do they interact? *American Journal of Physiology, 267*, H187–H194.

Judd, S. J. (1992). Pathophysiological mechanisms of stress-induced chronic anovulation. In K. E., Sheppard, J. H., Boublik, & J. W. Funder (Eds.), *Stress and reproduction* (pp. 253–265). New York: Raven Press.

Kaplan, J. R., Adams, M. R., Anthony, M. S., Morgan, T. M., Manuck, S. B., & Clarkson, T. B. (1995). Dominant social status and contraceptive hormone treatment inhibit atherogenesis in premenopausal monkeys. *Arterioscler Thromb Vasc Biol, 15*, 2094–2100.

Kaplan, J. R., Adams, M. R., Clarkson, T. B., & Koritnik, D. R. (1984). Psychosocial influences of female "protection" among cynomolgus macaques. *Atherosclerosis, 53*, 283–295.

Kaplan, J. R., Adams, M. R., Clarkson, T. B., Manuck, S. B., & Shively, C. A. (1991). Social behavior and gender in biomedical investigations using monkeys: Studies in atherogenesis. *Laboratory Animal Science, 41*, 334–343.

Kaplan, J. R., Adams, M. R., Koritnik, D. R., Rose, J. C., & Manuck, S. B. (1986). Adrenal responsiveness and social status in intact and overiectomized *Macaca fascicularis*, *American Journal of Primatology, 11*, 181–193.

Kaplan, J. R., Manuck, S. B., Adams, M. R., Weingand, K. W., & Clarkson, T. B. (1987). Inhibition of coronary atherosclerosis by propranolol in behaviorally predisposed monkeys fed an atherogenic diet. *Circulation, 76*, 1364–1372.

Kaplan, J. R., Manuck, S. B., Clarkson, T. B., & Prichard, R. W. (1985). Animal models of behavioral influences on artherogenesis. *Advances in Behavioral Medicine, 1*, 115–163.

Kaplan, J. R., Pettersson, K., Manuck, S. B., & Olsson, G. (1991). Role of sympathoadrenal medullary activation in the initiation and progression of atherosclerosis. *Circulation, 84* (Suppl. *VI*), VI-23–VI-32.

Kinch, R. A. H., Plunkett, E. R., Smout, M. S., & Carr, D. H. (1965). Primary ovarian failure. A clinicopathological and cytogenetic study. *American Journal of Obstetrics and Gynecology, 91*, 630–644.

LaVecchia, C., Decardi, A., Franceschi, s., Gentile, A., Negri, E., & Parazzini, F. (1987). Menstrual and reproductive factors and the risk of myocardial infarction in women under fifty-five years of age. *American Journal of Obstetrics and Gynecology, 157*, 1108–1112.

Loy, R. A., Loukides, J. A., & Polan, M. L. (1992). Ovarian steroids modulate human monocyte tumor necrosis factor alpha messenger ribonucleic acid levels in cultured human peripheral monocytes. *Fertility & Sterility, 58*, 733–739.

Ludmer, P. L., Selwyn, A. P., Shook, T. L., Wayne, R. R., Mudge, G. H., Alexander, R. W., & Ganz, P. (1986). Paradoxical vasoconstriction induced by acetylcholine in atherosclerotic coronary arteries. *New England Journal of Medicine, 315*, 1046–1051.

MacDonald, G. T. (1971). Reproductive patterns of three species of macaques. *Fertility & Sterility, 22*, 373–377.

MacMahon, B., Cole, P., & Brown, J. (1973). Etiology of human breast cancer: A review. *Journal of the National Cancer Institute, 50*, 21–42.

Mahoney, C. J., (1990). A study of the menstrual cycle in *Macaca irus* with special reference to the detectionof ovulation. *Journal of Reproductive Fertility, 21*, 153–163.

Manson, J. E. (1994). Postmenopausal hormone therapy and atherosclerotic disease. *American Heart Journal, 128*, 1337–1343.

Manuck, S. B., Kaplan, J. R., Adams, M. R., & Clarkson, T. B., (1989). Behaviorally elicited heart rate reactivity and atherosclerosis in female cynomolgus monkeys (Macaca fascicularis). *Psychosomatic Medicine, 51*, 306–318.

Manuck, S. B., Kaplan, J. R., & Matthews, K. A. (1986). Behavioral antecedents of coronary heart disease and atherosclerosis. *Arteriosclerosis, 6*, 2–14.

Manuck, S. B., Kaplan, J. R., Muldoon, M. F., Adams, M. R., & Clarkson, T. B. (1991). The behavioral exacerbation of atherosclerosis and its inhibition by propranolol. In P. M. McCabe, N. Schneiderman, T. M. Field, & J. S. Skylar (Eds.), *Stress, coping and disease* (pp. 51–72). Hillsdale, NJ: Lawrence Erlbaum Associates.

Manuck, S. B., & Polefrone, J. M. (1987). Psychophysiologic reactivity in women. In E. D. Eaker, B. Packard, N. K. Wenger, T. B., Clarkson, & H. A. Tyroler (Eds.), *Coronary heart disease in women* (pp. 164–171). New York: Haymarket Doyma.

Marrero, M. B., Paxton, W. G., Duff, J. L., Berk, B. C., & Bernstein, K. E. (1994). Angiotension II stimulates tyrosine phosphorylation of phospholipase C-_1 in vascular smooth muscle cells. *Journal of Biological Chemistry, 269*, 10935–10939.

Maseri, A., L'Abbate, A., Bardoli, G., Chierchia, S., Marzilli, M., Ballestra, A. M., Severi, S., Paradi, O., Biagini, A., Disante, A., & Pestola, A. (1978). Coronary vasospasm as a possible cause of myocardial infarction. A conclusion derived from the study of "preinfarction" angina. *New England Journal of Medicine, 299*, 1271–1277.

Maseri, A., Severi, S., DeNes, M., L'Abbate, A., Chierchia, S., Marzilli, M., Ballestra, A. M., Paradi, O., Biagini, A., & Disante, A. (1978) "Variant" angina: One aspect of a continuous spectrum of vasopastic myocardial ischemia: pathogenetic mechanisms, estimated incidence and clinical and coronary arteriographic findings in 138 patients. *American Journal of Cardiology, 42*, 1019–1035.

Matthews, K. A., Meilahn, E., Kuller, L. H., Kelsey, S. F., Caggiula, A. W., & Wing, R. R. (1989). Menopause and risk factors for coronary heart disease. *New England Journal of Medicine, 321*, 641–646.

McGill, H. C., Jr. (1968). *The geographic pathology of atherosclerosis.* Baltimore: Williams & Wilkins.

McGill, H. C., & Stern, N. P. (1979). Sex and atherosclerosis. *Atherosclerosis Reviews, 4*, 157–242.

Nappi, R. E., Petraglia, F., Genazzani, A. D., D'Ambrogio, G., Zara, C., & Genazzani, A. R. (1993). Hypothalamic amenorrhea: evidence for a central derangement of hypothalamic-pituitary-adrenal cortex axis activity. *Fertility & Sterility, 59*, 571–576.

Oliver, M. F. (1974). Ischaemic heart disease in young women. *British Medical Journal, 4*, 253–259.

Owens, J. F., Stoney, C. M., & Matthews, K. A. (1993). Menopausal status influences ambulatory blood pressure levels and blood pressure changes during mental stress. *Circulation, 88*, 2794–2802.

Palmer, J. R., Rosenberg, L., & Shapiro, S. (1992). Reproductive factors and risk of myocardial infarction. *American Journal of Epidemiology, 136*, 408–416.

Pettersson, K., Bejne, B., Bjork, H., Strawn, W. B., & Bondjers, G. (1990). Experimental sympathetic activation causes endothelial injury in the rabbit thoracic aorta via B1-adrenoceptor activation. *Circulation Research, 67*, 1027–1034.

Pike, M. C. (1987). Age-related factors in cancers of the breast, ovary and endometrium. *Journal of Chronic Diseases,* 40 (Suppl. II), 59S–69S.

Polan, M. L., Loukides, J., Nelson, P., Carding, S., Diamond, M., Walsh, A., & Bottomly, K. (1989). Progesterone and estradiol modulate interleukin-1 beta messenger ribonucleic acid levels in cultured human peripheral monocytes. *Journal of Clinical Endocrinology & Metabolism, 69*, 1200–1206.

Prior, J .C., Vigna, Y. M., Schechter, M. T., & Burgess, A. E. (1990). Spinal bone loss and ovulatory disturbances. *New England Journal of Medicine, 3232*, 1221–1227.

Proudler, A. J., Ahmed, A. I. H., Crook, D., Fogelman, I., Rymer, J. M., & Stevenson, J. C. (1995). Hormone replacement therapy and serum angiotension–converting-enzyme activity in postmenopausal women. *Lancet, 346*, 89–90.

Reid, I. A., Morris, B. J., & Ganong, W. F. (1978). The renin–angiotensin system. *Annual Reviews of Physiology, 40*, 377–410.

Reifenstein, E. C., Jr. (1946). Psychogenic or "hypothalamic" amenorrhea. *Medical Clinics of North America, 30*, 1103–1104.

Roberts, W. C., Durry, R. C., & Isner, J. M. (1982). Sudden death in Prinzmetal's angina with coronary spasm documented by angiography: Analysis of three necropsy patients. *American Journal of Cardiology, 50*, 203–210.

Rogers, T. B., & Lokuta, A. J. (1994). Angiotensin II signal transduction pathways in the cardiovascular system. *Trends in Cardiovascular Medicine, 4*, 110–116.

Russell, P., Bannatyne, P., Shearman, R. P., Fraser, I. S., & Corbett, P. (1982). Premature hyperg-onadotropic ovarian failure. Clinicopathological study of 19 cases. *International Journal of Gynecologic Pathology, 1*, 185–201.

Sack, M. N., Radar, D. J., & Cannon, R. O., (1994). Oestrogen and inhibition of oxidation of low-density lipoproteins in postmenopausal women. *Lancet, 343*, 269–270.

Sade, D. S. (1967). Determinants of dominance in a group of free ranging rhesus monkeys. In S. Altmann (Ed.), *Social communication among primates* (pp. 99–114). Chicago: University of Chicago Press.

Sade, D. S. (1973). An ethogram for rhesus monkeys. I. Antithetical contrasts in posture and move-ment. *American Journal of Physical Anthropology, 38*, 537–542.

Sade, D., Cushing, K., Cushing, P., Dunaif, J., Figueroa, A., Kaplan, J. R., Lauer, C., Rhodes, D., & Schneider, J. (1976). Population dynamics in relation to social structure of Cayo Santiago. *Yearbook of Physical Anthropology, 20*, 253–262.

Schneiderman, N. (1987). Psychophysiologic factors in atherogenesis and coronary artery disease. *Circulation, 76* (Suppl. 1), I-41–I-47.

Schuurs, A. H. W. M., & Verheul, H. A. M. (1990). Effects of gender and sex steroids on the immune response. *Journal of Steroid Biochemistry, 35*, 157–172.

Schwartz, S., Gadusek, C., & Sheldon, S. (1981). Vascular wall growth control: the role of endothe-lium. *Arteriosclerosis, 1*, 107–126.

Seibel, M. M., & Taymor, M. L. (1982). Emotional aspects of infertility. *Fertility & Sterility, 37*, 137–145.

Shively, C. A., Kaplan, J. R., & Adams, M. R. (1986). Effects of ovariectomy, social instability and social status on female *Macaca fascicularis* social behavior. *Physiol Behav, 36*, 1147–1153.

Silk, J. B., Clark-Wheatley, C., Rodman, P. S., & Samuels, A. (1981). Differential reproductive suc-cess and facultative adjustment of sex ratios among captive female bonnet macaques (*Macaca radiata*). *Animal Behavior, 29*, 1106–1120.

Speroff, L. (1993). The impact of oral contraception and hormone replacement therapy on cardio-vascular disease. In N. K. Wenger, L. Speroff, & B. Packard (Eds.), *Cardiovascular health and disease in women* (pp. 37–45). Greenwich, CT: LeJacq Communications.

Sprague, E. A., Troxler, R. G., Peterson, D. F., Schmidt, R. E., & Young, J. T. (1980). Effect of cor-tisol on the development of atherosclerosis in cynomolgus monkeys. In S. S. Kalter (Ed.), *The use of nonhuman primates in cardiovascular disease* (pp. 261–264). Austin: University of Texas Press.

Stamler, J., Pick, R., & Katz, L. N. (1956). Experiences in assessing estrogen antiatherogenesis in the chick, the rabbit, and man. *Annals of the New York Academy of Sciences, 64*, 596–619.

Stampfer, M. J., Colditz, G. A., Willett, W. C., Manson, J. E., Rosner, B., & Speizer, F. E. (1991). Postmenopausal estrogen therapy and cardiovascular disease. *New England Journal of Medicine, 325*, 756–762.

Starup, J., & Sele, V. (1973). Premature ovarian failure. *Acta Obstetrica Gynecologica Scandinavica, 52*, 259–268.

Stoney, C. M., Davis, M. C., & Matthews, K. A. (1987). Sex differences in physiological responses to stress and in coronary heart disease. A causal link? *Psychophysiology, 24*, 127–131.

Strawn, W. B., Bondjers, G., Kaplan, J. R., Manuck, S. B., Schwenke, D. C., Hansson, G. K., Shively, C. A., & Clarkson T. B. (1991). Endothelial dysfunction in response to psychosocial stress in monkeys. *Circulation Research, 68*, 1270–1279.

Suh, B. Y., Liu, J. H., Berga, S. L., Quigley, M. E., Laughlin, G. A., & Yen, S. S. (1988). Hypercortisolism in patients with functional hypothalamic amenorrhea. *J Clin Endocrinol Metab, 66*, 733–739.

Sullivan, J. M., Vander Zwaag, R., Lemp, G. F., Hughes, J. P., Maddock, V., Kroetz, F. W., Ramanathan, K. B., & Mirvis, D. M. (1988). Postmenopausal estrogen use and coronary athero-sclerosis. *Annals of Internal Medicine, 108*, 358–363.

Thom, T. J., (1987). Cardiovascular disease mortality among United States women. In E. D., Eaker, B. Packard, N. K. Wenger, T. B. Clarkson, & H. A. Tyroler (Eds.), *Coronary heart disease in women* (pp. 33–41). New York: Haymarket Doyma.

Trichopolous, D., Macmahon, B., & Cole, P. (1972). The menopause and breast cancer risk. *Journal of the National Cancer Institute, 48,* 605–613.

Troxler, R. G., Sprague, E. A., Albanese, R. A., Fuchs, R., & Thompson, A. J. (1977). The association of elevated plasma cortisol and early atherosclerosis as demonstrated by coronary angiography. *Atherosclerosis, 26,* 151–162.

Wagner, J. D., Clarkson, T. B., St. Clair, R. W., Schwenke, D. C., Shively, C. A., & Adams, M. R. (1991). Estrogen and progesterone replacement therapy reduces LDL accumulation in the coronary arteries of surgically postmenopausal cynomolgus monkeys. *Journal of Clinical Investigation, 88,* 1995–2002.

Walker, M. L., Gordon, T. P., & Wilson, M. E. (1983). Menstrual cycle characteristics of seasonally breeding rhesus monkeys. *Biology of Reproduction, 29,* 841–848.

Wenger, N. K. (1993). Coronary heart disease in women: An overview (myths, misperceptions, and missed opportunities). In N. K. Wenger, L. Speroff, & B. Packard (Eds.), *Cardiovascular health and disease in women* (pp. 21–29). Greenwich, CT: LeJacq Communications.

Williams, J. K., Adams, M. R., Herrington, D. M., & Clarkson, T. B. (1992). Short-term administration of estrogen and vascular responses of atherosclerotic coronary arteries. *Journal of the American College of Cardiology, 20,* 452–457.

Williams, J. K., Adams, M. R., & Klopfenstein, H. S. (1990). Estrogen modulates responses of atherosclerotic coronary arteries. *Circulation, 81,* 1680–1687.

Williams, J. K., Honoré, E. K., Washburn, S. A., & Clarkson, T. B. (1994). Effects of hormone replacement therapy on reactivity of atherosclerotic coronary arteries in cynomolgus monkeys. *Journal of the American College of Cardiology, 24,* 1757–1761.

Williams, J. K., Shively, C. A., & Clarkson, T. B. (1994). Determinants of coronary artery reactivity in premenopausal female cynomolgus monkeys with diet-induced atherosclerosis. *Circulation, 90,* 983–987.

Williams, R. B., Suarez, E. D., Kuhn, C. M., Zimmerman, E. A., & Schanberg, S. M. (1991). Biobehavioral basis of coronary-prone behavior in middle-aged men. Part I: Evidence for chronic SNS activation of Type As. *Psychosomatic Medicine, 53,* 517–527.

Wilson, M. E., Gordon, T. P., & Bernstein, I. S. (1978). Timing of births and reproductive success in rhesus monkey social groups. *Journal of Medical Primatology, 7,* 202–212.

Wu, C. H. (1990). Ovulatory disorders and infertility in women with regular menstrual cycles. *Current Opinion in Obstetrics and Gynecology, 2,* 398–404.

13

Comparative Effects of Age and Blood Pressure on Neuropsychological Test Performance: The Framingham Study

Merill F. Elias
University of Maine

Penelope K. Elias
Ralph B. D'Agostino
Boston University

Philip A. Wolf
Boston University School of Medicine

Hypertension is a risk factor for decline in cognitive functioning (Elias & Robbins, 1991a; Waldstein, Manuck, Ryan, & Muldoon, 1991) and it is possible that risk associated with poor performance increases disproportionately as one grows older (Wilkie & Eisdorfer, 1971; Wilkie, Eisdorfer, & Nowlin, 1976). Various models have been advanced to explain interactions of age with hypertension. Recently, Waldstein (1995) presented a life-span model. The prediction, based on this model, is that younger and older hypertensives will be more adversely affected by hypertension than will middle-aged individuals.

Earlier explanations of age by blood pressure interactions focused on individuals in late middle and old age (Wilkie & Eisdorfer, 1971). We refer to this collection of explanations of age by blood pressure interactions in older persons as the classic blood pressure–age interaction model (Elias, D'Agostino, Elias, & Wolf, 1995b) in order to distinguish it from the life-span model (Waldstein, 1995). In this chapter we focus on two questions: Does the existing literature support the classic blood pressure–age interaction model? What is the practical significance of blood pressure-related changes in cognitive functioning as opposed to age-related changes?

THE CLASSIC BLOOD PRESSURE–AGE INTERACTION MODEL

Functional and structural changes in brain, associated with primary biological aging (Busse, 1969) interact with changes in brain metabolism and neural degenerative processes associated with hypertension (Gifford, 1989; Phillips & Whisnant, 1992), thereby causing disproportionately greater cognitive decline in those who are both old and hypertensive. This is a simple statement of the classic blood pressure–age interaction model.

If, for heuristic purposes, one accepts the concept of primary biological aging as distinct from secondary aging, that is, adverse changes related to disease that accompany the aging process (see Busse, 1969; Elias, Elias, & Elias, 1990), then the classic blood pressure–age interaction model provides a useful guide for research on cognitive functioning in hypertensives who have reached late adulthood or old age.

Is There Empirical Support for the Model?

Longitudinal Studies. The classic blood pressure–age interaction model is supported by the results of two longitudinal studies. Wilkie, Eisdorfer, and Nowlin (1976) administered tests from the Wechsler Memory Scale on two occasions 6 1/2 years apart. Hypertensives, but not normotensives, exhibited statistically significant decline on Logical Memory–Immediate Recall and Visual Reproductions tests from the Weschler Memory Scale. The same result was observed from the performance scale of the Weschler Adult Intelligence Scale (WAIS) when Wilkie & Eisdorfer (1971) followed clearly hypertensive and normotensive, 60- to 69-year-old and 70- to 79-year-old individuals over a 10-year test–retest period. Sample size was very small in both studies and there were no controls for co-existing hypertension-related diseases or for the impact of antihypertensive medication on cognitive functioning.

Our longitudinal studies of hypertension using the WAIS and the Halstead–Reitan Neuropsychological Test Battery as outcome measures were stimulated by the work of Wilkie and Eisdorfer (1971), but involved several improvements in methodology: (a) larger sample size; (b) statistical control for treatment with antihypertensive drugs during longitudinal follow-up; (c) examination of relationships between untreated baseline blood pressure levels and subsequent longitudinal changes in cognitive functioning; (d) examination of the relationship of hypertension-associated diseases to cognitive ability.

Several of our studies clearly indicate that there is accelerated longitudinal decline in the presence of uncomplicated essential of hypertension and medically complicated hypertension. Higher blood pressure (systolic and diastolic), treated or untreated, is associated with more accelerated decline in fluid intellectual abilities.

One of these recent longitudinal studies (Elias et al., 1998a) employed 77 hypertensive and 63 normotensive individuals who were free from stroke, medically complicated hypertension, hypertension secondary to renal diseases, and other co-existing diseases, and who were not taking antihypertensive drugs at baseline (Examination 1). We also controlled statistically for antihypertensive medication after baseline (yes–no) and for the number of antihypertensive drugs taken during the 19-year longitudinal surveillance period that followed baseline blood pressure and cognitive evaluations with the WAIS.

Using a longitudinal growth curve method of analyses, a procedure that permits estimates of change over time even with missing longitudinal data points and also adjusts for attrition, we estimated decline over ten years of longitudinal surveillance for persons defined as hypertensive (untreated) or normotensive at Examination 1 (age range = 40–70 years). For a composite of WAIS scores measuring Visualization–Performance Ability (Block Design, Picture Arrangement, Picture Completion and Object Assembly) and for WAIS Digit Symbol Substitution test scores, persons who were hypertensive at baseline exhibited greater cognitive decline over the 19-year study period. Ever-Hypertensive versus Never-Hypertensive status, Examination 1 diastolic blood pressures averaged over all examinations were all significantly associated with longitudinal decline for the Visualization–Performance Ability composite score.

The pattern of change (in relation to blood pressure) was the same for each of the subtests of the WAIS constituting the Visualization–Performance composite score. That is, the higher the blood pressure, the greater the longitudinal decline in cognitive functioning. Only diastolic blood pressure, averaged over all longitudinal examinations, was significantly associated with longitudinal decline in psychomotor speed (Digit Symbol Substitution test scores). Neither hypertension nor any of the measures of blood pressure level were significantly associated with longitudinal decline in a Crystallized–Verbal Ability composite score. In general, associations between age and Visualization–Performance Ability were larger when blood pressure or hypertension was deleted from the regression model.

Results were the same when individuals who developed co-existing disease and complicated forms of hypertension after baseline (during the longitudinal follow-up) were brought into the analyses. The number of hypertension-related complications and co-existing diseases was significantly associated with cognitive decline on the Visualization–Performance composite score.

More recently, we have replicated these findings of associations among blood pressure level, hypertension and decline in cognitive functioning (Elias et al., 1998b, abstract) with a larger sample ($N = 466$; 25% hypertensive at Examination 1).

In addition to studies demonstrating longitudinal decline in WAIS scores, we conducted a study with a smaller number of subjects ($N = 53$) and a shorter longitudinal surveillance period (15 years). Increments in diastolic blood pressure (averaged over all examinations) were significantly associated with longitudinal decline on selected tests from the Halstead–Reitan Battery, specifically, the Finger Tapping Test–Non-Preferred Hand, WAIS Digit Symbol Substitution, the Category Test, and Trail Making Tests A and B (Elias, Robbins, & Elias, 1996).

In summary, it seems quite clear that chronic hypertension is associated with accelerated cognitive decline for fluid abilities and measures of speed of performance, but not crystallized verbal ability. It is also clear that rate of decline in cognitive functioning is related to blood pressure level, particularly the average blood pressure experienced over all longitudinal examinations. These longitudinal findings are consistent with the classic blood pressure–age interaction model, which predicts more accelerated change in cognitive functioning with advancing age as a function of hypertension or increments in blood pressure level.

Longitudinal studies of the blood pressure–age interaction model have one major limitation: It is not possible (for ethical and moral reasons) to deny hypertensive individuals treatment with antihypertensive drugs over the extended periods necessary for a meaningful longitudinal study (e.g., ideally, 10 years or more).

Therefore, to assess the combined effects of age and untreated hypertension on cognitive functioning for mature and elderly adults, we must turn to the cross-sectional literature. Here, samples have been considerably larger, and antihypertensive medication taking has been controlled either statistically or by excluding individuals who are taking antihypertensive drugs.

Cross-Sectional Studies. Cross-sectional studies are a poor substitute for longitudinal studies if the goal is to understand how hypertension affects rate of change over time. Nevertheless, from a population standpoint it is important to characterize the impact of hypertension on cognitive functioning for different age cohorts.

Two recent cross-sectional studies with the Framingham Heart Study population addressed the question of age cohort by blood pressure interactions within an age range we define as mature to elderly (55 to 89 years). Employing 2,123 individuals, 55 to 89 years of age at the time of neuropsychological testing, Farmer, White, Abbott, et al. (1987) found age by hypertension interactions for two of eight tests on the Kaplan–Albert Neuropsychological Test Battery. This battery (Farmer, White, Kittner, et al., 1987) includes tests of memory, abstract reasoning, and verbal fluency taken from the Weschler Adult Intelligence Scale (WAIS) and the Weschler Memory Scale (WMS). Table 13.1 lists the tests employed and summarizes their origins with respect to the WAIS or the WMS.

Findings by Farmer, White, Abbott, et al. (1987) were not consistent with the outcome predicted by the classic blood pressure–age interaction model. In fact, the outcome was opposite to the prediction. For study participants over 75 years of age, hypertension was associated with *better* performance on the Digit Span Forward test and the Logical Memory–Immediate Recall test. For individuals under 75 years of age, hypertension was associated with *lower* levels of performance for these two tests. Hypertension and increments in blood pressure were unrelated to any of the tests on the Kaplan–Albert battery when age groups were collapsed and the entire sample was used in the analyses ($N = 2,032$).

Several years later, we (Elias, Wolf, D'Agostino, Cobb, & White, 1993) repeated these analyses with the same study population and test battery (Table 13.1) used by Farmer, White, Abbott, et al. (1987) but made several changes in the analytic methods. These findings, and methodological dif-

TABLE 13.1
Summary of Tests Included in the Kaplan–Albert
Neuropsychological Test Battery and Their Origins[a]

Test	Origin
Logical memory–Immediate Recall	Wechsler Memory Scale, Form 2, Passage A
Visual Reproductions	Wechsler Memory Scale, Form 2
Paired Associate Learning	Wechsler Memory Scale, Form 1
Digit Span Forward and Digit Span Backward	Together form a subtest of the Wechsler Adult Intelligence Scale
Word Fluency	Multilingual Aphasia Examination
Similarities	Subtest of the Wechsler Adult Intelligence Scale
Logical Memory–Delayed Recall	Wechsler Memory Scale, Form 2, Passage A[b]

[a]For descriptions of these tests see Elias, Elias, et al., 1995; Elias, Wolf, D'Agostino, Cobb, & White, 1993; Farmer, White, Abbott, et al., 1987; and Farmer, White, Kittner, et al., 1987.
[b]Boston Variant: About 20 minutes after the Logical Memory–Immediate Recall test is given, the participant is asked to recall the first story read. This test is given after Visual Reproductions, Paired Associate Learning, Digit Span Forward, Digit Span Backward, Word Fluency, and Similarities tests have been given.

ferences between the two studies, have been discussed in detail in previous publications (Elias et al., 1993; Elias, Elias, Cobb, et al., 1995).

Briefly, Farmer, White, Abbott, et al. (1987) examined relations between diastolic and systolic blood pressure level and cognitive functioning with the expectation that the strongest associations between blood pressure and cognitive functioning would be seen if the two phenomena were assessed concurrently. Therefore, test performance scores were regressed on the average of one or two blood pressure measurements obtained at the beginning and end of the examinations in which neuropsychological testing occurred (Examinations 14 or 15). As noted previously, with the exception of significant age by blood pressure interactions for two test measures (opposite to the direction predicted by the classic blood pressure–age interaction model), Farmer, White, Abbott, et al. (1987) found no associations between blood pressure level (or hypertension) and cognitive functioning.

We felt that the Farmer, White, Abbott, et al. (1987) negative results may have been related to either or both of two aspects of their design: (a) There were too few blood pressure measurements; (b) the data analytic methods, ordinal logistic regression analyses, may have been insensitive to blood pressure–performance relationships. We (Elias et al., 1993) altered the design of our study accordingly. Multiple blood pressure measurements obtained on widely separated occasions prior to testing were used, and linear regression analyses were employed. We used the same statistical controls employed by Farmer et al. (1987)—age, gender, education, cigarette smoking and alcohol consumption, and antihypertensive medication—but added occupation as a control variable and tested a subset of individuals ($n = 1,038$) who were not treated for hypertension at any time during the study period.

Table 13.2 summarizes major design features of our analysis. The dependent variables (test scores) have already been defined in Table 13.1 and in text. Blood pressure was measured (once or twice) at each examination and was averaged over four or five biennial examinations (Examinations 4 to 8). This blood pressure measurement window was chosen (1956–1964) because relatively few hypertensive individuals in the sample (24%) were being treated with antihypertensive medications. The first three examinations (1950–1954) were not used in our study because blood pressure measurements declined during this period and did not stabilize and begin to rise until Examination 4 (Belander, Cupples, & D'Agostino, 1988). On the basis of blood pressure measurements taken during our blood pressure window (Examinations 4 to 8), three predictor

TABLE 13.2
Study Design Used to Determine Relations Between Indexes of Blood Pressure (Blood Pressure Level and Chronicity of Hypertension) in a Study of Stroke-Free Participants of the Framingham Heart Study

Study Years	Examinations	Study Event
1950–1954	1–3	Blood pressure declines and becomes less variable
1956–1964	4–8	Blood pressure measurement window[a]
1966–1974	9–13	Prediction interval (i.e., interval between blood pressure measurement and neuropsychological assessment)
1976–1978	14–15	Neuropsychological testing

Note. This table was adapted from a table published in "Untreated blood pressure level is inversely related to cognitive functioning: The Framingham Study," by M. F. Elias, P. A. Wolf, R. B. D'Agostino, J. Cobb, and L. R. White, 1993, American Journal of Epidemiology, 138, (6), p. 355. Copyright Johns Hopkins University School of Hygiene and Public Health. Used with permission.
[a]Average blood pressure level (systolic and diastolic mmHg) and chronicity of hypertension (proportion of examinations in which the individual was definitely hypertensive) were derived from Examinations 4, 5, 6, 7, and 8.

variables were formed: (a) averaged systolic blood pressure (mmHg), (b) averaged diastolic blood pressure (mmHg), and (c) chronicity of hypertension, that is, the proportion of examinations for which blood pressure was clearly in the hypertensive range using Framingham Study criteria (i.e., either a systolic blood pressure above 160 mmHg or a diastolic blood pressure above 95 mmHg). Test scores were regressed on these indexes of blood pressure and hypertension. As may be seen in Table 13.2, the blood pressure measurement window preceded neuropsychological testing by 12 to 14 years. Thus, neuropsychological test scores gathered at Examinations 14 or 15 (1976–1978) were regressed on blood pressure levels obtained at Examinations 4 through 8 (1956–1964).

Table 13.3 provides a summary of selected demographic characteristics for the study sample and presents information with respect to the predictor

TABLE 13.3
Selected Demographic Characteristics of the Full Sample and
Subsample of Individuals Employed in the Analysis of
Relations Between Blood pressure Indexes and Performance
on the Kaplan–Albert Neuropsychological Test Battery

Characteristic	Full Sample	Subsample (Untreated Exams 1 to 15)
N	1,702	1,038
n men	691	459
n women	1,011	579
Age in years (mean)	67	66
Age range	55–58	55–88
Mean diastolic BP	82	80
Range diastolic BP	56–120	56–98
Mean systolic BP	131	123
Range systolic BP	92–208	95–182
Hypertensive on one or more exams (%)	29	8
Smokers (%) > 0 cigarettes per day	22	26
Cigarettes per day		
Mean	4	5
Range	0–60	0–60
Taking antihypertensive medication	221	0

TABLE 13.3
(Continued)

Characteristic	Full Sample	Subsample (Untreated Exams 1 to 15)
Drinkers (%) > 1 oz/week	63	66
Alcohol (oz/week)		
Mean	3	3
Range	0–45	0–45
Education[a] in years (%)		
0	0.1	0.0
1–3	1.9	1.0
4–7	5.4	5.2
8	13.2	11.8
Attend HS	16.9	16.7
Graduate HS	31.0	30.4
Attend college	19.6	20.5
College graduate	7.4	8.5
Postgraduate	4.6	5.0
Occupation (%)[b]		
Unskilled	4.9	4.8
Skilled manual	12.0	11.4
Clerical sales	27.7	28.2
Administrative	21.4	20.2
Management	13.7	13.6
Professional	6.9	7.9

Note. Adapted from "Untreated blood pressure level is inversely related to cognitive functioning: The Framingham Study," by M. F. Elias, P. A. Wolf, R. B. D'Agostino, J. Cobb, and L. R. White, 1993, American Journal of Epidemiology, 138, p. 358, by permission of the authors and Johns Hopkins University. Copyright Johns Hopkins University, 1993.
[a]Highest level.
[b]Lifetime occupation at Examinations 14 and 15.

variables (blood pressure level and chronicity of hypertension) and the covariates (age, education, occupation, gender, cigarette smoking, alcohol consumption, and antihypertensive treatment for the full sample). Multiple linear regression analyses were used, and thus each regression coefficient obtained was adjusted for all other regression coefficients in the model. Participants in the full sample were free of stroke for the entire study period, and data were available for each of the covariates employed in the study. Individuals in the subsample met the same criteria as those in the full sample but were not treated for hypertension at any time during the study period. For the full sample, 1,702 individuals completed every examination in the battery; for the subsample, 1,038 individuals completed every test in the battery.

Although the period between blood pressure assessment (1956–1964) and neuropsychological testing (1976–1978) was very long, we hypothesized that a reliable blood pressure profile would predict test performance over a significant period. Our findings (Elias et al., 1993) were notably different from those reported by Farmer, White, Abbott, et al. (1987). We found no blood pressure by age interactions. Moreover, blood pressure levels and chronicity of hypertension were related to cognitive functioning for analyses that ignored age stratification and employed the full sample of 55- to 88-year-old study participants (Elias et al., 1993; Elias et al., 1995b). Essentially, increasing blood pressure and chronicity of hypertension were associated with lowered levels of performance on the composite of all eight test scores and the individual tests of Logical Memory–Immediate recall, Logical Memory—Delayed Recall, and Visual Reproductions ($N = 1,702$). This result was found when a control for hypertension (never treated vs. ever-treated during the study period) was added to the covariate set in the regression model and for a subgroup ($n = 1,038$) of individuals who had not been treated during the blood pressure measurement window or at any time during the entire study period.

We also performed a secondary analysis in which everyone who completed a test was permitted into the analysis for that test. In this case, two additional tests for the full sample, Paired Associate Learning and Digit Span Backward (Elias et al., 1995b), were significant.

In a subsequent study (Elias et al., 1995b) we performed a variety of analyses designed to more fully explore the possibility of age by blood pressure interactions for the Framingham sample and found none. The sample was slightly smaller than that employed in our original (Elias et al., 1993) analyses of these data ($N = 1,695$ vs. $N = 1,702$), but the demographic characteristics of the sample were highly similar to those described in Table 13.3.

There was no evidence that elderly individuals were more affected by increments in blood pressure level or chronic hypertension (defined later) than those of less advanced age (Elias et al., 1995b). We had expected that individuals in the oldest cohort of a three-age-group analysis (55 to 64; 65 to 74; 75 to 88) would be more vulnerable to the adverse effects of hypertension (or increments in blood pressure level) than would individuals in the younger two cohorts. Such was not the case. Moreover, statistically significant interactions were not observed for any of the test scores on the Kaplan–Albert battery when age was treated as a continuous variable in the interaction terms used to test the blood pressure by age and chronic hypertension by age interactions.

However, as previously found, higher blood pressure levels and chronic hypertension were related to lower levels of performance when age stratification was ignored and performance scores were averaged for persons of all ages (55 to 88 years), and this was true with control for antihypertensive medication use, alcohol consumption, cigarette smoking, education, age, gender, and occupational status (Elias et al., 1955a, 1995b). Similarly, increasing age was associated with lowered levels of performance when controlled for the indexes of blood pressure and all other covariates.

Given the orthogonal relationship between age and blood pressure level, and age and chronicity of hypertension, it is interesting to compare results for age (adjusted for the blood pressure indexes and all covariates) with the results for blood pressure (adjusted for age and all covariates). Regression coefficients obtained from these analyses are summarized in Table 13.4. The number of subjects involved in each analysis is shown because analyses were done separately for each test score and all individuals who completed each test were included.

Regression coefficients describing the magnitude of decline in performance scores related to ten mmHg increments in diastolic blood pressure, 10 mmHg increments in systolic blood pressure, and chronicity of hypertension are shown in one column of Table 13.4. Regression coefficients in another column describe magnitude of decline in performance in relation to 10-year increments in age. It is important to note that regression coefficients (β) for the blood pressure indexes are adjusted for age and all other covariates. Regression coefficients (β) for age are adjusted for the relevant blood pressure index and all other covariates. In other words, age was adjusted for diastolic blood pressure, systolic blood pressure, and chronicity of hypertension in separate sets of analyses. Each of these analyses also involved the other covariates (education, occupation, gender, alcohol consumption, cigarette smoking, and antihypertensive medication use [yes or no].

TABLE 13.4
Regression coefficients (beta) Expressing Relations Between
the Indexes of Blood Pressure and Test Scores and Between
Age (in 10-year increments) and Test Scores

Test Score	N	Adjusted β Values	
		Diastolic BP[a]	Age[b]
Logical Memory–Immediate Recall	1,789	−.1067***	−.2807****
Visual Reproductions	1,771	−.0871***	−.4546****
Paired Associate Learning	1,753	−.0587*	−.3411****
Digit Span Backward	1,800	−.0653*	−.1891****
Logical Memory Delayed	1,781	−.0749**	−.3267****
		Systolic BP[c]	Age[d]
Logical Memory–Immediate Recall	1,789	−.0510***	−.2609****
Visual Reproductions	1,771	−.0353*	−.4516****
Paired Associate Learning	1,753	−.0334*	−.3258****
Digit Span Backward	1,800	−.0201	−.1848****
Logical Memory Delayed	1,781	−.0445**	−.3082****
		Chronicity[e]	Age[f]
Logical Memory–Immediate Recall	1,789	−.2224**	−.2771****
Visual Reproductions	1,771	−.1794**	−.4615****
Paired Associate Learning	1,753	−.1021^	−.3333****
Digit Span Backward	1,800	−.0551	−.1823****
Logical Memory–Delayed Recall	1,781	−.1832*	−.3229****

Note. Data in this table are adapted from two tables in "Neuropsychological test performance, cognitive functioning, blood pressure and age: The Framingham Study," by M. F. Elias, R. B. D'Agostino, P. K. Elias, and P. A. Wolf, 1995, Experimental Aging Research, 21, p. 383–385, by permission of the authors and Taylor and Francis. Copyright Taylor and Francis 1995.
[a]Controlled for age and all other covariates.
[b]Controlled for diastolic blood pressure and all other covariates.
[c]Controlled for age and all other covariates.
[d]Controlled for systolic blood pressure and all other covariates.
[e]Controlled for age and all other covariates.
[f]Controlled for chronicity and all other covariates.
^p < .06; *p < .05; **p < .01; ***p < .001; ****p < .0001.

As may be seen in Table 13.4, diastolic blood pressure was inversely related to Logical Memory–Immediate Recall, Visual Reproductions, Paired Associate Learning, Digit Span Backward, and Logical Memory–Delayed Recall. Systolic blood pressure was related to Logical memory–Immediate Recall, Visual Reproductions, Paired Associate Learning, and Logical Memory–Delayed Recall. Chronicity of hypertension was related to the same four tests, although the association between chronic hypertension and Paired Associate Learning was marginal ($p < .06$).

Age was associated with poorer performance for each of these test scores and the remaining tests in the battery, Digit Span Forward, $\beta = -.1453, p < .0001$, Word Fluency, $\beta = -.1915, p < .0001$, and Similarities, $\beta = -.2612, p < .0001$.

As discussed previously, two aspects of differences in our design (Elias et al. 1993; Elias et al., 1995b) and the design used by Farmer, White, Abbott, et al. (1987) may have accounted for negative findings in their study and positive findings in ours. It is most likely that measurement of blood pressure over many examinations was the key to our positive findings. In fact, when Farmer and colleagues reanalyzed their data, using essentially the same design and methods (ordinal logistic regression) but including blood pressure measurements obtained over every examination during the entire study period (biennial Examinations 1 through 15), they found that chronic hypertension was associated with lowered levels of neuropsychological test performance (Farmer et al., 1990). Thus, it is clear that blood pressure–performance relationships can be detected via logistic regression analysis when reliable blood pressure profiles are obtained for study participants. Where this is the objective, multiple blood pressure measurements over widely separated occasions may be more important than multiple blood pressure measurements at a single occasion (Llabre et al., 1988).

In summary, for this large study population (Framingham Study participants) we found that rising blood pressure and hypertension have a negative effect on neuropsychological test performance (Elias et al., 1993), and this was true with age, education, gender, occupation, cigarette smoking, alcohol consumption, and antihypertensive medication controlled. However, we did not see the age by blood pressure level or age by hypertension interactions predicted by the classic age–blood pressure interaction model (Elias et al., 1993; Elias et al., 1995b).

Later in this chapter we offer some reasons as to why age by blood pressure and age by chronicity of hypertension interactions were not statistically significant. At this point we turn to the second question

addressed in this chapter: What is the practical significance of our findings? That is, are they of importance in terms of public health, or are they
trivial?

EPIDEMIOLOGICAL
SIGNIFICANCE OF BLOOD
PRESSURE AND
HYPERTENSION EFFECTS ON
COGNITIVE FUNCTIONING

Evidence From Linear
Regression Analyses

Examination of the magnitude of the regression coefficients in Table 13.4
is instructive with respect to the issue of epidemiological significance of
associations between blood pressure and test performance. The interpretation of these regression coefficients is straightforward. coefficients for diastolic blood pressure (Table 13.4) indicate decline in performance (in z score
units) associated with 10 mmHg increments in blood pressure. Coefficients
for chronicity of hypertension (Table 13.4) indicate the decline in performance associated with a diagnosis of hypertension at every examination during the blood pressure measurement window (vs. never being diagnosed
hypertensive), and coefficients for age indicate the decline in performance
associated with 10-year increments in chronological age. Because the test
scores were converted to standard scores (z scores) prior to the analysis, z
$= [[X] - X]/SD$ (Downey & Starry, 1977), decline in performance can be
interpreted in units of one standard deviation. Thus, for example, Logical
Memory test scores declined by $-.11$ standard deviation units ($\beta = -.1067$)
for every 10 mmHg increment in diastolic blood pressure (Table 13.4) but
declined by a little more than one quarter standard deviation unit
($\beta = -.2807$) in relation to 10-year increments in age.

As would be expected, the effects of sustained hypertension (chronic
hypertension) were more dramatic. In fact, for Logical Memory–Immediate
Recall (Table 13.4), decline associated with chronic hypertension
($\beta = -.2224$) approached the level of decline associated with 10-year increments in age ($\beta = -.2807$).

Obviously the scaling of increments of blood pressure (10 mmHg) in
relation to increments in age (10 years) is arbitrary. We are comparing
apples and oranges when we compare 10 mmHg increments in diastolic

blood pressure with 10-year increments in age; but the comparison has heuristic value. Ten mmHg increments in blood pressure have a meaningful clinical implication, and 10-year increments in age are biologically and psychologically meaningful. Although changes in performance associated with 10 mmHg increments in blood pressure were quite modest in relation to changes associated with chronic hypertension and age, it is certain that blood pressure levels can rise more than 10 mmHg if untreated.

Evidence From Logistic Regression Analyses

Although regression coefficients are useful indexes of the practical significance of associations between risk factors and outcome measures, epidemiologists often express relations between risk factors and outcome measures (e.g., blood pressure and stroke) as odds ratios. This method of data analysis seemed particularly appropriate to the question we posed about the epidemiological significance of our findings. Therefore, we reanalyzed the Framingham Study data using a multiple binary logistic regression procedure (Elias et al., 1995a). Odds ratio estimates are derived by exponentiating the regression coefficients obtained (Hosmer & Lemeshow, 1989).

As was the case for our linear regression analyses summarized earlier in this chapter, statistical controls for age, education, gender, education, occupation, cigarette smoking, and alcohol consumption were employed. For each of the dependent variables (test scores), three analyses using logistic regression analyses were performed—one with systolic blood pressure, one with diastolic blood pressure, and one with chronicity of hypertension as the predictor variable. Each analysis included the set of covariates listed previously and utilized a sample of 1,695 individuals. In this case analyses were performed with equal numbers of subjects for each test score; that is, a requirement for inclusion in the study was the completion of all tests in the Kaplan–Albert battery (Elias et al., 1995a).

Definition of the Dependent Variables. Rather than recording the specific z score obtained by each individual, as in linear regression analysis, we expressed an individual's score as a binary outcome: good performance and poor performance. Two different criteria were used for good and poor performance and were applied in separate analyses. In one set of analyses, good versus poor performance was defined for each of the eight test scores as a z score in the upper (good) or lower (poor) half of the distribution of z scores. In the other set of analyses, good performance was defined as a score in the upper 75th percentile of the distribution of z scores, and "very" poor performance was defined as a score in the lower 25 percentile.

These definitions of good and poor performance are not entirely arbitrary. Performance above and below the 50th percentile is often used as an index of acceptable and unacceptable performance on scholastic aptitude tests, and performance below the 25th percentile is often thought of as particularly deficient.

Findings. As was true for the linear regression analyses performed, interactions of the blood pressure and chronicity of hypertension with gender and age were not significant.

Findings for the parent sample of 1,695 subjects (55 to 88 years of age) are shown in Table 13.5. Data are expressed as odds ratios associated with performing in the lower 50th percentile of the distribution of test scores for each 10 mmHg increment in diastolic blood pressure level, 20 mmHg increments in systolic blood pressure, chronicity of hypertension (always vs. never hypertensive), and 10-year increments in age. These are the independent odds associated with each of the predictors. Regression coefficients for diastolic blood pressure, systolic blood pressure, and chronicity of hypertension were controlled for age and all other covariates in the model. Conversely, age was controlled for diastolic blood pressure and all other covariates in the model. As for the linear regression analyses previously discussed, the idea was to compare performance decrements associated with 10 mmHg increments in diastolic blood pressure, 20 mmHg increments in systolic blood pressure, chronicity of hypertension, and 10-year increments in age.

Table 13.5 summarizes data only for those tests that have been consistently associated with blood pressure level or chronic hypertension in our previous studies (Elias et al., 1993; Elias et al., 1995a, 1995b). As in the previous analyses, all other tests were nonsignificant for the blood pressure and chronicity of hypertension variables.

Because regression coefficients with respect to age–performance associations were highly similar regardless of whether systolic blood pressure, diastolic blood pressure, or chronicity of hypertension were included in the regression model (controlled), results for age are presented only for the analyses in which diastolic blood pressure and all variables in the covariate set were included in the model. Relations

TABLE 13.5
Odds of Performing in the Bottom 50th Percentile
of the Distribution of Test Scores and in 95% Confidence
Limits for Diastolic Blood Pressure, Systolic Blood Pressure,
and Chronicity, and for Selected Tests of the Kaplan–Albert
Battery for Which Statistically Significant Results
Were Obtained[a]

Variable	Odds Ratio	95% CI
Diastolic BP[b]		
Logical Memory–Immediate Recall	1.13**	1.01–1.27
Visual Reproductions	1.12**	1.00–1.26
Digit Span Backward	1.12*	1.00–1.26
Logical Memory–Delayed Recall	1.14**	1.02–1.29
Systolic BP[c]		
Logical Memory–Immediate Recall	1.15**	1.07–1.37
Visual Reproductions	1.13*	1.00–1.28
Digit Span Backward	1.06	0.93–1.07
Logical Memory–Delayed Recall	1.16**	1.02–1.32
Chronicity (0.00 vs. 1.00)[d]		
Logical Memory–Immediate Recall	1.44**	1.00–2.08
Visual Reproductions	1.41*	1.00–2.04
Digit Span Backward	1.20	0.82–1.76
Logical Memory–Delayed Recall	1.53**	1.06 –2.24
Age[e]		
Logical Memory–Immediate Recall	1.69****	1.45–1.97
Visual Reproductions	2.57****	2.20–2.99
Digit Span Backward	1.27***	1.08–1.48
Logical Memory—Delayed Recall	1.77****	1.52–2.07

Note. Adapted from "Blood pressure, hypertension, and age as risk factors for poor cognitive performance," by P. K. Elias, R. B. D'Agostino, M. F. Elias, and P. A. Wolf, 1995, *Experimental Aging Research*, 21, p. 409, by permission of the authors and Taylor and Francis. Copyright Taylor and Francis 1995.
[a]Analysis was for the full sample (N = 1,695). Tests shown on this table were significant beyond the .10 level for the analyses using diastolic blood pressure and age as predictors. Asterisks following the odds ratios indicate the significance levels of the Wald Chi-Square test in these analyses.
[b]Odds ratios are for increments in diastolic blood pressure of 10 mmHg.
[c]Odds ratios are for increments in systolic blood pressure of 20 mmHg.
[d]Odds ratios are for the proportion of visits never hypertensive (0.00) versus the proportion of visits always hypertensive (1.00).
[e]Odds ratios are for increments of 10 years of age.
$*p < .10; **p < .05; ***p < .01; ****p < .001.$

between diastolic blood pressure and cognitive functioning were statistically significant for all four test measures. Thus, for example, the odds of performing in the lower 50th percentile of the distribution of Logical Memory–Immediate Recall scores for individuals who were hypertensive on every examination (vs. never hypertensive) during the blood pressure measurement window were 1.44 to 1. Odds of poor performance associated with 10 mmHg increments in diastolic blood pressure and 20 mmHg increments in systolic blood pressure were 1.13 to 1 and 1.15 to 1, respectively. However, the highest risk of poor performance was associated with age. Odds ratios ranged from 1.27 to 2.57 for 10-year increments in chronological age (see Table 13.5).

Table 13.6 shows the odds of performing in the bottom quartile of the distribution of test scores for the various risk factors. The magnitudes of the odds ratios are similar to those shown in Table 13.5, although fewer associations are statistically significant. In general, the highest level of risk of poor performance is associated with 10-year increments in age and a diagnosis of hypertension on every examination during the blood pressure measurement window.

As reported by Elias et al. (1993), the addition of an antihypertensive medication (yes or no) covariate at any time during the study had no effect on these findings. In fact, antihypertensive medication use was not significantly associated with any of the test scores (Elias et al., 1993; Elias et al., 1995b).

The data shown in Tables 13.5 and 13.6 were based on analyses done with the parent sample ($N = 1,695$). Elias et al. (1995a) did not present data for the subsample of individuals who were never treated for hypertension (see Table 13.3). There were too few hypertensives in the never-treated subsample ($n = 1,038$) for a meaningful analysis of chronicity of hypertension. However, it was possible to perform logistic regression analyses with respect to blood pressure level. Compared to the parent sample, fewer significant associations were observed for the subsample of never-treated hypertensives ($n = 1,038$), but the odds of performing in the lower 50th percentile were somewhat higher than those observed for the parent sample. For example, the results for 10 mmHg increments in diastolic blood pressure were: Logical Memory–Immediate Recall (odds ratio = 1.20; CI = 1.02 to 1.52, $p < .05$), Logical memory–Delayed Recall (odds ratio = 1.22; CI = 1.00 to 1.49, $p < .01$; and Digit Span Backward (odds ratio = 1.29; CI = 1.06 to 1.58, $p < .01$). Similar results were obtained when the odds of performing in the lower 25th percentile were calculated.

TABLE 13.6

Odds of Performing in the bottom 25th Percentile of the Distribution of Test Scores and in 95% Confidence Limits for Diastolic Blood Pressure, Systolic Blood Pressure, and Chronicity, and Age for Tests in the Kaplan–Albert Battery for Which Significant Effects Were Found[a]

Variable	Odds Ratio	95% CI
Diastolic BP[b]		
Logical Memory–Immediate Recall	1.14**	1.00–1.28
Visual Reproductions	1.12*	0.99–1.27
Digit Span Backward	0.93	0.83–1.04
Logical Memory–Delayed Recall	1.17***	1.03–1.32
Systolic BP[c]		
Logical Memory–Immediate Recall	1.12	0.98–1.29
Visual Reproductions	1.08	0.94–1.24
Digit Span Backward	1.00	0.88–1.14
Logical Memory–Delayed Recall	1.17**	1.03–1.34
Chronicity (0.00 vs. 1.00)[d]		
Logical Memory–Immediate Recall	1.62**	1.11–2.38
Visual Reproductions	1.29	0.88–1.90
Digit Span Backward	1.02	0.71–1.48
Logical Memory–Delayed Recall	1.41*	0.97–2.05
Age[e]		
Logical Memory–Immediate Recall	1.87****	1.59–2.21
Visual Reproductions	2.71****	2.28–3.21
Digit Span Backward	1.26***	1.08–1.46
Logical Memory–Delayed Recall	1.83****	1.57–2.16

Note. Adapted from "Blood pressure, hypertension, and age as risk factors for poor cognitive performance," by P. K. Elias, R. B. D'Agostino, M. F. Elias, and P. A. Wolf, 1995, *Experimental Aging Research,* 21, p. 410, by permission of the authors and Taylor and Francis. Copyright Taylor and Francis 1995.

[a]Analysis was for the full sample ($N = 1,695$). Tests shown on this table were significant beyond the .10 level for the analyses using diastolic blood pressure and age as predictors and the criterion of falling in the lower 25th percentile. Asterisks following the odds ratios indicate the significance levels of the Wald Chi-Square test in these analyses using the criterion of falling in the lower 25th percentile.

[b]Odds ratios are for increments in diastolic blood pressure of 10 mmHg.

[c]Odds ratios are for increments in systolic blood pressure of 20 mmHg.

[d]Odds ratios are for the proportion of visits never hypertensive (0.00) versus the proportion of visits always hypertensive (1.00).

[e]Odds ratios are for increments of 10 years of age.

*$p < .10$; **$p < .05$; ***$p < .01$; ****$p < .001$.

GENERAL DISCUSSION

Blood Pressure by Age and Hypertension by Age Interactions

Our studies with the Kaplan–Albert Neuropsychological Test Battery have produced no evidence in support of the classic blood pressure–age interaction model for persons ranging in age between 55 and 88 years. Given the sample sizes involved and controls for antihypertensive medication (as a covariate and with all persons who ever received antihypertensive medication excluded), it is unlikely that these results can be attributed to inadequate power to test blood pressure level by age interactions or to the confounding effects of antihypertensive medication treatment.

It is important to emphasize that our data speak only to interactions of blood pressure (or chronic hypertension) with age cohort membership. They do not permit conclusions with respect to rates of change in cognitive functioning in relation to blood pressure level. There are a variety of reasons why our cross-sectional data cannot be generalized to age change in relation to blood pressure level or chronic hypertension.

For example, it is possible that failure to find that elderly individuals are more cognitively disadvantaged by hypertension (or rise in blood pressure) than younger individuals is related to a survivorship phenomenon. Obviously, elderly persons in the Framingham Study cohort have survived risk factors and disease(s) related to mortality, morbidity, or disability. It has been shown that survivorship is positively associated with cognitive functioning prior to terminal drop (Siegler, 1975). Selective volunteering may also play a role in negative findings with respect to age cohort by blood pressure interactions. Framingham Study participants were not required to take the Kaplan–Albert battery and thus may represent a selective subset of individuals who agreed to be tested cognitively. Individuals who detect changes in their own cognitive functioning, objectively or subjectively, may not volunteer for studies involving neuropsychological measures. This self-selection bias toward better performing participants may increase with a diagnosis of hypertension and advanced chronological age. Consequently, poorer performing individuals may be increasingly underrepresented in samples of elderly participants or hypertensives (or both). The validity of these survivor and sample-bias hypotheses is not easily verified in cross-sectional studies. The same individuals are not followed over time. Longitudinal studies are necessary to evaluate the effects of differential rates of attrition on rate of change as a function of hypertensive diagnostic status, increasing blood pressure level, and increasing age.

There have been a few longitudinal studies employing individuals over 60 years of age. Wilkie and Eisdorfer (1976) and Wilkie et al. (1976) found a higher rate of decline in performance on the WAIS and tests of memory for hypertensive than for normotensive individuals over a 10-year test–retest interval, but samples were very small, participants were taking antihypertensive medication, and there was no control for the medication variable in these studies.

In our own longitudinal studies with young and middle aged hypertensive and normotensive individuals (Elias et al., 1989; Elias et al., 1990; Schultz et al., 1989), we have found lower levels of neuropsychological test performance for small samples of hypertensives treated with antihypertensive medications, but no interactions of blood pressure status and rate of change over a 10-year period. The confounding of medication and diagnostic status is not unique to our longitudinal studies or to work by Wilkie and her colleagues (Wilkie & Eisdorfer, 1971; Wilkie et al., 1976). It has been impossible, for ethical and moral reasons, to deny hypertensives treatment in order to participate in longitudinal studies over significant segments of the adult years. Thus, drug treatment constitutes a significant barrier to longitudinal studies over meaningfully long periods. This "treatment barrier" does not negate the value of characterizing change over time for treated hypertensives. These studies have ecological validity given the contemporary emphasis on aggressive diagnosis and treatment of hypertension. However, analyses of influences of antihypertensive medication on change in cognitive functioning over time is more easily recommended than accomplished. Very large samples are required, and in the absence of a clinical trial methodology it is virtually impossible to control drug classes and levels over significant periods.

Moreover, longitudinal designs are not free from inherent methodological limitations. They are vulnerable to bias related to (a) shrinking sample sizes with advancing age, and (b) selective attrition of those who perform more poorly, are ill, or both (Elias & Robbins, 1991b; Siegler & Botwinick, 1979). However, a variety of methods are available for evaluating and attenuating the influence of attrition in longitudinal studies (Collins & Horn, 1991; McArdle, Hamagami, Elias, & Robbins, 1991; Rogosa, Brandt, & Zimowski, 1982; Willett, 1988/1989).

Blood Pressure Effects

Age by blood pressure interactions aside, it is clear that increasing levels of blood pressure and chronic hypertension are associated with lower average levels of cognitive functioning for tests placing demands on attention, mental flexibility, learning, memory, and abstract reasoning (Waldstein, 1995; Waldstein, Manuck, et al., 1991; Waldstein, Ryan, Manuck, Parkinson, & Bromet, 1991). These findings have been explained in terms of hypertension-related changes in brain structure and function (e.g., Elias & Robbins, 1991a; Waldstein, 1995; Waldstein, Manuck, et al., 1991). Although hypotheses regarding social–psychological variables as mediators between hypertension (or blood pressure) and cognitive functioning have been advanced (Elias, Robbins, & Schulz, 1987), they have gained less support than pathophysiological explanations (Elias & Robbins, 1991a; Waldstein, 1995; Waldstein, Manuck, et al., 1991). Whereas pathophysiological models emphasize pathophysiological processes as directly intervening between blood pressure and cognition, Elias et al. (1993) and Waldstein, Manuck, et al. (1991) have suggested a third explanation, that is, "a neuro-degenerative process or processes may cause lowered levels of performance and increased blood pressure level, in the absence of a direct pathophysiological link between performance and blood pressure level" (Elias et al., 1993, p. 362). Models explaining poorer performance by hypertensives in terms of pathophysiological correlates of hypertension are compelling, but more studies are needed to confirm this link. Magnetic resonance imaging (MRI) studies show promise in this regard (Salerno et al., 1992; van Swieten et al., 1991).

Epidemiological Significance

From an epidemiological and clinical perspective, it is important to understand the implications of changes in cognitive functioning in relation to increments in blood pressure (or chronic hypertension). It is clear that risk of below average levels of performance (see Table 13.5) and very poor performance (see Table 13.6) associated with 10 mmHg increments in diastolic blood pressure and 20 mmHg increments in systolic blood pressure were modest. Moreover, the relatively wide confidence intervals for odds (see Tables 13.5 and 13.6) indicate that intra-individual variation in risk was considerable in the Framingham Study sample. These data and findings with respect to the Halstead–Reitan Neuropsychological Test Battery (Elias, Robbins, Schultz, Streeten, & Elias, 1987) suggest that within limits, clinically significant increments in blood pressure (10 mmHg increments in diastolic and 20 mmHg increments in systolic) are not associated with clinically significant cognitive dysfunction. However, it seems safe to assume that most readers of this chapter would prefer not to embrace even this level of increased risk of lowered cognitive functioning. Furthermore, even slight increases in risk are epidemiologically significant (i.e., they have important implications for decline in cognitive functioning at a population level).

Obviously, untreated blood pressure levels can rise beyond 10 mmHg diastolic and 20 mmHg systolic. Further, sustained high blood pressure (chronic hypertension) is of epidemiological and clinical importance (i.e., it is of practical concern both for large populations and for treatment of the individual patient). The odds of performing in the lowest quartile of the distribution of scores for chronic hypertensives were 1.62 and 1.41 for the Logical Memory Tests (Table 13.6).

Traditionally, reduction of the risk for vascular disease and events (stroke) is the foremost concern in the treatment of hypertension. Maintenance of maximally high levels of cognitive functioning is very likely an important by-product of aggressive treatment. This is only true to the extent that one is at lower risk in relation to treatment than in relation to hypertension. It is probably not unreasonable to argue that in proper dosages and with the correct matching of type of hypertension with medication prescribed (see Streeten & Anderson, 1988), some classes of antihypertensive medications either have no effect on cognitive functioning or result in improved functioning (Muldoon, Manuck, Shapiro, & Waldstein, 1991; Muldoon, Waldstein, & Jennings, 1995). However, the final verdict is far from in. Some antihypertensive medications have had adverse effects on cognitive functioning in clinical trials and in studies using case-cohort methods (Muldoon, Manuck, Shapiro, & Waldstein, 1991; Muldoon et al., 1995). Obviously, nondrug avenues of treatment and prevention of hypertension (diet, exercise, weight control, and healthy lifestyle) are important alternatives to drug treatment.

ACKNOWLEDGMENTS

Statistical analyses and preparation of this chapter were supported in part by research grants 5-R37-AG03055-19 (National Institute on Aging), to Merrill F. Elias; 1-K01-AG0646-03 (Special Career Emphasis Award from the National Institute on Aging) to Penelope K. Elias; and research grants 2-R01-AG08122-11 (National Institute on Aging); 5-R01-NS-17950-18 (National Institute of Neurological Disorders and Stroke), and contract number N01-HC 38038 (National Heart, Lung, and Blood Institute) to Philip A. Wolf.

REFERENCES

Belanger, R. A., Cupples, L. A., & D'Agostino, R. B. (1988). Section 36. Means at each examination and inter-examination consistency of specified characteristics; Framingham Heart Study, 30-year follow-up. In W. B. Kannel, P. A., Wolf, & R. J. Garrison (Eds.), *The Framingham Heart Study: An epidemiological investigation of cardiovascular disease* (NIH Publication No. 88-2970. Bethesda, MD: National Institutes of Health, Public Health Service.

Busse, E. W. (1969). Theories of aging. In E. W. Busse & E. Pfeiffer (Eds.), *Behavior and adaptation in later life* (pp. 11–32). Boston: Little Brown.

Collins, L. M., & Horn, J. L. (Eds.). (1991). *Best methods for the analysis of change.* Washington, DC: American Psychological Association.

Costa, P. T., & Shock, N. A. (1990). New longitudinal data on the question of whether hypertension influences intellectual performance. In M. F. Elias & D. H. P. Streeten (Eds.), *Hypertension and cognitive processes.* Mt. Desert, ME: Beech Hill Publishing.

Downey, N. M., & Starry, A. R. (1977). *Descriptive and inferential statistics.* New York: Harper & Row.

Elias, P. K., D'Agostino, R. B., Elias, M. F., & Wolf, P. A. (1995a). Blood pressure, hypertension, and age as risk factors for poor cognitive performance. *Experimental Aging Research, 21,* 369–391.

Elias, M. F., D'Agostino, R. B., Elias, P. K., & Wolf, P. A. (1995b). Neuropsychological test performance, cognitive functioning, blood pressure and age: The Framingham Study. *Experimental Aging Research, 21,* 393–417.

Elias, M. F., Elias, P. K., Cobb J., D'Agostino, R. B., White, L. R., & Wolf, P. A. (1955). Blood pressure affects cognitive functioning: The Framingham studies revisited. In J. E. Dimsdale & A. Baum (Eds.), *Quality of life and behavioral medicine research* (pp. 121–143). Hillsdale, NJ: Lawrence Erlbaum Associates.

Elias, M. F., Elias, P. K., & Elias, J. W. (1990). Biological and health influences on behavior. In J. E. Birren & K. W. Schaie (Eds.), *Handbook of the psychology of aging* (pp. 79–102). New York: Academic Press.

Elias, M. F., & Robbins, M. A. (1991a). Cardiovascular disease, hypertension, and cognitive function. In A. P. Shapiro & A. Baum (Eds.), *Behavioral aspects of cardiovascular disease* (pp. 249–285). Hillsdale, NJ: Lawrence Erlbaum Associates.

Elias, M. F., & Robbins, M. A. (1991b). Where have all the subjects gone? Longitudinal studies of disease and cognitive function. In L. M. Collins & J. L. Horn (Eds.), *Best methods for the analysis of change* (pp. 264–275). Washington, DC: American Psychological Association.

Elias, M. F., Robbins, M. A., & Schultz, N. R., Jr. (1987). Influence of hypertension on intellectual performance. Causation or speculation? In J. W. Elias & P. H. Marshall (Eds.), *Cardiovascular disease and behavior* (pp. 107–149). Washington, DC: Hemisphere.

Elias, M. F., Robbins, M. R., Schultz, N. R., Jr., Steeten, D. H. P., & Elias, P. K. (1987). Clinical significance of cognitive performance by hypertensive patients. *Hypertension, 9,* 192–197.

Elias, M. F., Schultz, N. R., Robbins, M. A., & Elias, P. K. (1989). A longitudinal study of neuropsychological performance by hypertensives and normotensives: A third measurement point. *Journal of Gerontology: Psychological Sciences, 44,* 25–28.

Elias, M. F., Wolf, P. A., D'Agostino, R. B., Cobb, J., & White, L. R. (1993). Untreated blood pressure level is inversely related to cognitive functioning: The Framingham Study. *American Journal of Epidemiology, 138,* 353–364.

Farmer, M. E., Kittner, S. J., Abbott, R. D., Wolz, M., Wolf, P. A., & White, L. R. (1990). Longitudinally measured blood pressure, antihypertensive medication use, and cognitive performance: The Framingham Study. *Journal of Clinical Epidemiology, 43,* 475–480.

Farmer, M. E., White, L. R., Abbott, R. D., Kittner, S. J., Kaplan, E., Wolz, M. M., Brody, J. A., & Wolf, P. A. (1987). Blood pressure and cognitive performance: The Framingham study. *American Journal of Epidemiology, 126,* 1103–1114.

Farmer, M. E., White, L. R., Kittner, S. J., Kaplan, E., Moes, E., McNamara, P., Wolz, M. M., Wolf, P. A., & Feinleib, M. (1987). Neuropsychological test performance in Framingham: A descriptive study. *Psychological Reports, 60,* 1023–1040.

Gifford, R. W. (1989). Core organ effects: Part II. Cerebral. In H. A. Punzi, & W. Framenbaum (Eds.), *Clinical cardiovascular therapeutics: Vol. 1. Hypertension* (pp. 65–81). Mt. Kisco, NY: Futura.

Hosmer, D. W., & Lemeshow, L. (1989). *Applied logistic regression.* New York: Wiley.

Llabre, M. M., Ironson, G. H., Spitzer, S. B., Gellman, M. D., Weidler, D. J., & Schneiderman, N. (1988). How many blood pressure measurements are enough? An application of generalizability theory to the study of blood pressure reliability. *Psychophysiology, 25,* 97–106.

McArdle, J. J., Hamagami, A., Elias, M. F., & Robbins, M. A. (1991). Structural modeling of mixed longitudinal and cross-sectional data. *Experimental Aging Research, 17,* 29–51.

Muldoon, M. F., Manuck, S. B., Shapiro, A. P., & Waldstein, S. R. (1991). Neurobehavioral effects of antihypertensive medications. *Journal of Hypertension, 9,* 549–559.

Muldoon, M. F., Waldstein, S. R., & Jennings, J. R. (1995). Neuropsychological consequences of antihypertensive medications. *Experimental Aging Research, 21,* 353–368.

Phillips, S. J., & Whisnant, J. P. (1992). Hypertension and the brain. *Archives of Internal Medicine, 157,* 938–945.

Rogosa, D., Brandt, D., & Zimowski, M. (1982). A growth curve approach to the measurement of change. *Psychological Bulletin, 90,* 726–748.

Salerno, J. A., Murphy, D. G. M., Horwitz, B., DeCarli, C., Haxby, J. V., Rappoport, S. I., & Schapiro, M. B. (1992). Brain atrophy in hypertension: A volumetric magnetic resonance imaging study. *Hypertension, 20,* 340–348.

Sands, L. P., & Meredith, W. (1992). Blood pressure and intellectual functioning in late mid-life. *Journal of Gerontology, 47,* P81–P84.

Schultz, N. R., Jr., Elias, M. F., Robbins, M. A., Steeten, D. H. P., & Blakeman, N. (1989). A longitudinal study of performance of hypertensive and normotensive subjects on the Wechsler Adult Intelligence Scale. *Psychology and Aging, 4,* 496–499.

Siegler, I. C. (1975). The terminal drop hypothesis: Fact or artifact? *Experimental Aging Research, 1,* 169–174.

Siegler, I. C., & Botwinick, G. W. (1979). A long term longitudinal study of intellectual ability of older adults. The matter of selective subject attrition. *Journal of Gerontology, 34,* 242–245.

Streeten, D. H. P., & Anderson, G. H., Jr. (1988). Hypertension: Relating drug therapy to pathogenetic mechanisms. *Progress in Drug Research, 32,* 175–193.

Waldstein, S. R. (1995). Hypertension and neuropsychological function: A lifespan perspective. *Experimental Aging Research, 21,* 321–352.

Waldstein, S. R., Manuck, S. B., Ryan, C. M., & Muldoon, M. F. (1991). Neuropsychological correlates of hypertension: Review and methodologic considerations. *Psychological Bulletin, 110,* 451–468.

Waldstein, S. R., Ryan, C. M., Manuck, S. B., Parkinson, D. K., & Bromet, E. G. (1991). Learning and memory function in men with untreated blood pressure elevation. *Journal of Consulting and Clinical Psychology, 59,* 513–517.

Wilkie, F. L., & Eisdorfer, C. (1971). Intelligence and blood pressure in the aged. *Science, 172,* 959–962.

Wilkie, F. L., & Eisdorfer, C., & Nowlin, J. B. (1976). Memory and blood pressure in the aged. *Experimental Aging Research, 2,* 3–16.

Willett, J. B. (1988/1989). Questions and answers in the measurement of change. *Review of Research in Education, 15,* 345–422.

van Sweiten, J. C., Geyskes, G. G., Drix, M. M. A., Beeck, B. M., Ramos, L. M. P., van Latum, J. C., & van Gijn, J. (1991). Hypertension in the elderly is associated with white matter lesions and cognitive deficits. *Annals of Neurology, 30,* 825–830.

14

Uncertain Health Effects of Cholesterol Reduction in the Elderly

Matthew F. Muldoon
University of Pittsburgh School of Medicine

Jay R. Kaplan
Bowman Gray University School of Medicine

Stephen B. Manuck
University of Pittsburgh

Coronary heart disease (CHD) remains the leading single cause of death in the United States, and elevated serum cholesterol is the most widely recognized risk factor for myocardial infarction and CHD death. Furthermore, a large body of experimental evidence supports acceptance of hypercholesterolemia as a causal and reversible (i.e., treatable) agent in coronary artery arthersclerosis. Acknowledging the potential benefit of, and widespread need for, cholesterol-lowering interventions, the National Cholesterol Education Program has issued guidelines for the treatment of severe as well as mild hypercholesterolemia, particularly in persons with other CHD risk factors (Summary of the second report of the National Cholesterol Education Program, 1993). According to recent estimates, some 52 million adults (29% of the population) qualify for targeted dietary treatment (Sempos et al., 1993). Assuming a 10% reduction in cholesterol with diet modification, it is estimated that 7%, or 13 million would also require long-term drug therapy to reach their goal reductions in cholesterol level. Because cholesterol levels tend to increase with age, a preponderance of the general population targeted for dietary and phamacologic treatment is over 65 years of age.

Justification for such widespread and long-term cholesterol-lowering interventions rests largely on evidence from randomized clinical trials of cholesterol reduction—both primary and secondary prevention trials (which enroll healthy individuals and persons having manifest CHD, respectively). However, meta-analyses have raised doubts about the wisdom of current recommendations (Davey-Smith & Pekkanen, 1992; Muldoon, Manuck, & Matthews, 1990). The six major, randomized, primary prevention trials completed before 1990 had a total of nearly 120,000 subjects, predominantly men between 40 and 60 years of age, and involved the use of cholesterol-lowering diets, drugs, or both for an average of 5 years. Whereas treatment reduced CHD mortality by a modest 15%, this CHD benefit was offset by an increase in non-CHD mortality. Specifically, cancer deaths increased by 43%, and nonillness mortality (NIM; deaths from suicides, accidents, and violence) increased by a striking 76%. In absolute terms these opposing treatment effects negated one another, and total mortality was essentially unchanged.

Many investigators consider these latter findings to be spurious. First, there were relatively few deaths in each trial, and the cancer and NIM excesses reach statistical significance only on meta-analysis. Second, no biologic mechanism is readily available to explain any increase in non-CHD deaths with cholesterol lowering. Finally, recently completed trials using a new class of cholesterol-lowering agents (the HMG CoA reductase inhibitors) have revealed a significant reduction in heart disease mortality without any notable increase in non-CHD deaths (Shepherd et al., 1995; Randomised, 1994).

Nonetheless, the meta-analyses of clinical trials do raise doubts about the net health effects of cholesterol reduction in initially healthy, nonelderly men. How cholesterol lowering affects the elderly is even less clear because few such individuals have been enrolled in trials completed to date. In the absence of such data, this chapter examines the probable impact of cholesterol-lowering interventions in the elderly on CHD, non-CHD, and NIM based on information derived from epidemiologic observations, clinical studies, and populations samples with psychological assessments. The focus is on persons free of heart disease (i.e., primary prevention), because a net health and longevity benefit of cholesterol reduction from secondary prevention has been established.

CHOLESTEROL AND AGING

Total serum cholesterol levels gradually rise from childhood through adulthood. Cross-sectional studies indicate that cholesterol tends to peak in both sexes at around age 60 (Fig. 14.1; Fulwood et al., 1986), With further aging, cholesterol levels tend to decline (Ettinger et al., 1992). Prospective data corroborate these age and gender patterns, and the data further reveal that body mass index changes in parallel with cholesterol levels (Wilson, Anderson, Harris, Kannel, & Castelli, 1994). Therefore, the rise in cholesterol during adulthood and the fall after age 60 may be attributable, in part, to weight change. Although there is evidence that hypocholesterolemia (cholesterol < mg/dl) increases in prevalence between 65 and 85 years of age (Manolio et al., 1992), other data suggest that individuals who reach age 80 in good health tend to have "normal" cholesterol levels—without overrepresentation of either hypo- or hypercholesterolemia (Schaefer et al., 1989).

Given these age-related changes in serum lipids, it is clear that application of the National Cholesterol Education Program guidelines will identify more middle-aged-to-elderly than nonelderly individuals for cholesterol-lowering treatment. In this regard, Sempos and colleagues have estimated that among men and women in age groups 55–64, 65–74, and over 74, fully 50% are candidates for cholesterol reduction (Sempos et al., 1993).

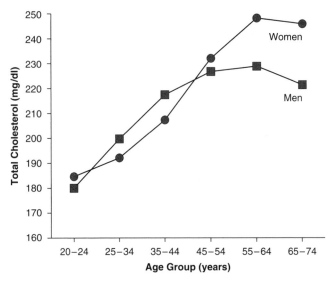

FIG. 14.1.   Mean serum cholesterol levels by sex and age. Data from the second National health and Nutrition Examination (Fulwood, 1986).

A public health demonstration project evaluated the efficacy of community-based cholesterol-lowering interventions in elderly individuals (Greenblatt-Ives, Kuller, & Traven, 1993). Some 1,200 ambulatory, non-institutionalized men and women 65 to 79 years of age with serum cholesterol levels over 240 mg/dl were randomly assigned to health screenings and promotion services at local hospitals and clinics, or to a control group. The intervention was provided in free appointments, which were attended by approximately half the intervention group subjects. Results revealed that after 2 to 3 years, neither the intervention group as a whole nor those actually attending the intervention sessions had lower cholesterol levels than those of the control group. Only active drug treatment significantly reduced serum cholesterol concentration. The authors concluded that aggressive treatment (i.e., with drugs) is required to meaningfully lower cholesterol in elderly, hypercholesterolemic individuals.

CORONARY HEART DISEASE

In young and middle aged men, relative hypercholesterolemia is known to convey increased risk of heart disease. Furthermore, the relationship between cholesterol and CHD risk is graded (Stamler, Wentworth, & Neaton, 1986), and high cholesterol remains a risk factor in men with manifest CHD (Pekkanen et al., 1990) and in countries where the mean cholesterol concentration is relatively low (Chen et al., 1991). In addition, elevated serum cholesterol has been associated with preclinical atherosclerotic plaques in the carotid, femoral and coronary arteries (Giral et al., 1991; Pathological, Determinants of Atherosclerosis in Youth Research Group, 1990).

Separation of total cholesterol into lipoprotein fractions has permitted important refinement of the relationship between serum lipids and atherosclerotic disease. Low density lipoprotein (LDL) cholesterol, although closely correlated with total cholesterol, appears to be a stronger predictor of CHD. Equally impressive is the robust and independent, inverse relationship between high density lipoprotein (HDL) cholesterol and CHD, whereas the role of elevated triglyceride levels in coronary atherosclerosis remains controversial. Recent data suggest that HDL and triglycerides assume more importance in women than men and, conversely, that elevated LDL cholesterol is an inconsistent predictor of heart disease in women (Manolio et al., 1992; Miller-Bass, Newschaffer, Klag, & Bush, 1993).

In both genders, the relationship between either total or LDL cholesterol and CHD risk declines substantially with age. Among the 316,099
white men screened for the Multiple Risk Factors Intervention Trial and
followed for 12 years, the slope of increasing relative risk with increasing cholesterol flattens noticeably between ages 35–39 and 55–57 (Fig.
14.2; Neaton & Wentworth, 1992). This declining relative risk with aging
is now well recognized but is offset, in part, by the high absolute incidence of CHD in the elderly. The term "attributable risk" denotes the
actual number of CHD events in a population that are attributable to
serum cholesterol levels; the magnitude of attributable risk reflects the
net influence of both relative risk and overall disease rate in the population. According to some calculations, the attributable risk of hypercholesterolemia increases with aging.

Nonetheless, several published reports indicate that sometime between
age 60 and 80 the increased risk of CHD associated with hypercholesterolemia falls to zero, in both relative or absolute terms. Among such
studies, analysis of the Framingham heart Study data (Kronmal, Cain, Ye,

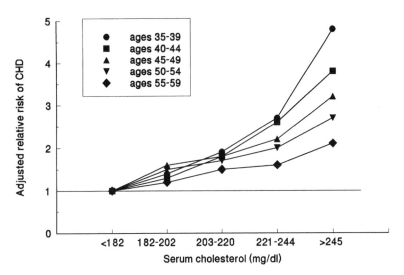

FIG. 14.2.   Age-specific relative risk estimates by quintile of
serum cholesterol. Data from 12-year follow-up of 316,099 white
men age 35 to 57 years at baseline who were screened for the
Multiple Risk Factors Intervention Trial. Reprinted from "Health
effects of serum cholesterol reduction: The potential for good and
the potential for harm," by M.F. Muldoon, L.J. Bonci, V. Rodriguez,
J.R. Kaplan, and S.B. Manuck, 1994, Medicine, Exercise, Nutrition,
and Health, 3, p. 75.

& Omenn, 1993) revealed that "The relationship with CHD mortality was significantly positive at ages 40, 50, and 60 years but attenuated with age until the relationship was positive but insignificant at age 70 years and negative but insignificant at 80 years." In the Lipid Research Clinics Follow-Up Study, whereas individuals age 30 to 59 years and dying from CHD had higher cholesterol levels than did survivors of similar age, those between 60 and 79 years succumbing to heart disease had cholesterol levels indistinguishable from those of elderly subjects not dying from heart disease (Grover, Palmer, & Coupal, 1994). Similar null findings in an elderly sample have been reported for prevalent heart disease (Ettinger et al., 1992). In a representative community sample of 1,000 adults over 70 years of age living in New Haven, Connecticut, a total serum cholesterol level over 240 mg/dl did not convey increased risk of CHD mortality in men or women—in fact, the most CHD deaths tended to occur in individuals with a cholesterol level under 200 mg/dl (Krumholz et al., 1994). Among elderly hypertensive participants (mean age 72 years) in trial of antihypertensive medication, cholesterol level was a significant *inverse* predictor of heart disease mortality (Staesson et al., 1990).

The declining value cholesterol as a risk factor for heart disease in the elderly has several possible causes. First, changes in the arterial wall with aging may reduce its vulnerability to the pathogenic effects of hypercholesterolemia. Second, as a result of selective survival, persons with high cholesterol levels who reach old age may be resistant to the effects of their hypercholesterolemia. Third, weight loss (as may occur from many chronic diseases) lowers cholesterol levels and may confound cholesterol–CHD relationships. Harris, Feldman, et al. (1992) examined this latter hypothesis in a national sample of approximately 2,200 men and women age 65 to 74 years and found that in fact among elderly not reporting weight loss, the relationship between cholesterol level and CHD was as strong as in younger individuals. This suggests that high cholesterol may continue to be a CHD risk factor in the healthy elderly.

NON-CHD AND TOTAL MORTALITY

Compared to research relating serum cholesterol to CHD, whether cholesterol level correlates with, or contributes to, non-CHD illness and death has received little attention, either in epidemiologic research or in laboratory investigations. This is beginning to change following the publication of data revealing inverse relationships between serum cholesterol levels and non-CHD mortality. Figuring most prominently is the Report of the Conference on Low Blood Cholesterol: Mortality Associations (Jacobs et al., 1992). In this cooperative analysis of 19 prospective cohorts comprised of approximately 650,000 men and women, Jacobs and colleagues examined a variety of causes of death among participants with low cholesterol levels, defined as less than 160 mg/dl, in relation to those with cholesterol levels between 160 and 199 mg/dl. In hypercholesterolemic men, the risk of cancer death was increased by approximately 20%, respiratory death by 16%, and digestive disease death by 55%, and the risk of death from residual medical causes increased by about 60%.

Whether these associations reflect causal relationships, or epiphenomena, or are owing to confounding, remains highly controversial. Controlling for smoking, alcohol consumption, and weight seems to leave the findings unaltered. These low-cholesterol–mortality associations also persist after excluding deaths occurring during the first 5 years of follow-up (in an attempt to remove persons from analysis who had any pre-existing serious illness). As note earlier, meta-analysis of randomized, primary prevention clinical trials has revealed an increase in non-CHD mortality, with cancer deaths increased by approximately 40% over the average 5-year treatment period. Again, however, trials using statin-class medications have not found an increase in non-CHD mortality with cholesterol lowering.

The reciprocal epidemiologic associations described previously merge to create a complex and nonlinear relationship between cholesterol level and total mortality. In men, high levels of cholesterol are associated with increased overall mortality owing to elevates rates of cardiovascular disease, and low cholesterol levels are associated with increased mortality because of elevated rates of death from noncardiovascular causes, including cancer, liver and lung diseases, and NIM. The cholesterol–total mortality pattern consequently assumes a Ushape (Fig. 14.3; Jacobs et al., 1992). In women, total mortality tends to decline with increasing cholesterol levels, without an identifiable rise even in individuals with frank hypercholesterolemia (Jacobs et al., 1992; Miller-Bass et al., 1993). Using data from the Honolulu Heart Study, Frank, Reed, Grove, and Benfante (1992) modeled the effect of widespread cholesterol reduction and concluded that none of three intervention strategies modelled would significantly after total mortality—that is, heart disease reductions would be offset by increases in non-CHD mortality.

Low-cholesterol–non-CHD mortality associations appear to be stronger in the elderly than in middle aged adults (Harris, Kleinman, Makuc, Gillum, & Feldman, 1992). To the extent that the risk of heart dis-

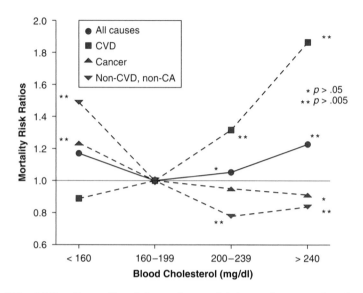

FIG. 14.3. Proportional hazards model hazard rate ratios for cause-specific mortality relative to total cholesterol 160–199 mg/dl. Data from 12-year follow-up of 350,977 men age 35–57 years at baseline (Jacobs, 1992). Excludes deaths occurring less than 5 years after study baseline. Adjusted for age, diastolic blood pressure, cigarette smoking, body mass index, and alcohol consumption (where available). CVD indicates cardiovascular disease, and CA indicates cancer. * and ** indicate $p < .05$ and $p < .005$, respectively compared with total cholesterol 160–199 mg/dl. Reprinted from "Health effects of serum cholesterol reduction: The potential for good and th potential for harm," by M.F. Muldoon, L.J. Bonci, V. Rodriguez, J.R. Kaplan, and S.B. Manuck, 1994, *Medicine, Exercise, Nutrition and Health, 3,* p. 79.

ease attributable to hypercholesterolemia declines after age 70, the U-shaped total mortality curve tends to become negative. Five small studies of elderly nursing home residents and one clinical trial of antihypertensive medications in patients age 60 or over found cholesterol level to be inversely related to all-cause mortality (Forette, Tortrat, & Wolmark, 1989; Rudman et al., 1988; Rudman, Mattson, Feller, & Nagraj, 1989; Staesson et al., 1990; Verdery & Goldberg, 1991). More edifying, however, is the analysis by Kronmal et al. (1993) of Framingham Heart Study data. The authors studied changes in cholesterol–mortality associations between 40 and 80 years of age using Cox proportional hazard regression to adjust for covariates and other risk factors. As illustrated in Fig. 14.4, total mortality increases with advancing age as expected. Notably, high

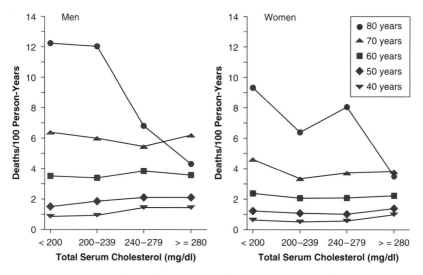

FIG. 14.4.   Crude total mortality within age categories by sex and serum cholesterol interval. Data from the Framingham Heart Study (Kronmal et al., 1993).

cholesterol transitions from being an indicator of increased mortality risk in persons 40 years of age to being as apparent marker of good prognosis in the very old. Using these same data to model the effects of a 50 mg/dl reduction in cholesterol on cause-specific and total mortality (Fig. 14.5), we see that the projected health benefits enjoyed by young adults are lost in the elderly, in whom life expectancy may actually be shortened by cholesterol reduction.

The critical assumption made in these latter analyses is that low or lowered cholesterol levels cause non-CHD deaths. Many investigators contend, however, that low cholesterol is merely a marker (or epiphenomenon) reflecting poor health or chronic disease in some portion of the population—and that the portion grows with aging. For example, in nursing home studies low cholesterol has been linked to mild anemia, enteral feedings, and high while cell count, suggesting that hypercholesterolemia is an index of protein-calorie malnutrition and infection (Rudman et al., 1988; Rudman et al., 1989; Verdery & Goldberg, 1991). Some epidemiologic data suggest that the association between low cholesterol level and total mortality is confounded by falling cholesterol level, itself a predictor of mortality risk (Anderson, Castelli, & Levy, 1987), or is limited to persons with low activity levels and recent weight loss (Davey-Smith, Shipley, Marmot, & Rose, 1992; Harris, Kleinman, et al., 1992).

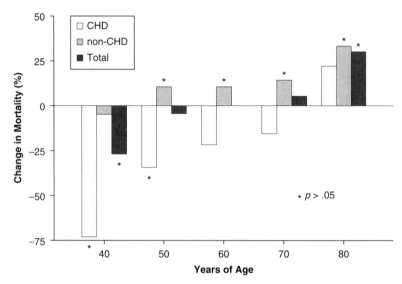

FIG. 14.5.   Percentage change in mortality associated with a 50
mg/dl decline in cholesterol by age group and cause of death.
Estimated from a Cox model adjusting for sex, blood pressure,
body mass index, and smoking. Data from Kronmal (1993).

Although not entirely consistent, there is evidence that compared to
those with normal cholesterol levels, elderly hypercholesterolemic individuals have poorer overall health and, somewhat surprisingly, a greater
prevalence of diabetes (Franzblau & Criqui, 1984; Greenblatt-Ives,
Bonino, Traven, & Kuller 1993; Manolio et al., 1993). On the other hand,
among women nursing home residents, low cholesterol was associated
with increased mortality after controlling for age, weight, renal function,
plasma proteins, and prevalent cancer (Forette et al., 1989). Similarly,
Kronmal's findings were not materially changed by excluding deaths
occurring in the first 4 years after cholesterol level determination, adjustment for falling cholesterol, and exclusion of subjects with very low cholesterol (< 160/mg/dl; Kronmal et al., 1993).

NON-ILLNESS MORTALITY

Finally, evidence has recently emerged indicating that low or lowered cholesterol may be associated with increased mortality from suicides, accidents, and violence. Indeed, this literature has expanded substantially since
a comprehensive review in 1993 (Muldoon et al., 1993). Extensive epidemiologic studies by Jacobs et al. (1992), Lindberg, Rastam, Gullberg,

and Eklund (1992), and Neaton and Wentworth (1992) each found that men with particularly low serum cholesterol levels experienced elevated mortality from suicides, accidents, and violence (Fig. 14.6). A similar relationship appears to exist in women, although it is not statistically significant. Published negative studies either tend to be smaller than the positive investigations (Pekkanen, Nissinen, Punsar, & Karvonen, 1989) or to have examined populations with high average cholesterol levels (Vartiainen et al., 1994). In studies reporting subcategories of NIM separately, suicide in particular is associated with naturally low cholesterol levels (Lindberg et al., 1992; Neaton & Wentworth, 1992). Primary, prevention cholesterol-lowering trials completed before 1990 have revealed a 70% increase in NIM among treated men. Trials employing cholesterol-lowering diets find an increase in NIM (Muldoon et al., 1990) whereas those using statin-class medications have not.

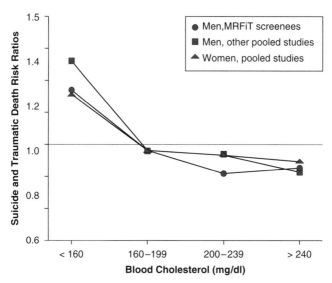

FIG. 14.6.   Hazard rate ratios for suicide and trauma mortality relative to total cholesterol 160–199 mg/dl. Data from 9 to 30 year follow-up of (a) 350,977 men screened for the Multiple Risk Factors Interventions Trial, (b) 172,760 men from 18 other pooled studies, and (c) 124,814 women from 11 pooled studies (Jacobs, 1992). Excludes deaths occurring less than 5 years after study baseline. Adjusted for age, diastolic blood pressure, cigarette smoking, body mass index, and alcohol consumption (where available). Reprinted from "Health effects of serum cholesterol reduction: The potential for good and the potential for harm," by M.F. Muldoon, L.J. Bonci, V. Rodriguez, J.R. Kaplan, and S.B. Manuck, 1994, *Medicine, Exercise, Nutrition and Health, 3*, p. 82.

Several questions regarding mechanism immediately emerge; indeed, this purported association between serum lipid levels and "behavioral" mortality is as perplexing as any of the cholesterol–non-CHD illness associations yet discussed. Were we to discover that hypercholesterolemia co-occurs with behaviors such as alcoholism, or with psychopathology such as depression, factors known to be associated with suicide and violence, then the epidemiologic findings might have some credible basis. Still, important questions regarding direction of causality would remain. Alternatively, if controlled experiments of cholesterol lowering were to reveal some treatment effects on precursors of suicide and risk-taking behavior, then psychological models and neurophysiological mechanisms could be developed and explored. Such research is important to the health of the elderly, particularly elderly men, because of their high suicide rate (Holinger, 1987).

Neurobehavioral Correlates
of Low or Lowered Cholesterol

The first paper describing analyses of cholesterol levels and depression in a nonpatient sample appeared in 1993. Several other reports followed, with several enrolling elderly subjects. Morgan, Palinkas, Barrett-Connor, and Wingard (1993) studied a group of 1,020 men between 50 and 89 years of age. Categorical depression defined as a Beck Depression Index ≥ 13 was associated with hypocholesterolemia in men over age 70, whereas no relationship was observed in younger men. Control for indices of poor physical health (number of chronic diseases, number of medications, exercise) did not alter the findings.

A follow-up study used the Center for Epidemiologic Studies' Depression Scale in nearly 4,000 elderly men and women (Brown et al., 1994). Although it replicated the earlier findings of increased depression with low cholesterol level primarily in the very elderly, this second investigation found that multivariate analysis including self-report general health and physical functioning substantially weakened the association. The meaning of the latter finding is unclear to the extent that depression and self-reported general health are anticipated to covary. A third study enrolling an elderly population cohort failed to find any relationship between serum cholesterol level and depression (McCallum, Simons, Simons, & Friedlander, 1994).

Two nonelderly population samples were studied with either a simple emotional health questionnaire (Lindberg, Larsson, Setterlind, & Rastam, 1994) or the Minnesota Multiphasic Personality Inventory (Freedman et al., 1995). The former, but not the latter, found low cholesterol to be associated with depression. Glueck and colleagues (1994) reported that 203 individuals hospitalized with major depression had much lower cholesterol concentrations than did age- and sex-matched controls, although data on diet and weight were lacking. Similar trends were observed in some (Maes et al., 1994; Oxenkrug, Branconnier, Harto-Traux, & Cole, 1983), but not all (Swartz, 1990), similar studies of patients with depression. preliminary evidence suggests that schizophrenic patients may have unusually low cholesterol levels, particularly if the patients are withdrawn or drug resistant (Brice, 1935; Reveley, Zafar, & Dursunm, 1994; Sletten, Nilsen, Young, & Anderson, 1964).

Serum cholesterol levels averaged 192 mg/dl among 331 suicide attempters, compared with 210 mg/dl in 331 nonpsychiatric controls matched for age, sex, an drug and alcohol abuse ($p < 0.001$; Gallerani et al., 1995). In psychiatric patient groups, low serum cholesterol has been associated with suicidal ideation or prior attempts (Modai, Valevski, Dror, & Weizman, 1994; Sullivan, Joyce, Bulik, Mulder, & Oakley-Browne, 1994) and serious suicide attempts in men (Golier, Marzuk, Leon, Weiner, & Tardiff, 1995). Nonetheless, negative studies exist (Fritze, Schneider, & Lanczik, 1992), and none has controlled for dietary factors or specifically examined suicidal impulses in the elderly.

With respect to the epidemiologic link between cholesterol level and trauma mortality, hostility and anger as personality traits are more typically related to hyper- rather than to hypercholesterolemia (Dujovne & Houston, 1991; Marmot, 1991; Waldstein, Polefrone, Muldoon, & Manuck, 1993; Weidner, Sexton, McLellan, Connor, & Matarazzo, 1987). However, actual acts of aggression have been associated with low serum cholesterol. hatch and colleagues found low cholesterol levels among jailed prisoners (Hatch et al., 1966), and Vikkunen reported that among homicidal offenders, those with habitual violence while under the influence of alcohol had lower cholesterol levels than did other offenders (Virkkunen, 1983). Subsequent brief reports lend support to these findings (Hillbrand & Foster, 1993; Spitz, 1994; Virkkunen & Penttinen, 1984). Finally, antisocial personality disorder was associated with relative hypocholesterolemia in two of three studies (Freedman et al., 1995; Stewart & Stewart, 1981; Virkkunen, 1979).

Experimental evidence concerning the neurobehavioral effects of cholesterol reduction is limited to a series of dietary investigations in nonhuman primates and several clinical studies. Kaplan and colleagues have published three appears in which cynomolgus macaques were fed either a "luxury" (cholesterol-elevating) died or "prudent" (cholesterol-lowering) diet. The first study revealed that among a variety of behaviors sampled over 22 months in adult males, only contact aggression differed between dietary conditions ($p > 0.03$), with prudent diet monkeys initiating more aggression than luxury diet monkeys (Kaplan, Manuck, & Shively, 1991). In a second study, the fenfluramine challenge test was employed as an indirect measure of brain serotonergic activity, and the investigators found the hypothesized lower prolactin responses to fenfluramine among prudent diet animals (Muldoon, Kaplan, Manuck, & Mann, 1992). Finally, relative to their high cholesterol diet counterparts, juvenile male and female monkeys consuming a low cholesterol diet were observed to be more aggressive and less affiliative and to have lower cerebrospinal fluid concentrations of 5-hydroxyindoleacetic acid (the serotonin metabolite; Kaplan et al., 1994).

With respect to cholesterol lowering in the clinical setting, four uncontrolled reports indicate that cholesterol-lowering drugs may increase depression (Duits, 1993; Ernst, 1994; Ketterer, Brymer, Rhoads, Krafts, & Goldberg, 1994; Lechleitner, 1992). Conversely, preliminary evidence from placebo-controlled, double blind studies suggests that such treatment does not alter self-reported quality of life (Downs, Oster, & Santanello, 1993), or increase hostility (Kostis, Rosen, & Wilson, 1994; Strandberg et al., 1994). Interesting preliminary evidence associates cholesterol-lowering medication with a mild decline in some aspects of neuropsychological performance (Muldoon, 1997; Roth, 1992). In related research, two unblinded investigations of elderly patients with severe hypertriglyceridemia found that treatment with gembrozil improved depression scores (Glueck et al., 1993) and dementia ratings (Rogers, Meyer, McClintic, & Mortel, 1989).

CONCLUSION

CHD is the leading cause of death in persons over 65 years of age (U.S. Senate Subcommittee on Aging, 1991), and cholesterol reduction is the most widely recognized preventive strategy for reducing the burden of CHD. Current treatment recommendations target individuals with known heart disease, hypercholesterolemia, and multiple other risk factors. Many elderly meet one of these criteria such that recent estimates indicate that more than 60% of the elderly population are advised to engage in long-term cholesterol-lowering interventions (Garber, 1991). Nonetheless, as outlined here, there are numerous reasons to cautiously approach cholesterol lowering in the elderly.

Does hypercholesterolemia promote coronary atherosclerosis in the elderly? Whether yes or no, is cholesterol lowering effective in preventing CHD events in the elderly? Are the cutpoints for treatment used in nonelderly adults also appropriate guidelines for individuals over 65 years of age? Can we afford to pay for the treatment of so many millions of individuals?

In terms of total health and well-being, what is the optimal cholesterol level, and does this value change with age? Because non-CHD causes of death have been linked to low serum cholesterol, might relative hypercholesterolemia correspond with "nutritional robustness" and provide some adaptive advantage in resisting life-threatening non-CHD illness (Jacobs, Muldoon, & Rastam, 1995)? If so, does cholesterol lowering increase non-CHD morbidity or mortality, or both? Does low or lowered cholesterol affect mood or impulse control, and does treatment cause more depressive illness or suicide? What is the net balance between beneficial and adverse health effects of such cholesterol lowering in the elderly?

In one sense, the last decade has brought substantial advances in researchers' broadening appreciation of the roles of serum lipids in health and disease. However, with many lines of research still in their infancies, this new knowledge has done more to expand the list of questions than to provide answers. This may be more true of the elderly than of any other segment of the population. At present, differences of opinion exist regarding the role of cholesterol lowering to prevent CHD in the elderly. Some advise widespread cholesterol-lowering interventions (LaRosa, 1995). However, treatment costs would be great and other CHD risk reducing interventions may be more cost-effective (Avins, 1996). We espouse the conclusion of Garber, Littenberg, Sox, Wagner, and Gluck (1991) in their review of the cost and health consequences of cholesterol screening in the elderly:

> If guidelines that were developed for the general adult population were strictly applied to the elderly, billions of dollars will be spent each year for an intervention whose effectiveness has not been tested. We can be more confident of the success of our efforts to improve and to prolong the lives of older Americans if we devote our resources to interventions whose effectiveness is not in doubt. (p. 1094)

ACKNOWLEDGMENTS

Supported in part by National Institutes of Health grants HL 46328 and HL 40962.

REFERENCES

Anderson, K.M., Castelli, W.P., & Levy, D. (1987). Cholesterol and mortality. *Journal of the American Medical Association, 257* (16), 2176–2180.

Avins, A.L., Browner, W.S. (1996). Lowering risk without lowering cholesterol: Implications for national cholesterol policy. Ann Intern Med 125:502–506.

Boston, P.F., Durson, S.M., Zafar, M.A. Serum cholesterol and treatment-resistance in schizophrenia. Biol Psychiatry 1996;40:452–543.

Brice, A.T. (1935). The blood fats in schizophrenia. *Journal of Nervous and Mental Disease, 81* (6), 613–632.

Brown, S.L., Salive, M.E., Harris, T.B., Simonsick, E.M., Guarankik, J.M., & Kohout, F.J., (1994). Low cholesterol concentrations and severe depressive symptoms in elderly people. *British Medical Journal, 308,* 1328–1332.

Chen, Z., Peto, R., Collins, R., MacMahon, S., Lu, J., & Li, W. (1991). Serum cholesterol concentration and coronary heart disease in population with low cholesterol concentrations. *British Medical Journal, 303,* 276–282.

Davey-Smith, G., Shipley, M.J., Marmot, M.G., & Rose, G. (1992). Plasma cholesterol concentration and mortality. *Journal of the American Medical Association, 267,* 70–76.

Davey-Smith, G.D., & Pekkanen, J. (1992). Should there be a moratorium on the use of cholesterol lowering drugs? *British Medical Journal, 304,* 431–434.

Downs, R., Oster, G., & Santanello, N.C. (1993). HMG CoA reductase inhibitors and quality of life. *Journal of the American Medical Association, 269* (24), 3107–3108.

Duits, N. (1993). Depressive symptoms and cholesterol-lowering drugs. *The Lancet, 341,* 114.

Dujovne, V.F., & Houston, B.K. (1991). Hostility-related variables and plasma lipid levels. *Journal of Behavioral Medicine, 14* (6), 555–565.

Ernst, E., Saradeth, T., Seidl, S., Resh, K.L., & Frischenschlager, O. (1994). Cholesterol and depression. *Archives of Internal Medicine, 154,* 1166.

Ettinger, W.H., Wahl, P.W., Kuller, L.H., Bush, T.L., Tracy, R.P., Manolio, T.A., Borhani, N.O., Wong, N.D., & OïLeary, D.H. (1992). Lipoprotein lipids in older people. *Circulation, 86* (3), 858–869.

Forette, B., Tortrat, D., & Wolmark, Y. (1989). Cholesterol as risk factor for mortality in elderly women. *The Lancet,* 868–870.

Frank, J.W., Reed, D.M., Grove, J.S., & Benfante, R. (1992). Will lowering population levels of serum cholesterol affect total mortality? *Journal of Clinical Epidemiology, 45* (4), 333–346.

Franzblau, A., & Criqui, M.H. (1984). Characteristics of persons with marked hypercholesterolemia: A population-based study. *Journal of Chronic Disease, 37* (5), 387–395.

Freedman, D.S., Byers, T., Barrett, D.H., Stroup, N.E., Eaker, E., & Monroe-Blum, H. (1995). Plasma lipid levels and psychologic characteristics in men. *American Journal of Epidemiology, 141,* 507–517.

Fritze, J., Schneider, B., & Lanczik, M. (1992). Autoaggressive behavior and cholesterol. *Neuropsychobiology, 26,* 180–181.

Fulwood, R., Kalsbeck, W., Rifkind, B., Russell-Briefel, R. Muesing, R., LaRosa, J., & Lippel, K. (1986). *Total serum cholesterol levels of adults 20–74 years of age* (Vital and Health Statistics, Publication No. (PHS): pp. 86–1686). Washington, DC: U.S. Department of Health and Human Services.

Gallerani, M., Manfredini, R., Caracciolo, S., Scapoli, C., Molinari, S., & Fersini, C. (1995). Serum cholesterol concentrations in parasuicide. *British Medical Journal, 310,* 632–636.

Garber, A.M., Littenberg, B., Sox, H.C., Wagner, J.L., & Gluck, M. (1991). Costs and health consequences of cholesterol screening for asymptomatic older Americans. *Archives of Internal Medicine, 151,* 1089–1095.

Giral, P., Pithois-Merli, I., Filitti, V., Levenson, J., Plainfosse, M.C., Mainardi, C., & Simon, A.C. (1991). Prevention Cardio-casculaire en Medecine du Travail METRA Group. Risk factors and early extracoronary atherosclerotic plaques detected by three-site ultrasound imaging in hyperc-holesterolemic men. *Archives of Internal Medicine, 151,* 950–956.

Glueck, C.H., Tieger, M., Kunkel R., Hamer, T., Tracy, T., & Spiers, J. (1994). Hypercholesterolemia and affective disorders. *American Journal of Medical Science, 308* (4), 218–225.

Glueck, C.H., Tieger, M., Kunkel, R., Tracy, T., Spiers, J., Streicher, P., & Illig, E. (1993). Improvement in symptoms of depression and in an index of life stressors accompany treatment of severe hypertriglyceridemia. *Biological Psychiatry, 34*, 240–252.

Golier, J.A., Marzuk, P.M., Leon, A.C., Weiner, C., & Tardiff, K. (1995). Low serum cholesterol level and attempted suicide. *American Journal of Psychiatry, 52* (3), 419–423.

Greenblatt-Ives, D., Bonino, P., Traven, N.D., & Kuller, L.H. (1993). Morbidity and mortality in rural community-dwelling elderly with low total serum cholesterol. *Journal of Gerontology, 48* (3), M103–M107.

Greenblatt-Ives, D., Kuller, L.H., & Traven, N.D. (1993). Use and outcomes of a cholesterol-lowering intervention for rural elderly subjects. *American Journal of Preventive Medicine, 9* (5), 274–281.

Grover, S.A., Palmer, C.S., & Coupal, L. (1994). Serum lipid screening to identify high-risk individuals for coronary death. *Archives of Internal Medicine, 154*, 679–684.

Harris, T., Feldman, J.J., Kleinman, J.C., Ettinger, W.H., Makuc, D.M., & Schatzkin, A.G., (1992). The low cholesterol–mortality association in a national cohort. *Journal of Clinical Epidemiology, 45*, 595–601.

Harris, T., Kleinman, J.C. Makuc, D.M., Gillum, R., & Feldman, J.J. (1992). Is weight loss a modifier of the cholesterol–heart disease relationship in older persons? Data from the NHANES I epidemiologic follow-up study. *Annals of Epidemiology, 2*, 35–41.

Hatch, F.T., Reissell, P.K., Poon-King, M.W., Canellos, G.P., Lees, R.S., & Hagopian, L.M. (1966). A study of coronary heart disease in young men. *Circulation, 33*, 679–703.

Hillbrand, M., & Foster, H. G. (1993). Serum cholesterol levels and severity of aggression. *Psychological Reports, 72*, 270.

Holinger, P.C. (1987). *Violent deaths in the United States.* New York: Guilford.

Jacobs, D. R., Blackburn, H., Higgins, M., Reed, D., Iso, H., McMillian, G., Neton, J., Nelson, J., Potter, J., Rifkind, B., Rossouw, J., Shekelle, R., & Yusuf, S. (1992). Report of the conference of low blood cholesterol: Mortality associations. *Circulation, 86*, 1046–1060.

Jacobs, D. R., Muldoon, M. F., & Rastam, L. (1995). Low blood cholesterol, nonillness mortality, and other nonatherosclerotic disease mortality: A search for causes and confounders. *American Journal of Epidemiology, 141*, 518–522.

Kaplan, J.R., Manuck, S.B., & Shively, C. (1991). The effects of fat and cholesterol on social behavior in monkeys. *Psychosomatic Medicine, 53*, 634–642.

Kaplan, J.R., Shively, C.A., Botchin, M.B., Morgan, T.M., Howell, S.M., Manuck, S.B., Muldoon, M.F., & Mann, J.J. (1994). Demonstration of an association among dietary cholesterol, central serontonergic activity and social behavior in monkeys. *Psychosomatic Medicine, 56*, 479–484.

Ketterer, M.W., Brymer, J., Rhoads, K., Kraft, P., & Goldberg, A.D. (1994). Lipid-lowering therapy and violent death: Is depression a culprit? *Stress Medicine, 10*, 233–237.

Kostis, J.B., Rosen, R.C., & Wilson, A.C., (1994). Central nervous system effects of HMG CoA reductase inhibitors: Lovastatin and pravastatin on sleep and cognitive performance in patients with hypercholesterolemia. *Journal of Clinical Pharmacology, 34*, 989–996.

Kronmal, R.A., Cain, K.C., Ye, Z., & Omenn, G.S. (1993). Total serum cholesterol levels and mortality risk as a function of age. *Archives of Internal Medicine, 153*, 1065–1073.

Krumholz, H.M., Seeman, T.E., Merill, S.S., Mendes de Leon, C.F., Vaccarino, V., Silverman, D.I., Tsukahara, R., Ostfeld, A.M., & Berkman, L.F. (1994). Lack of association between cholesterol and coronary heart disease mortality and morbidity and all-cause mortality in persons older than 70 years. *Journal of the American Medical Association, 272* (17), 1335–1340.

LaRosa, J. C. (1995). Should high lipid levels in very old patients be lowered? *Aging & Drugs, 6*, 85–90.

Lechleitner, M., Hoppichler, F., Konwalinka, G., Patsch, J.R., & Braunsteiner, H. (1992). Depressive symptoms in hypercholesterolemic patients treated with pravastatin. *The Lancet, 340*, 910.

Lindberg, G., Larsson, G., Setterlind, S., & Rastam, L. (1994). Serum lipids and mood in working men and women in Sweden. *Journal of Epidemiology Community Health, 48*, 360–363.

Lindberg, G. Rastam, L., Guillberg, B., & Eklund, G.A. (1992). Low serum cholesterol concentration and short term mortality from injuries in men and women. *British Medical Journal, 305*, 277–279.

Maes, M., Delanghe, J., Meltzer, H.Y., Scharpe, S., DìHondt, P., & Cosyns, P. (1994). Lower degree of esterification of serum cholesterol in depression: Relevance for depression and suicide research. *Psychiatrica Scandinavica, 90*, 252–258.

Malenka, D.J., & Baron, J.A. (1981). Cholesterol and coronary heart disease. *Archives of Internal medicine, 149*, 1981–1985.

Manolio, T.A., Ettinger, W.H., Tracy, R.P., Kuller, L.H., Borhani, N.O., Lynch, J.C., & Fried, L.P. (1993). Epidemiology of low cholesterol levels in older adults. *Circulation, 87* (3), 728–737.

Manolio, T.A., Pearson, T.A., Wenger, N.K., Barrett-Connor, E., Payne, G. H., & Harlan, W. R. (1992). Cholesterol and heart disease in older persons and women. *Annals of Epidemiology, 2*, 161–176.

Marmot, M.G., Davey-Smith, G., Stansfield, S., Patel, C., North, F., Head, J., White, I., Brunner, E., & Feeney, A. (1991). Health inequalities among British civil servants: The Whitehall II study. *The Lancet, 337*, 1387–1392.

McCallum, J., Simons, L., Simons, J., & Friedlander, Y. (1994). Low serum cholesterol is not associated with depression in the elderly: Data from an Australian community study. *Australia and New Zealand Journal of Medicine, 24*, 561–564.

Miller-Bass, K., Newschaffer, C.J., Klag, M.J., & Bush, T.L. (1993). Plasma lipoprotein levels as predictors of cardiovascular death in women. *Archives of Internal Medicine, 53*, 2209–2216.

Modai, I., Valevski, A., Dror, S., & Weizman, A. (1994). Serum cholesterol levels and suicidal tendencies in psychiatric inpatients. *Journal of Clinical Psychiatry, 55* (6), 252–254.

Morgan, R.E., Palinkas, L.A., Barret-Connor, E.L., & Wingard, D.L. (1993). Plasma cholesterol and depressive symptoms in older men. *The Lancet, 34*, (341), 75–79.

Muldoon, M.F., Bonci, L.J., Rodriguez, V., Kaplan, J.R., & Manuck, S.B. (1994). Health effects of serum cholesterol reduction: The potential for good and the potential for harm. *Medicine, Exercise, Nutrition and Health, 3*, 74–90.

Muldoon, M.F., Kaplan, J.R., Manuck, S.B., & Mann, J.J. (1992). Effects of a low-fat diet on brain serontonergic responsivity in cynomolgus monkeys. *Biological Psychiatry, 31*, 739–742.

Muldoon, M.F., Manuck, S.B., & Matthews, K.A. (1990). Effects of cholesterol lowering on mortality: A quantitative review of primary prevention trials. *British Medical Journal, 301*, 309–314.

Muldoon, M.F., Rossouw, J.E., Manuck, S.B., Glueck, C.J., Kaplan, J.R., & Kaufmann, P.G., (1993). Low or lowered cholesterol and risk of death from suicide and trauma. *Metabolism, 42* (Suppl. 1), 45–56.

Muldoon, M.F., Ryan, C.M., Flory, J.D., Matthews, K.A., Manuck, S.B. Effects of cholesterol reduction on cognitive performance *American Heart Association 70th Scientific Sessions*, Orlando, FL, November 9-12, 1997. *Circulation* 1997:96 (suppl 1): 405.

Neaton, J.D., & Wentworth, D. (1992). Serum cholesterol, Blood pressure, cigarette smoking, and death from coronary heart disease. *Archives of Internal Medicine, 152*, 56–64.

Oxenkrug, G.F., Branconnier, R.J., Harto-Traux, N., & Cole, J.O. (1983). Is serum cholesterol a biological marker for major depressive disorder? *American Journal of Psychiatry, 140*, 7.

Pathological Determinants of Atherosclerosis in Youth Research Group. (1990). Relationship of atherosclerosis in young men to serum lipoprotein cholesterol concentrations and smoking. *Journal of the American Medical Association, 264*, 3018–3024.

Pekkanen, J., Linn, S., Heiss, G., Suchindran, C.M., Leon, A., Rifkind, B.M., & Tyroler, H.A. (1990). Ten-year mortality from cardiovascular disease in relation to cholesterol level among men with and without preexisting cardiovascular disease. *New England Journal of Medicine, 322*, 1700–07.

Pekkanen, J., Nissinen, A., Punsar, S., & Karvonen, M.J. (1989). Serum cholesterol and risk of accident or violent death in a 25-year follow-up. *Archives of Internal Medicine, 149*, 1589–1591.

Randomised trial of cholesterol lowering in 4444 patients with coronary heart disease: The Scandinavian Simvastatin Survival Study. (1994). *The Lancet, 334*, 1383–1389.

Rogers, R.L., Meyer, J.S., McClintic, K., & Mortel, K.F. (1989). Reducing hypercholesterolemia cerebral perfusion. *Angiology*, 40: 260–269.

Roth T., Richardson, G.R., Sullivan, J.P., Lee, R.M., Merlotti, L., & Roehrs, T. Comparative Effects of pravistatin and lovastatin on nighttime sleep and daytime performance. Clin Cardiol 1992; 15: 426–432.

Rudman, D., Mattson, D.E., Feller, A.G., & Nagraj, H.S. (1989). A mortality risk index for men in a Veterans Administration extended care facility. *Journal of Parenteral Enteral Nutrition, 3* (2), 1989–1995.

Rudman, D., Mattson, D.E., Nagraj, H.S., Feller, A.G., Jackson, D.L., Caindec, N., & Rudman, I. W. (1988). Prognostic significance of serum cholesterol in nursing home men. *Journal of Pareteral Eterel Nutrition, 12* (2), 155–158.

Schaefer, E.J., Moussa, P.B., Wilson, P.W., McGee, D. Dallal, G., & Castelli, W.P. (1989). Plasma lipoproteins in healthy octogenarians: Lack of reduced high density lipoprotein cholesterol levels: Results from the Farmingham Heart Study. *Metabolism, 38* (4), 292–296.

Sempos, C.T., Cleeman, J.I., Caroll, M.D., Johnson, C.L., Bachorik, P.S., Gordon, D.J., Burt, V.L., Briefel, R.R., Brown, C.D., Lippel, K., & Rifkind, B.M. (1993). Prevalence of high blood cholesterol among U.S. adults. *Journal of the American Medical Association, 269* (23), 3009–3014.

Shepherd, J., Cobbe, S.M., Ford, I., Isles, C.G., Lorimer, A.R., MacFarlane, P.W., McKillop, J.H., & Packard, C.J. (1995). Prevention of coronary heart disease with pravastatin in men with hypercholesterolemia. *New England Journal of Medicine, 333* (20), 1301–1307.

Sletten, I.W., Nilsen, J.A., Young, R.C., & Anderson, J.T. (1964). Blood lipids and behavior in mental-hospital patients. *Psychosomatic Medicine, 26*, 261–266.

Spitz, R.T., Hillbrand, M., & Foster, H.G. (1994). Serum cholesterol levels and frequency of aggression. *Psychological Reports, 74*, 622.

Staesson, J., Amery, A., Birkenhager, W., Bulpitt, C., Clement, D., de Leeuw, P., Deruyttere, M., De Schaepdryver, A., Dollery, C., Fagard, R., Fletcher, A., Forrete, F., Forte, J., Henry, J., Koistinen, A., Leonetti, G., Nissinen, A., O'Brien, E., O'Malley, K., Pelemans, W., Petrie, J.C., Strasser, T.K., Terzoli, L., Thijs, L., Tuomilehto, J., Webster, J., Williams., B.O. (1990). Is a high serum cholesterol level associated with longer survival in elderly hypertensives. *Journal of Hypertension, 8*(8), 755-761.

Stamler, J., Wentworth, D., & Neaton, J.D., (1986). Is relationship between serum cholesterol and risk of premature death from coronary heart disease continuous and graded? Journal of the *American Medical Association, 256*, 2823–2828.

Stewart, M.A., & Stewart, S.G. (1981). Serum cholesterol in antisocial personality. *Neuropsychobiology, 7*, 9–11.

Strandberg, T.E., Raikokonen, K., Partinen M., Pihl, S., Vanhanen, H., & Miettinen, T.A. (1994). Associations of cholesterol lowering by statins with anger and hostility in hypercholesterolemic men. *Biological Psychiatry, 35*, 575–577.

Sullivan, P.F., Joyce, P.R., Bulik, C.M., Mulder, R.T., & Oakley-Browne, M. (1994). Total cholesterol and suicidality in depression. *Biological Psychiatry, 36*, 472–477.

Summary of the second report of the National Cholesterol Education Program (NCEP) expert panel on detection, evaluation, and treatment of high blood cholesterol in adults (Adult Treatment Panel II). (1993). *Journal of the American Medical Association, 269*, 3015–3023.

Swartz, C.M. (1990). Albumin decrement in depression and cholesterol decrement in mania. *Journal of Affective Disorders, 19*, 173–176.

U.S. Senate Subcommittee on Aging. (1991). *Aging America* (Publication No. 273). Washington, DC: U.S. Department of Health and Human Services.

Vartiainen, E., Puska, P., Pekkanen, J., Tuoumilehto, J., Lonnqvist, J., & Ehnholm, C. (1994). Serum cholesterol concentration and mortality from accidents, suicide, and other violent causes. *British Medical Journal, 309*, 445–447.

Verdery, R.B., & Goldberg, A.P. (1991). Hypercholesterolemia as a predictor of death: A prospective study of 224 nursing home residents. *Journal of Gerontology, 46* (3), M84–M90.

Virkkunen, M. (1979). Serum cholesterol in antisocial personality. *Neuropsychobiology, 5,* 27-30.

Virkkunen, M. (1983). Serum cholesterol levels in homicidal offenders. *Neuropsychobiology, 10,* 65–69.

Virkkunen, M., & Pettinen, H. (1984). Serum cholesterol in aggressive conduct disorder: A preliminary study. *Biological Psychology, 19,* 435–439

Waldstein, S.R., Polefrone, J., Muldoon, M.F., & Manuck, S.B., (1993). Relationship of cardiovascular reactivity and anger expression to serum lipid concentrations in healthy young men. *Journal of Psychosomatic Research, 37,* 249–256.

Weidner, G., Sexton, G., McLellarn, R., Connor, S.L., & Matarazzo, J.D. (1987). The role of Type A behavior and hostility in an elevation of plasma lipids in adult women and men. *Psychosomatic Medicine, 49* (2), 136–145.

Wilson, P.W., Anderson, K.M., Harris, T., Kannel, W.B., & Castelli, W.P. (1994). Determinants of change in total cholesterol and HDL-C with age: The Framingham Study. *Journal of Gerontological Medical Science, 49* (6), M252–M257.

Author Index

Grover, S. A., 230, *241*
Gruchow, H. W., 180, *193*
Gruys, E., 112, *116*
Guarankik, J. M., 236, *240*
Guillberg, B., 234, 235, *242*
Gulpitt, C. J., 51, *56*
Gumbrecht, G., 142, *149*
Guschwan, M., 86, *106*
Gutherie, D., 146, *149*
Guyre, P. M., 93, *106*
Gwyther, L., 76, *81*

H

Hackett, T. P., 167, *176, 177*
Hagapian, L. M., 235, *241*
Hallen, J., 112, *115*
Hallstrom, T., 48, *55*
Halter, J. B., 142, 145, *149, 151*
Hamagami, A., 219, *223*
Hamer, R. M., 167, *177*
Hamer, T. 235, *241*
Hamilton, M. E., 86, *106*
Hamm, P., 32, *41*
Hamm, T. E., Jr., 180, *193*
Handa, R. J., 86, *106*
Handwerger, B. S., 90, 97, *104*
Haney, T. L., 136, 137, 138, 140, *149*
Hankinson, S. E., 180, *193*
Hannet, I., 62, *68*
Hansson, G. K., 188, *196*
Hardy, R. R., 88, *105*
Harell, R. E., 136, 137, *151*
Harker, J., 110, *117*
Harlan, E. S., 143, 144, 151
Harlan, W. R., 227, 228, *242*
Harlow, S., D., 76, *81*
Harralson, T. L., 144, *151*
Harring, K., 157, 160, *176*
Harris, J. R., 9, 11, 13, *14*
Harris, T. B., 227, 230, 231, 233, 236, *240, 241, 243*
Hart, T., 146, *149*
Harth, M., 77, *81*
Hartka, E., 145, *150*
Harto-Traux, N., 235, *242*
Hastillo, A., 167, *177*
Hata, N., 86, *106*
Hatch, F. T., 235, *241*
Hauger, R., 71, 73, 77, *81*
Havik, O. E., 167, *176, 177*

Hawrylowicz, C., 100, *107*
Haxby, J. V., 220, *223*
Hay, J., 71, *81*
Hayakawa, K., 88, *105*
Haynes, S. G., 181, 182, *193*
Head, J., 235, *242*
Hecker, M. H. L., 46, 47, *55*
Heckhausen, J., 122, 124, *131, 132,* 156, *177*
Heidrich, S., 159, 164, *177*
Heijtink, R. A., 78, *82*
Helgeson, V. S., 156, 160, *177*
Heller, D. A., 10, 11, 13, *14*
Heller, R. F., 180, *193*
Hellman, S., 173, *176*
Helzer, J. E., 145, *149*
Henderson, A. S., 6, *14*
Hennekens, C. H., 46, 53, *55, 57,* 180, *193*
Henry, J., 230, 232, *243*
Herbert M., 121, *132*
Herbert, P., 53, *55*
Herbert, T. B., 69, 70, 73, *81*
Hermann G., 93, 98, 99,100, 102, *105*
Herrick, S. E., 126, *131*
Herrington, D. M., 187, *197*
Hertzog, C., 6, *14*
Hessen, M. T., 63, *68*
Higgins, M., 179, *193,* 231, 234, 235, *241*
Higgins, P., 121, 128, *131*
Higley, J. D., 147, *150*
Hilgers, K. F., 190, *194*
Hillbrand, M., 235, *241, 243*
Hiramatusu, S., 85, *107*
Hirokawa, K., 86, 88, 91,*105, 107*
Hjortland, M. C., 46, *55*
Ho, H. Z., 10, *14*
Hoffman, J. T., 126, *131*
Holbrook, N. J., 64, *68*
Hollinger, P. C., 236 *241*
Holman, H. R., 121, 126, *132*
Holsboer, F., 145, *150*
Holt, K., 157, 160, *176*
Homma Y., 91, *107*
Honoré, E. K., 187, *197*
Hopkins, J., 96, *105*
Hoppichler, F., 238, *241*
Horn, J. L., 219, *222*
Horvath, J. A., 92, *103*
Horwatt, K., 96, *106*
Horwitz, B., 220, *223*
Hosmer, D. W., 213, *223*
Houston, B. K., 46, 47, *55,* 235, *240*
Howell, S. M., 238, *241*

Subject Index